I0756143

Magnolia Tree

Tales of a Gypsy Flowercaster

Tales of a Gypsy Flowercaster

Short Stories From the Long Life of a Romani Designer

DANNY VANO MILLER

Written with Tom Grant

Bello Chaphoro Press
VISALIA, CALIFORNIA

Published by Bello Chaphoro Press
Visalia, California

ISBN 979-8-218-50511-0

Library of Congress Control Number: 2024913370

First edition: 2026

Printed and bound in the United States of America

Illustrations by Danny Vano Miller

Bello Chaphoro Press logo and book design by Tom Grant

Cover images generated using Microsoft AI Image Generator

Danny Vano Miller and Tom Grant are pseudonyms. Some names and other identifying details have been changed to protect the privacy of various individuals. In some instances, the chronology or circumstances of events may have been altered somewhat.

Visit us at BelloChaphoro.com

For my Kunni

and

for Leo

ACKNOWLEDGMENTS

Tom Grant extends his heartfelt thanks to A. I. Bing of Redmond, Washington, for the latter's spot-on suggestions, software usage tips, and informative answers to queries.

Contents

1

First Things First

"Hey, Uncle Danny!" my nephew Sammy called out excitedly, just a few minutes after starting to flip through the fat notebook containing my handwritten memoirs. "What were you thinking? You gotta refer to us as *Roma, Romani,* or *Romanies*, not *Gypsies. Gypsy* is just insulting and straight-out racist! It's used as a slur against Roma, like when rednecks use the n-word to refer to Black folks. It comes from a place of prejudice, bigotry, and persecution!"

Hahaha! This wasn't the first time during my born-again-Gypsy nephew's visit that I rolled my eyes. I was stuck in my wheelchair for maybe another few weeks. There was no escape. Damn dopehead driver!

Sammy was on a roll. "Uncle, you need to set the *gadje* (non-Roma) straight and not feed their prejudices. And leave out the negative stuff about my cousins, calling them thieves and dopeheads. That just perpetuates the myths and stereotypes."

Oh, boo-hoo! Jeez, I missed my business partner, Mike Cohen, so much! He was at an interior design convention in San Diego. While Mike was away, I worked quite a bit on several of the short stories that make up my memoirs, and I was really looking forward to him coming home and giving me some decent feedback. Mike is mildly autistic, and like other autistic people that I know, he's pretty upfront with his opinions, blunt even. He really struggles if someone tries to get him to lie or sugarcoat the truth. I guess you could say that being honest and direct is his natural communication style.

At first, I guess I took some of what Mike calls "constructive criticism" too personal. I wanted to hear how good my stories were, not how I wasn't saying things right. Or not how changing things around or cleaning up my writing a bit might make it better. "Well, Danny, you asked," Mike would say, "and I'm just telling you what I think!" On the other hand, it didn't take me long to realize that whenever Mike *did* tell me that he liked this or that in my writing, he meant it and wasn't just trying to avoid hurting my feelings.

Anyway, now I respect Mike's opinions and ideas about my writing and everything else. He's a brilliant man, the smartest man I know who is so nice about it.

I should have known better than to share my life story with Sammy, but Mike was going to be gone for another week or so, and I really wanted to run my latest chapter by someone. Sammy had been pestering me for a long time to let him read some of my new stuff. "Don't start in on me, Sammy. You college kids all sound alike: 'Downtrodden peoples of the world unite! Free Willy! Smash the Franistani oppressors!' Hahaha! What a load of crap!"

I tried reasoning with my nephew: "I want to get my life story out there, Sammy. So the title has to attract people's attention and get them interested. The way to do that is to use words that they're familiar with. My memoirs are about the life and career of a *Gypsy* designer. Most gadje wouldn't have a clue what a *Romani* designer is. I'd like to have folks read my book and maybe want to learn more about us Roma."

"Well, Uncle Danny, at least let me or Mike or someone else go through and correct your spelling and grammar."

"Look, Sammy," I said, "Mavis, the new temp gal you met last week, will be working more hours starting next Monday. Mavis is going to start putting everything on the laptop, and she says that the word processing program she uses will highlight possible misspelled words as she types. But how I say things stays just like it is. I write like I speak. Folks seem to understand me just fine."

And on and on we went, until Sammy threw up his hands in frustration and got up and said that he had to be going. "Uncle Danny, I love you, but right now you're being stubborn, and you're making me *munca* (ill)! What you do outta me sometimes, Uncle!"

Well, no apologies to you, Sammy! Seeing as how I'm too old and banged up to join in the fight to right even one of the world's wrongs, I think I'll just continue to call myself a Gypsy, tell Gypsy stories, talk about my Gypsy heritage, my Gypsy friends, my Gypsy family, and share all of my Gypsy wisdom and memories with anyone who will listen! I figure that I, Danny Miller, own the term *Gypsy*! I use it proudly to refer to myself and other Gypsies, whether I'm talking to Gypsies or to non-Gypsies. I like the word *Gypsy*, and, as far as I'm concerned, it's a good word, a fine word. It's a word that everyone already knows. It's used by some very fine people, and ok, by some pretty awful people too.

A lot of bumpkins still have negative feelings about Gypsies, and they express their prejudices in situations that don't necessarily involve real Gypsies. When someone thinks that he's been ripped off or gotten a bad deal, he might sputter and bitch about getting "gypped." Someone who can't manage to hold down a job for long or settle down anywhere for any length of time—who packs up and moves around a lot—is often said to "live like a Gypsy." Large cities from time to time have campaigns to eliminate "gypsy cabs," unlicensed private vehicles operating illegally as taxi cabs, relied on by so many folks in poor neighborhoods with bad public transportation.

I know that I'm rattling on and on, but I just don't think

that insisting on the use of a "correct" term for *Gypsy* is going to change how bigots see Gypsies, any more than newer, more politically-correct language has changed the opinions of stupid people about any other group that has been discriminated against.

I hope that people who read or listen to my life story will come away with a positive impression of me as a person and of Gypsy people in general. And for folks who have heard a lot of bigoted crap about Gypsies, maybe learning something good about Gypsies from the Gypsy horse's mouth will help set them straight!

Like I told Sammy, I'm really anxious to get my story out there for people to read. It hasn't been easy for me. A couple of years before Sammy's visit, I had thrown out a bunch of my writing notebooks after my son Earl (aka "Earl the Pearl") called me one afternoon when I was at Mike's and my little vacation place up in Three Rivers, California. Earl was probably the last person I would want to read my life story before I had a chance to change names, dates, and places in the final, typewritten manuscript I hoped to submit to book publishers.

The day Earl called, Mike was away on a business trip, and Earl wanted to know if Mike was going to be home, because if he wasn't, Earl wanted to stop by and talk to me about helping him get started in a new paving business. "That big fuckin' queer," Earl spat into the phone, "he better watch out! I'll work him over real good for calling the cops on me the last time I was there!"

Those two never did get along, because Mike knew that whenever Earl visited, he was one hundred percent trying to get money out of me. And if Earl pulled some scam on me, he knew that I wouldn't go to the cops, because keeping our children out of jail is one of the many ways we Gypsies coddle and spoil our kids and protect them from the unfortunate consequences of the bad decisions they make all the time.

Well, I just didn't know what to do. Earl was on his way over to pitch God-only-knows-what-kind-of hare-brained, drug-fueled paving scheme. I was still in a wheelchair after knee surgery and was weeks away from being able to hop in my truck and make a getaway before Earl showed up. I didn't know any of our neighbors well enough yet to ask them if they could hold onto my notebooks while Earl was visiting me. I was afraid that Earl would find my writing notebooks when he rifled through my stuff.

We'd often get into shouting matches when he'd track me down and demand money to buy drugs, or a new truck, or hire a better criminal defense attorney. Well, he wouldn't come right out and say he needed money to get high, but he would show up looking like hell, all sweaty and smelling like he had gotten sick on himself. I knew what he wanted was money for a fix.

So I panicked and did something really stupid: Before Earl got there, I tossed the whole bunch of notebooks into the incinerator and burned them with the trash. I guess if I hadn't been so panicked, I would have just tossed the notebooks into the incinerator and *not* burned them! Well, anyway, my work is safe from now on. My new assistant scans my handwritten pages and copies the scans to an external hard drive before she inputs them, so there's always a backup.

Let me tell you a little more about myself and my background before you tackle reading my stories. I'll begin with the basics and try to clear up some misconceptions about Gypsies.

I'm an American Gypsy with one foot in the *gadjo* (non-Roma) world. Gypsy men these days dress pretty much like other men here in the U.S., I guess. Gypsy girls and women still tend to dress more conservative than non-Gypsies, wearing longer skirts, for example. In terms of complexion, some American Gypsies look like our cousins from India and have dark skin and eyes and black hair. Other Gypsies, like English Gypsies, are lighter complected and tend to look more like the people they have lived among for a long time. As for me, I have a dark complexion and a cool accent. I used to have thick, wavy, black hair; now it's thick, wavy, and silver.

When I was more active physically and meeting more people, there were dark-complected folks who took one look at me, walked over to me, like maybe to ask directions, and started speaking their own lingo. Italians used to do that; Mexicans did that; Arabs and dark-skinned Jewish guys from the Middle East did that; Greeks and Turks did that—a lot. Mike, my longtime business partner, did that once many years ago on a busy New York City street corner. That's how we met!

On the other hand, for many years now, as far back as grade school, other folks I've met have asked me if I'm Italian or Mexican or whatever. I've always been proud to answer that I'm a Gypsy. Most folks are genuinely happy to finally meet a *real* Gypsy.

When I tell people I meet that I'm a Gypsy, they often ask where I'm from originally. Both of my parents' families came to America in the early 1900s. I was born here in America, in Columbus, Ohio, the first person in my family to be born in a hospital. But, as is the case with other Gypsies, my ancestors were probably refugees fleeing armies invading the areas where they lived in India over a thousand years ago. Their descendants eventually arrived in Eastern Europe and spread out to other parts of the world.

Many Gypsies ended up as slaves when they reached what is now part of Romania. My dad's people left Romania and settled in Bosnia after the slaves were freed in the mid-1850s. Because of their unique culture influenced by Romanian customs, even today these people are often referred to as *Romanian Gypsies.* In Bosnia, the men worked as animal trainers, horse traders, farmers, metal workers, carpenters, musicians, and traveling-show (carnivals, circuses, touring theater companies, etc.) people. The women were mostly wives, mothers, homemakers, caregivers, and seamstresses, as well as traveling-show workers, and entertainers. Once they arrived in the United States, Gypsy men and women adapted their traditional skills to their new life in America.

In recent times, as older occupations have declined, some Romanian Gypsy men have found employment in the modern economy, working as car mechanics, auto body repairmen, or as construction workers. Some continue to work in traveling shows and amusement parks. Many Romanian Gypsies, both men and women, are now self-employed, making use of their skills in various trades.

Many of my mother's people were very talented and creative. Back in Italy, they were actors, singers, musicians, and stage decorators who had worked for generations in the grand theaters and opera houses of Naples and Venice. Some even produced their own plays which they performed in traveling theaters.

But there were hard times, too, and there was a lot of prejudice and discrimination against the Gypsy community in Italy. In smaller towns especially, if a Gypsy was accused of a serious crime, the locals would often band together to attack Gypsies and try to drive them out of town.

My mom's parents, Manfri and Rosa Vano, were newlyweds anxious to escape the prejudices of the Old World and find a better life for themselves in America. They settled in Chicago, in a neighborhood on the Near West Side that was already coming to be known as Little Italy. Some of my mom's family members who had been living in Chicago for a while had already become well-known and respected set designers, musicians, singers, live-theater managers, and artists. The men among the newer arrivals worked as tinkers, craftsmen, painters, repairmen, woodworkers, carpenters, as well as traveling-show workers and performers. Some of the descendants of these Italian-Gypsy newcomers have become well-known sports figures, actors, authors, artists, designers, and musicians.

Women mostly stayed at home. They were homemakers, raised the kids, did the cooking, cleaning and washing, sewed the family's clothing, linens, etc., and took care of older relatives. But some women had special skills that the traveling shows made good use of. They designed and decorated theatrical sets, event spaces, and performance stages. It was usually women who helped plan special events like weddings and birthdays and did the shopping, decorating, cooking, and baking. Others became popular entertainers and big-top performers.

When my mom's parents arrived in Chicago, they lived for a while with some relatives, but before they started a family, they wanted to leave Chicago and start a new life on their own, just the two of them.

Like so many Gypsies from other parts of Europe, *Nonna* (Grandmother) Rosa and *Nonno* (Grandfather) Manfri explored their new country by joining one of the many carnivals traveling all over the United States. These carnivals had food booths, freak shows, rides, and game booths—where folks could buy a chance to win a prize. Some of these carnivals had a bandstand and offered entertainment and live music for dancing and a large space for weddings and other special events. Some of them featured name acts when they played larger venues. A lot of carnival goers preferred the carnival stage to the stuffy and often cramped city theaters where vaudeville and musical acts usually performed.

Some Gypsies stayed on the road with the circus or carnival season after season. Others left after a while to start their own traveling show, or to lead what Gypsies call a "settled" (non-itinerant) life.

After years on the carnival circuit, Nonno Manfri and Nonna Rosa had enough money saved up to put together their own traveling tent show. My grandparents had learned a lot from the years spent traveling the different show circuits. They wanted to create a family-oriented traveling show, one that would showcase their family's musical and creative talents and appeal to people of all ages.

The Vano Family Travelling Theatre became known for its theatrical productions, vaudeville acts, and good quality Italian and American food in an elegant and beautifully decorated sit-down restaurant setting. I guess it was sort of an early dinner-theater idea that became very popular in smaller towns in the Midwest and South. The stages for the plays and musical acts were decorated with handmade flowers, foliage, and trees.

The dinner pavilion in my grandparents' traveling show was known for the elegant and extravagant artificial flower arrangements placed throughout the dining room. Nonna Rosa and my aunties and cousins made every single stem, flower, and all of the lush foliage entirely by hand. Some flowers were tinted exotic colors. The bandstand and stages for the plays and musical acts were decorated with simpler arrangements of beautiful natural-looking artificial flowers and foliage—again, all handmade by my family.

That's how I got my start in the business of making by hand

flowers and almost anything else growing in a garden. I guess you could even say that I was born into it! Before I could read and write, I was put to work making crepe-paper roses and other flowers for our musical and theatrical productions, as well as for weddings and other special events that we hosted on site.

As I remember, my first attempt at making crepe-paper flowers didn't work out so good! My great-aunt Flodia reached out and grabbed my shoulder one afternoon as I chased my little sister Rosie around the backstage work area. I can't remember exactly how old I was, but up to that point in my young life, I had gotten away with pretending not to really understand what the Big People around me were saying to me, especially if they had angry looks on their faces. But this time, my sad puppy face and crocodile tears didn't work their usual charm. I was stopped in my tracks, my shoulder hurting from the tight grip of my auntie's bony fingers.

"You, little man. Stop wriggling and stay put!" Auntie Flodia had a strong and deep voice, and an accent like Bela Lugosi's in *Dracula*. For such a tiny little person, Auntie Flodia sounded like she could cause some serious damage if I didn't do exactly what she wanted. "Useless, except to be nuisance, like bug. You just take up space. Come here, make flowers. Here, I show you how. I go slow, just for you," she said, plopping some hand-trimmed crepe-paper streamers down on the work table in a little pile. "Here, here, Mr. Danny. You watch. Watch my pretty fingers."

I fumbled around with a streamer, but it kept slipping from my hand, landing on the table, over and over. Finally, Auntie Flodia grabbed the fingers of my right hand and worked the crepe paper over and around and between the fingers until I could make the same movements on my own.

Years later, when I saw the movie *The Miracle Worker*, one scene really stuck in my mind: It was that scene where Annie Sullivan teaches Helen Keller the word *water* by spelling *w-a-t-e-r* onto one of Helen's hands while working the old-fashioned water-pump handle up and down over and over to splash water onto Helen's other hand. That reminded me of my auntie grabbing my right hand and moving my fingers exactly like she moved her own until I finally caught on!

After just a few days, my auntie was showing my little paper flowers to everyone who walked into her *atelier* (workshop, studio). From then on, we were best pals!

In the space of what seems now like not much time at all, I could make a rose or a carnation; a magnolia bud or a full bloom took a little longer, but not much. It wasn't long before I started creating my own made-up, "fantasy flowers" in a variety of colors and materials. They looked like real flowers, but they were from my imagination.

Even when I was still a young boy, sometimes when we stopped in a town where we had family, I would watch my dad and the other men build outdoor furniture from birch and other local wood. Over time, they taught me the carpentry and wood-working skills that would be so important in my years in display design and production design.

By the time I was about eight years old, Nonna Rosa and Nonno Manfri were getting tired of traveling around so much and dealing with everything involved in the running of a traveling show. They finally decided to retire. With my dad's folks, they bought a large house in Cicero, Illinois, a suburb of Chicago. My mom and dad weren't interested in taking on so much responsibility, so my mom's oldest brother, Benno, took over running the traveling dinner show. As soon as Uncle Benno learned the ropes, my folks moved in with my grandparents, and my dad went back to work with his brother Gheorghe in the awning and outdoor furniture business that they had started a few years after they arrived in America.

When we first moved to Cicero, and before I was old enough to explore my new city on my own, I really missed the hustle and bustle of the traveling theater and seeing all of the different cities and regions of the United States. But the design bug had bit me, and I continued to add to what I had learned on the road. Almost every day, my mom let me grab some change from the emergency fund that she kept in an old teapot up on a kitchen shelf. I'd run to the corner five-and-dime and buy as much crepe paper as I could afford, then run home and think of new flowers to make.

All through my school years, I made flowers, trees, garlands, and stage sets for plays and other events at school, as well as for neighborhood and family celebrations. I continued to do carpentry and woodworking and to create my fantasy flower displays whenever I returned to the road and even after eventually deciding to lead a settled life.

I began my long career in display design by creating window and interior retail displays in Los Angeles. Later I worked mostly in Chicago and the New York City area. I designed and installed window and interior displays and customized seasonal decor for major department and luxury-goods stores and performance venues.

I returned periodically to Los Angeles, where I helped design and install interior and exterior décor for the 1960 Academy Award ceremonies. Later in my career, I supervised the design and construction of sets, props, and other visual elements for theatrical, motion picture, and television productions. I eventually became an art director/managing partner at Affinity Design, a well-respected and award-winning display-design and production-design company located in Chicago.

Everything I have accomplished, despite many misadventures and missteps along the way, is built upon my very first attempts to master the art of *faux floristry* (making artificial flowers) when I was just a young boy zigzagging across the United States in a traveling theater show. Learning how to make artificial flowers by hand and using these fantasy flowers in arrangements opened up a whole new world to me, a world that grew larger and more interesting as I gained more experience and relied more and more on my own imagination for ideas and inspiration.

I'm hoping that you, dear reader, will enjoy these stories about my life in that new world!

Danny Vano Miller
Carmel-by-the-Sea, California
August 14, 2017

2

Jews and Gypsies, Oh My!

Detour

I graduated from the eighth grade in June 1942, and turned fourteen in July. I was no longer legally required to stay in school and could work full time in my family's successful awning and lawn furniture business in Chicago. Working with my dad every day, I realized that he just wasn't all that happy living and working in a big noisy city or staying in one place for too long. He talked a lot about how much he missed our life on the road.

The longer we lived in Chicago, the more my dad wanted to take a break from slogging through the piles of winter snow that seemed to grow deeper over the years. Our friends Esther and Sammy Haddad out in Los Angeles were always trying to lure my folks back to L.A. to take advantage of the night life and fine weather. Their most recent invitation was to spend Christmas vacation with them at their ranch in Encino, in the L.A. area.

We had a family powwow, and after my brothers and sisters had heard only a few stories about the train trip our folks and I took to Los Angeles back in 1939 to attend Esther and Sammy's wedding, the vote was unanimous: The Miller family was going to spend a sunny and warm California Christmas on a real ranch!

Didn't seem like no time at all. Thanksgiving came and went. Finally, we were on our way, The Wandering Miloradovitches, as some of my mom's cousins called us—like we were a circus act or something! My family always seemed to be doing our own thing, and this time around, we were heading toward the bright lights and smelly air of Los Angeles.

We dropped off some boxes of food and outgrown clothes at my sad-sack Aunt Binnie's trailer in a rundown, weed-and-dog-infested Gypsy trailer court in the little town of Perris, in Riverside County, California. Like members of other ethnic groups living in the Perris area, most of the Gypsies were honest and hard-working folks, and had nice modern trailers or houses. Others always seemed to be running some sort of grift, like doing shoddy roofing or paving jobs. Some had been worn down by hard work and were real poverty people: desperate, trying to make it through hard economic times by hook or by crook.

Before the war, there was day-labor work in the local fruit and nut orchards that barely paid enough to buy food, cover the rent, and put enough gas in the work trucks to keep them running. But a lot of the real go-getter Gypsy men picked up temporary work that led to full-time work as house painters, construction workers, mechanics, even gardeners.

The war had already brought a lot of changes, and younger Gypsies were heading toward larger cities to find work in aircraft plants or other industries involved in the war effort. And there were quite a few, even whole families, that had been recruited down at the welfare office to pull up stakes and move to a new town that the federal government was building in Tennessee. There were a lot of good-paying construction jobs there, and free housing.

Aunt Binnie's youngest son, Hamm, was one of the local Perris guys recruited by the government construction program. He wasn't told all that much about the job in Tennessee, only that he would be working at some place called the Clinton Engineer Works, but he was ready to go as soon as he received his train ticket. Hamm was all excited because he'd never been on a train before. He told my folks about his new job, and they went down to the welfare office to talk to the government recruiters there and find out more.

Mom and Dad liked what they heard and signed up to work back in Tennessee. My folks weren't given train tickets because they received some kind of stipend to return home to pick up our trailer, new car, my brothers and sisters, and head for Tennessee. Two of my dad's younger nephews, Mulo and Dervo, had also signed up for jobs in Tennessee and were going to take along their dump trucks and more road construction equipment. Their dad, my uncle Charlie, was now without his two best workers. He soon decided to join Mulo and Dervo and signed up at a government recruitment center in Indianapolis to work in Tennessee. Uncle Charlie brought along the rest of his family, a new trailer, a work truck, and an old flatbed truck.

It wasn't until the summer of 1943 that the place where we were living and working in Tennessee was renamed Oak Ridge. Most people living in the area thought it was a military base or engineering complex. It was only much later, after the first atomic bomb was dropped on Hiroshima, Japan, that we found out that Oak Ridge was one of the places where the atomic bomb was developed. Not tested or anything, but some big uranium enrichment plants were at Oak Ridge. It was where the fuel for the very first atomic bomb was enriched. All this was super hush-hush, and each worker was only told what he or she needed to know to do each specific assigned job.

While my folks were busy on the phone telling Esther and Sammy and everyone back home about the change in plans, I was on my own for a couple of days. There didn't seem to be a lot going on in Aunt Binnie's trailer court. Most of the younger men had already left to find work elsewhere. When I was out wandering around by myself, I got spooked by the hungry stares from the scraggly packs of dogs that seemed to be everywhere.

The only bright spot was seeing my cousin Luna again. She

was just sixteen but seemed a lot older. Luna read a lot of books and was probably the first artsy type I met. Her saving grace was that she didn't like boys *that way.* So Luna had plenty of time to devote to her talents and other and better things than landing a husband and becoming a hopeless trailer-bound drudge. Luna was a real talented singer, and she played guitar and ukulele. She was a gifted artist and made beautiful sketches and drawings of people and animals. Years later, while going to art school in L.A., she earned a pretty decent living doing quick but real detailed ink drawings of passers-by on the street.

Luna would tug on my sleeve to get my attention, proudly show me her latest little masterpiece, and tell me how different her life was going to be someday in "the *real* Paris, the Paris spelled with one *r*." That finally happened some years later, not long after the war was over. Luna made some beautiful sketches of young street Gypsies in Paris, and took some wonderful photographs of people and places in a Paris coming back into its own after the awful German occupation.

My folks and I said our *adoos* (goodbyes) to Aunt Binnie and her brood and headed back to Chicago. We had a lot to do before leaving for Tennessee!

All About Miss Esther Bornstein

I was anxious to get a head start on what my over-active young mind was hoping would be a real adventure back in Tennessee. I was sad though that we wouldn't have time to stop in Los Angeles and spend some time with Esther and Sammy Haddad and the friends we had made when we went out to California back in 1939 for Miss Esther and Sammy's wedding. Miss Esther had come over from Germany in 1926 to live with a grand-aunt and grand-uncle in Ohio and go to school here in the States. With everything happening in Germany, she wound up just staying put in the U.S.

Miss Esther had finished high school and college in Ohio and was now working in Hollywood, California, as a legal secretary at a big fancy movie-star law firm in the Taft Building at Hollywood and Vine. She worked under her maiden name, so even at work, Miss

Esther was addressed as Esther, Miss Esther, or Miss Bornstein. Miss Esther's husband, Sammy, was a Canadian guy who had settled in Los Angeles and ran a successful electrical contracting business. In person, in the flesh, Sammy was just as Miss Esther had described him in the many letters she had written to me and my folks about her new life in California. Sammy was a charmer: He was handsome, well-spoken, and well-mannered, but not a dandy or stuck up. He was like a guy out of a classy Hollywood movie, but with a good sense of humor and a lot of really neat stories to share. Anyhoo, I really had been looking forward to seeing Miss Esther and Sammy again.

My folks and I had met Miss Esther back in the early thirties in Christiansburg, Ohio, on the day my niece Nettie George was born. In fact, it was the circumstances around Nettie's birth that brought the Bornstein and Miller families together years ago.

Back then, in 1933, we were on the road with my mom's parents' traveling theater, passing through Champaign County, Ohio, on our way to winter quarters in South Carolina. I was five years old and a real handful, into all sorts of silly shenanigans and good-natured mischief. My parents were often at their wits' end: scolding me, chasing after me, trying to bribe me with a treat or a new toy to settle down and behave.

The only person who could handle me and put the brakes on my bad behavior was Great-Aunt Flodia, who had got me started making paper and silk flowers before I was even four years old. Whenever my folks put me in the timeout corner in our dining room, Auntie Flodia would come and grab me—a cigarette dangling from her lips—drag me back to the theater's workroom, sit me down, dump a pile of crepe paper streamers onto the work table in front of me, and say really sweet things like "you eat after you make two dozen roses," or, my favorite, that I did my best to live up to: "no rest for wicked little man." Hahahaha!

We were just outside a little village called Christiansburg when my sister Kezia went into labor and was having a real difficult time. My dad told me the whole story years later: Some Mennonite folks in a horse-drawn buggy were alongside our column of traveling-show wagons, trailers, trucks, vans, and buses. My brother-in-law, Hank George, ran over to the buggy and explained what was going on and asked if there was a midwife or doctor nearby.

A young man leaned forward in the buggy to talk to Hank and pointed down the road, then made a movement to the right with his left hand. Hank came over to our truck and told my dad that we had lucked out, that there were two doctors, a husband and wife, who had been delivering babies for over forty years and lived just up the road and to the right, at a place called Duck Farm.

Hank ran back to his and Kezia's *vardo* (house wagon), pulled out of the column of traveling-show vehicles and headed down the road toward where the doctors lived. My dad grabbed my little brother Tony and me, lifted us up into the back of his work truck, and we took off to follow Hank and Kezia's vardo. Gosh, all we saw as far as the eye could see was farmland filled with row after row of corn and what looked like tall grass.

After going just a short distance, Hank turned off into a wide driveway on the right that ran alongside a large farmhouse. He pulled over just to the side of the farmhouse, jumped out of the vardo and ran around to the front porch. Hank was yelling as he hurried up the steps and knocked kinda frantic-like until a nice lady answered. She came to the edge of the porch and directed us down the road a bit.

Soon enough, we saw a fancy wooden sign that said Duck Farm in beautifully carved lettering. We drove through the large open metal gates and headed down a long paved tree-lined drive that ended at the front of a big old rambling shingle-style house. There was a parking area on the right side of the house, in front of a one-story annex where a sign indicated that this was the place where Dr. Laura Bornstein and Dr. Max Bornstein had their practice.

A nurse took Mom and Kezia back into the examination area, and the rest of us made ourselves comfortable in the waiting room, which was set up like a regular parlor or living room. After a while, Dr. Laura came out to the waiting area and told us that Kezia was resting comfortably but would have to have some help from her and Dr. Max when the baby was on its way.

The French doors on the left side of the room quietly opened, and a very tall young woman, who was like the tallest girl I had ever seen, came into the waiting room. She was light-complected and gangly, and her beautiful thin face was surrounded by wavy bobbed auburn hair. I can still see that face, traced with fine detail into my memory all those years ago. The smiling young woman introduced herself as Esther Bornstein, a niece who had moved to Ohio from Germany to live with her grand-aunt and grand-uncle, Dr. Laura Bornstein and Dr. Max Bornstein.

"Well, you know, this is going to take some time," Miss Esther said. "Don't worry, Mr. George. Your lovely wife is going to have the best of care. Never mind sitting here smoking up a storm and worrying. Won't you let me give you gentlemen and the kiddies a little tour of Duck Farm and show you what makes it so special?"

Off we went on a walking tour of the farmyard and beyond. We headed back through the French doors and navigated through a maze of big and small rooms and zigzagging hallways to the other side of the house. Finally, we were back outside in the bright sunshine.

Wow! It was so noisy! There must have been dozens of pigs in large pens next to a small barn, so many—too many—pigs, goats, and cows, and all sorts of other farm critters. Miss Esther laughed and said, "Well, this is what happens when no one has money to pay for a doctor! Like other doctors in these parts, Auntie Laura and Uncle Max will let folks pay for their services with farm-grown food and livestock. We're Jews, so what we can do with pigs has its limits, definitely!"

I didn't really understand what Miss Esther was getting at, and my dad and Hank just made "I dunno" faces at each other. All I was thinking in my little five-year-old pea brain was that we Gypsies love to eat pit-roasted pig meat every chance we get, for holidays and wakes and whatnot. And here we were, surrounded by a year's worth of pigs, all fat and ready to be roasted. Mmmmmmm!

"We've asked the rabbis in Columbus all sorts of questions about what we can or can't do with the pigs. We know, of course, that we can't eat them. But can we sell them, trade them, or give them away? Is it okay to let the farmer next door, who's not Jewish, take one now and then for food for his family? Not that Mr. Robinson doesn't do that already; and sometimes he takes a truckload to local livestock auctions. But, there's always a lot of pigs left, and what are we supposed to do with them?

"Rabbis are supposed to be smart, and you'd think that they could agree on something, but none of them can come up with an answer that makes any sense. And they argue with one another even when they're trying to tell us what we should do. So we just keep collecting pigs and more pigs. In the meantime, Duck Farm is becoming more of a Pig Farm!" Hank and my dad laughed, then we continued on our walk, heading down a gravel road that ran all neat and tidy through a large fallow field.

I was still too busy fantasizing pit-roasted pork feasts to listen to anything that the Big People were talking about as we made our way through the fields. Years later, my mom told me that after only a short while, the good doctors had given up expecting the squabbling rabbis to ever come up with a solution to their pig problem. The Bornsteins just kept hoping against hope that times would get better, and folks would be able to pay with cash instead of with pigs.

Meanwhile, they looked the other way whenever their neighbor and former tenant farmer, Homer Robinson, backed his big cattle trailer into the farmyard and drove off to the county livestock auction with a load of squealing and groinking piggies.

Miss Esther's aunt and uncle had let our entire procession of Gypsy wagons, trucks, trailers, and cars make camp in an uncultivated field which had large patches of gravel and some little cabins for itinerant farm hands. There was running water, showers, toilets, and a wash house with a couple of old wringer washers and laundry tubs. There was even a large horse-drawn chuck wagon that took meals to the field hands during planting and harvest seasons.

Amish, Mennonite, and Jewish farmers were usually real good about letting Gypsy folks just passing through set up camps in their fields. If the farmers needed any extra manpower for harvesting crops, raising barns, taming horses, or tending livestock—whatever—the Gypsy men were more than willing to lend a hand.

On Saturday nights when there were Gypsies camping in the clearing, Max Bornstein and his sons and friends would pack a horse cart with food, drink, toys for the kiddies, violins, clarinets, accordions, and other musical instruments and head out to the Gypsy camp. The Gypsy men and boys would help build a roaring fire, and all hopped-up on good food and plenty of drink, the Bornsteins and the Gypsies would make music together into the small hours of the new day. Both my dad and Dr. Max were really good musicians, and kept things hopping at the jam sessions, my dad on his guitar or fiddle and Dr. Max on his fiddle.

Sometimes the Gypsies could hear Gypsy riffs in the *klezmer music* (Eastern European Jewish folk melodies) that the Bornsteins and their friends were playing. And now and then, the klezmer guys would hear what sounded like snippets of klezmer rhythms in the Gypsy songs and dances. Even today, when I listen to klezmer music, I can pick up on some of the Gypsy guitar riffs that got added to the klezmer music through the years.

The day after Miss Esther took us on a short tour of Duck Farm, my sister gave birth to a healthy, noisy, and fat baby girl, my niece Nettie. Dr. Max recommended bed rest, and after that, taking it easy for a few days before we started back on the road. My folks had enjoyed meeting the Bornsteins so much that we actually wound up staying a week or so.

My dad and Max Bornstein had hit it off right away, and Dr. Max got really excited when Dad told him that he would leave him a half case of real Canadian whiskey to help him relax after tending to his patients all day. This was during Prohibition, and I guess the local moonshine was pretty awful. Prohibition ended just a few months after our stay at Duck Farm, but by then, Dr. Max had developed a real liking for Canadian whisky.

The day after my niece Nettie was born, Miss Esther offered to show us more of the farm. Hank pulled Tony and me in a small farm wagon, and off we went. We headed through the farmyard and out across the open fields, stopping to check out some of the old stone and shingle buildings that could only be reached after a long hike.

Miss Esther and two of Homer Robinson's daughters, Bessie and May, trudged ahead, outpacing our little group, then turned and waited for us to catch up, slowing down and walking alongside us again as we stumbled along the uneven paths. Hank remarked how well Miss Esther seemed to get along with Gypsy folks. "Oh, you're not the first Gypsy people that I've met!" she shot back.

"Back home in Breslau, my parents often let Gypsies passing through our area bring their wagons and livestock into our fields. I used to sit staring out the window of the classroom that had been set up in our house for my brothers and sisters and me. How I envied the Gypsy kids riding their horses across the fields, the girls' hair blowing in the wind. I could hear their laughter and bright voices from the classroom where I had to study one boring book after another. The Gypsy kids seemed so carefree and happy!

"From time to time, my older brother and sisters and I would take baskets of food and toys down to the Gypsy camps. We felt that we had a lot in common with the Gypsies, since many Christian Germans consider both Jews and Gypsies to be outsiders. There are railway stations with signs on the platforms that say, 'Jews are unwanted here.' And Gypsies as well aren't welcome."

"Golly, Miss Esther," Bessie Robinson said, "that's just *simpy,* (foolish, simple-minded) about those signs, you know? Don't Jewish folks look like everybody else over there? I mean, aren't all of you *white*?" Hank and the other Big People had a good laugh over that!

My sister Kezia was feeling a lot better by the end of the week. The baby was doing fine, not fussy at all, and smiled and made gurgling noises a lot. Miss Esther and Dr. Laura gave Nettie a beautiful layette with little pink ribbons all over the tiny outfits and bibs and whatnot, and they stayed with Nettie whenever Kezia wanted to go out and get some air and explore the gardens at Duck Farm.

We were getting ready to continue on our way to winter quarters, but I'll tell you, I already knew that I was really going to miss Dr. Laura and Dr. Max, the Saturday night get-togethers, Duck Farm, and most of all, Miss Esther. The day before we left Duck Farm and headed to South Carolina, Miss Esther came by our family vardo, carrying a beautifully wrapped flat box. I reached up to grab it, hoping that it didn't contain underwear or socks. Miss Esther giggled and lifted the box up over my head.

"This isn't for you, Mr. Danny. I've spoiled you enough already!" Miss Esther grabbed my hand and said, "Come on, kiddo, let's go see Auntie Flodia. I want to thank her for the beautiful silk flower arrangement she made for the office sitting room. I've never seen anything lovelier!" As we entered Auntie Flodia's workroom, she hopped up and hurried over to grab my free hand. "Oh, Miss Esther, what has the little man done now? Here, I'll take him off your hands. He just needs quiet time."

"Oh, my goodness, Auntie, Danny has been my little treasure. I just came by to thank you for the beautiful flower arrangement you made for the sitting room. This is for you." Miss Esther handed Auntie Flodia the gift box, and Auntie smiled and turned it every which way before she opened it. She took her time, being careful not to tear the fancy gift wrap. "Miss Esther, what beautiful hankies! This embroidery is so good! I love all the pretty flowers! And this is fine Irish linen, the very best there is. You have a good hand, Miss Esther. Thank you, my dear!"

"Oh, Auntie, I didn't do the embroidery. I can barely darn a stocking! I have two left hands unless I'm typewriting or taking shorthand! Auntie Laura, Celia Robinson and I got those handkerchiefs for you over in Columbus. But I feel honored that you think I could sit still long enough to do such beautiful work. That's one reason Mr. Danny and I became such good friends. Us against the world, you might say. We just can't stay still!"

"If you say so, Miss," Auntie Flodia said, looking away. "I tell you one thing. I never seen nobody take so quick to making crepe-paper flowers as Mr. Danny. Show the nice lady, little man, show her the magic that you can do with your hands!" I crawled up onto one of the two chairs that Auntie Flodia brought from the back of her atelier. Miss Esther stood there beside the worktable and watched as I grabbed at the pile of creme-colored crepe paper streamers and quickly made a dozen or so roses of different sizes. She stood there wide-eyed, almost like frozen, and finally grabbed the edge of the worktable and eased herself down into the other chair.

Auntie Flodia fussed over the roses, straightening petals here and there, finally attaching a fine handmade leafy stem to each of the roses. Auntie Flodia arranged the roses into a small bouquet, tied a ribbon around them and wrapped them in a fancy paper doily that looked as if it was made of real lace.

"Here you are, little man! Is pretty bouquet you make for special new friend." I looked up into Auntie's face and grinned as I took the bouquet from her wrinkled and skinny hands. I slid out of my chair and went over to Miss Esther. "Miss, these are for you, for being my good friend and never making me stand in the corner." Auntie Flodia and Miss Esther both laughed, and Miss Esther reached down and gave me the best grown-up hug I'd ever had.

The next morning, before the rooster's crow, we were on the road again, heading toward winter quarters in South Carolina. There would be a lot of hustle and bustle for the Big People to get caught up in: repairs to be made, new theater sets to be built, concession stands to be refitted and repurposed, big-top tryouts, and dinner-theater auditions.

But winter quarters wouldn't be all work and no play: There would be weddings and other carny events, Saturday-night dances, jam sessions, and carny romances for sure. All happening hidden away from the winter outside, under the almost-high-as-the-sky metal zigzag ceilings of the giant old dirigible hangars.

Well, I guess all this was much ado about nothing of interest to a spoiled little boy daydreaming and nightdreaming about his time spent in the company of Miss Esther Bornstein at Duck Farm, in the village of Christiansburg, Champaign County, Ohio.

3

The Trials of Grand-Uncle Stefan

Whenever I look back at everything that happened when I was young, what I remember most is being on the road a lot, often missing school, even after my folks left my Italian grandparents' traveling show when I was eight years old. Good news or bad, a trip planned months ahead or undertaken on a moment's notice, we threw stuff into the back of the work truck and headed off to visit family near or far: to celebrate a wedding, a birth, an anniversary, to visit a sick relative in the hospital, to attend a family member's funeral or his or her *pomana* (memorial meal). And my dad would take me out of school fairly often to go with him to help out on a short-term job somewhere, maybe a blacktop or asphalt job, making lawn furniture, doing the ladder work on an out-of-town awning job—any of these things in order to raise some cash for travel expenses, a family celebration, a new truck, or new trailer.

It was on these trips that I learned a lot about my family's history, customs, and beliefs. I also learned to avoid trying to reason with some really ignoramus family members who often loudly and stupidly argued among themselves about almost everything! My aunties and cousins bickered about Gypsy customs, religion, politics, and anything else they knew very little about. They would debate everything from what happened to the English Gypsy girl who had a 'colored' baby in 1924 to how much bra padding a girl could wear to weddings and other gatherings and still be considered a decent girl. They just seemed to like to hear themselves talk. Like so many other aspects of Gypsy life, some Gypsies' attitudes, beliefs, and opinions—even the ability to get through life without crashing again and again—are often influenced by their ignorance and lack of education.

My folks always tried to stay out of and rise above the many petty arguments, jealousy, gossip, etc. They both made an effort to find out as much as possible about a situation before weighing in on it. My dad especially was very respected in the family and was often asked for advice on how to handle and help settle a difficult or sensitive family matter.

Just a few months after the official end of World War II and our return to Chicago from Oak Ridge, Tennessee, my dad received a phone call from his youngest brother, Vern, who lived in Urbana, Ohio. My grand-uncle Stefan, Mosha Dragosh Miloradovitch's oldest brother, had suffered a series of heart attacks, one after the other in just a few days, and was in a hospital over in Columbus.

Uncle Stefan was a hard-working man. He ran a successful construction business and was also a master woodworker, making fine furniture to order. He was so stubborn that we knew all along that he would never slow down without a little nudge from the Man Upstairs. My mom and dad had already lost more than a few aunts and uncles and cousins in the last few years. My great-grandparents and all of their brothers and sisters had died years ago. Now, it seemed like my great-grandparents' offspring, who had come to America when they were still relatively young, were going pretty fast.

I was on my way out to our work truck when Dad motioned

to me to come and listen in on the phone. Boy, did I get an earful! Uncle Vern sounded pretty upset. "Brother, I apologize for not calling sooner, but we was waitin' for somethin' definite to tell you and the wife. I know that you and Elena would like to be here for Uncle Stefan, and I'm beggin' you to come and be here for me too. The nieces and cousins are drivin' me fuckin' crazy with all of their arguin'. Uncle Stefan and the nurses and doctors are real upset too with all the shenanigans. I can't tell you how many times we've been thrown out of the ward or the whole hospital! The noisy bitches that got us thrown out make all nice and start cryin' and say that they'll be quiet and behave back inside, so the nurses finally give in and let us back in to visit Uncle Stefan. Help me, bro! I'm feelin' munca, doin' real poorly, and I'm afraid that I'm gonna wind up in a hospital bed right soon!"

So Dad left his brother Gheorghe in charge of the awning and lawn furniture business, threw a couple of mattresses, some clothes, pots and pans, and whatnot into the big work truck, and off we went, driving all day to Columbus, Ohio, from Chicago.

Uncle Vern had said to go ahead and stay at Uncle Stefan's place. Some of my cousins, in town to visit Uncle Stefan, had pried open a side door of the large house and crashed upstairs there for a few days before word got back to Uncle Vern. He shooed out the freeloaders, told us the place was a mess from all of the remodeling, but said that we were more than welcome to stay there.

We weren't sure which bedrooms we were supposed to use, so we made do up in the attic, part of which was in the process of being converted into a huge mahogany-paneled billiards room and two large bedrooms, each with a full bath. Uncle Stefan loved billiards—pool, whatever you want to call it—and before he settled down and married Aunt Irene, he had become somewhat of a legend in bars and pool halls throughout the South and Midwest. Uncle Stefan had moved a lot of furniture up to the attic already, so it wasn't hard to get settled in. Other than clothes and such, a lot of stuff we had brought with us from Chicago just stayed in the truck until later.

Aunt Irene was a *gadji*, a non-Gypsy girl, and a nice Jewish girl to boot! Uncle Stefan gave up his wandering, unsettled life on the traveling show circuit shortly after beginning to court Aunt Irene. He soon put down roots in Columbus with his beautiful bride and prospered in his father-in-law's construction business. Aunt Irene helped her mom keep the books and manage the payroll. She and Uncle Stefan were successful because of their hard work and, according to Uncle Stefan, because they were never able to have kids.

Aunt Irene passed away before her folks did. She had been their only child, but they loved Uncle Stefan like a son. When Aunt Irene's dad passed away, Uncle Stefan inherited the beautiful family home and the construction business. He continued for many years to put in long hours on site, at the office, and in his wood-crafting shop.

To me, Uncle Stefan seemed like a pretty calm and collected old guy, but he didn't hide his dislike for the nutcases he crossed paths with at family gatherings. When Aunt Irene was still alive, he would stand next to the dining room doorway after family dinners, shake a few hands, give some of the better-behaved little kids duty pats, then disappear through the doorway and head out to whatever he had been working on in his wood shop.

After Aunt Irene passed away, the family gatherings were few and far between. Uncle Stefan was jealous of the calm and quiet of his home. If someone he didn't like much showed up unannounced, he'd just ignore them and go about his business. I heard stories that if folks just wouldn't go away and kept ringing the doorbell or started banging on the door, Uncle Stefan would pour pans of water down on them from the second floor.

That first evening at Uncle Stefan's, we invited over some of Dad's local family members and friends, planning to head out to the hospital early the next day. Some cousins and my dad's buddies Silky Sam, Oil Can Harry and his wife, Dinka, stopped by. My dad made the ones who'd had a lot to drink stay over. So we dragged the extra mattresses out of the truck and up some pretty steep stairs and plopped them down in the billiards room. We all fell asleep soon enough, warmed by the fire burning quietly in the ornate fireplace, and tired from the long drive and all of the yakking and catching up.

At about 3 a.m., we were all awakened by a loud crash, a deep thud, and what sounded like broken glass hitting the floor. We seen that the huge wall mirror opposite the large bay window had slammed into a table on its way to the floor. Three of us managed to turn over the heavy mirror, only to find dried water splotches all over the back. It looked like the braided picture-hanging wire had rusted in a couple of spots, and had corroded enough to give way under the weight of the heavy mirror.

But we also seen something else: a little piece of paper attached with cellophane tape to the back of the mirror. There it was, in my cousin Luba's second-grade public school stick-letter scrawl: "luba wan dis." "Wow, she must have had help gettin' to the back of the mirror," my little brother Gussie said.

"Naw, mebbe she was filled with the spirit, the spirit of greed," my dad's buddy Oil Can Harry added, and we all had a good laugh. We looked around at one another and didn't need no Vulcan mind-meld to figure out what to do next. We pulled all of the furniture away from the walls, checked out the back of anything hanging on the walls, and, lo and behold, almost every friggin' thing in the room that wasn't nailed or screwed down had one of them little pieces of paper, with either Luba's name, or Brenda's, or Minda's, or Laraine's—four of Uncle Stefan's least favorite grand-nieces!

We shook our heads and laughed. I was tryin' to picture how fat-ass Luba and her shiftless Skinny-Bones-Jones husband, Burl, were gonna get that heavy mirror into their little trailer and hang it without doin' some serious damage to themselves, the mirror, and the trailer.

But not so fast, greedy bitches! We spent a few minutes gathering up all of the little pieces of paper that we could find and plopped them down on top of the old roll-top desk in the corner. "Hey!" Harry called out, grabbing a handful of the paper scraps. "Let's not toss these; how 'bout we mix 'em all up and switch 'em around? Mebbe move some of the furniture, and leave the back of that broken mirrow facing out.

That way when Uncle Stefan gits back home, he'll at least know who was in here messin' with his stuff."

I rummaged around in the roll-top desk drawers and found a couple rolls of cellophane tape. Hyped up on coffee and cola, we mixed up the labels one more time and started taping them back on everything, after adding some "editorial comments" of our own. My brother Gussie came up with a new label for the overstuffed chair: "Luba hopes her big butt will fit in this." Hahahaha! We all had a good laugh and finished sticking the labels back on just before the caffeine buzz wore off.

Early the next morning, when we headed over to see Uncle Stefan and finally found the hospital he was in, it was obvious right away that Gypsies had started to arrive and settle in. There were trailers and rigs of all sizes parked along the road, all jumbled up with cars and delivery vans and trucks. Some folks were already pitching tents on the hospital grounds.

Later that first day, there was quite a commotion when a couple of local cops tried to stop some of the men from digging a pig roasting pit right in the middle of the hospital's front lawn. When we were leaving, I noticed that the same cops were busy helping to set up the cooking area and were dragging tables into the food tents. Two other cops were stripped to the waist and were hauling off the dirt from the fire pits in wheelbarrows. I guess the promise of plenty of good food and a generous *meeta* (bribe) had persuaded the officers to pitch in.

People were tired and hungry after driving all that way and were happy when some of the food was finally ready. By lunch time the next day, even a lot of the doctors and nurses and other hospital workers were lining up for some fine meals of pork, potatoes, vegetables, and fresh-baked bread.

One of Uncle Stefan's nurses told my folks that a doctor had donated two pigs that a farmer over near Urbana gave him for birthing his and his wife's first baby. The good doc had seen a bunch of Gypsy guys digging the fire pits in the hospital's front lawn, and he had a couple of his farm hands slaughter the pigs and bring them over.

I'm not sure that there was medical insurance back then, but many Gypsies were superstitious about any kind of insurance, believing that having it might bring bad luck. Uncle Vern said that Uncle Stefan and Aunt Irene's family were pretty much pay-as-you-go with the doc they went to for anything serious, like broken bones or whatnot. Uncle Vern had given the hospital all of the money in his wallet when Uncle Stefan went in. Even though the hospital admissions lady said not to worry, that they would send a bill at some point, one thing seemed pretty certain to Uncle Vern and my dad: Uncle Stefan wasn't going to get no good care without a lot of money at the ready.

Later, after we had visited Uncle Stefan for a while, Dad got a gang together to make some birch outdoor chairs and tables and other furniture that would be popular with the local swells living in big houses with nice wide front verandas. We set up workshops on the hospital grounds, in the nearby campgrounds, and in the pastures that the Amish, Jewish, and Mennonite farmers opened to us. Despite the groups all over the hospital grounds and camped out in the hospital lobby and hallways, the locals and the visitors were getting along real good.

Some of the menfolk drove around looking for daywork, offering to break in horses and do blacksmith work. Car and truck repairs were also popular. The women and kids went door-to-door in the town, selling all sorts of handmade stuff. I was put to work making paper roses and foliage, which turned out to be real popular when we went peddling.

Anyway, when we finally found the ward where Uncle Stefan was, there seemed to be a lot of high-pitched commotion over by what turned out to be his bed. The menfolk were basically pretty quiet, said their hellos to Uncle Stefan, then quickly moved away and stood or sat at the end of the ward, smoking and quietly talking among themselves.

But it was a whole different story with the womenfolk. They were standing around Uncle Stefan's bed like a hopped-up brood of hens, yelling and talking over one another. A nurse and a couple of orderlies finally approached the gaggle of harpies around Uncle's bed. I'm not sure what the nurse said, but the women quieted down quite a bit. As Uncle Vern, my folks and I approached Uncle Stefan's bed, it looked like he had managed to nod off despite the noise. His eyes were closed, and, to me, anyway, his breathing seemed pretty regular and relaxed.

"Danny, it's been terrible awful," Uncle Vern said, getting up on his tippy toes to whisper in my right ear. "You missed the worst part. The nurses and orderlies threw all of us out for a couple of hours! The ladies was just all talking at once. Luba got so excited that she dropped a lit match, one of them big ones, on Uncle's bed covers and almost set him on fire! I can't believe they let that bitch back in!

"Jeez," Uncle Vern continued, straightening up. "Here we go again." The ladies were starting to talk loud again, and mill around, bumping into each other and Uncle Stefan's bed, which I guess nobody had locked the wheels on, because it slammed into a chair, then hit the wall. Cousin Laraine was the loudest. That shrill voice of hers cut right to the bone, just like when the nuns in grammar school used to scrape the chalkboard with their fingernails to quiet us down. So Uncle Vern asked Cousin Laraine to pipe down, for Uncle Stefan's sake.

"You shut your trap, Vern Miller!" Cousin Laraine snapped back, "You can't order me around. You ain't my fadder, and I don't take crap from my husband, you, or anybody else!"

"Say, Cousin Laraine," Cousin Flodia chimed in, "I like them mules you wearing. Where'd you get 'em?"

"At Monkey Wards in Nashville."

"That ain't right, Laraine. You got 'em at the Hebrew department store," Cousin Totie said. "I was with you."

"No you wasn't, and these is new mules. You went with me just that one time to Monkey Wards when I got me some new house slippers. I told Henry to buy me some decent house slippers, but instead, he bought me a flimsy robe that made me look like a Nashville floozy."

"No, I was with you, Laraine," Cousin Totie insisted. "I told you your dog would go after them little dangly thangs on them mules. And he did! He chewed up both them mules, made a meal out of 'em. That's why we went back with Cousin Tanya and bought these here new ones, after the dog chewed up the first pair."

Cousin Totie went on and on. "And I remember it was the big Hebrew department store 'cause Cousin Tanya and I was lookin' at the folks workin' there and checkin' out how big some people's nose was. We was playin' 'Who's a Jew?' "

Laraine poked at the air with a bony finger. "I remember now! On the way back home, we stopped at Piggly Wiggly to buy us some roasting chickens. They was a buck each, and I had to borry thirty cent from Tanya. Jeez Louise, I thought she'd never let me forget that. Told folks my kids would starve if it wasn't for her!"

"No, Sister," Lizzie interrupted, "we was at Winn-Dixie, and them scrawny little roasters was fifty cent a pound. Highway robbery! And I told him as much."

"Who, Sister?"

"Who d'ya think? That fat Wop butcher at Winn-Dixie who's always makin' eyes at me. I told him where he could shove them fifty-cent-a-pound chickens!"

"But, Cousin, wasn't we over at Hills?" Cousin Genta asked.

"No," Totie snarled, "we was at Piggly Wiggly, and them roasters was a dollar twenty-five for the bigger ones."

"Cousin, them roasters was two for two bucks."

"No, Sister, that was for the big Cornish hens," Aunt Margie shouted, pushing her way to the front of the group.

Cousin Genta chimed in, "Ain't no such thing as a *big* Cornish hen. They's all little."

"Aargh!" All of a sudden, Uncle Stefan jerked upright in the bed, moaned loudly, then started yelling at the women to get the hell out. Some nurses ran over with a couple of orderlies and pushed all of us out into the hallway. The women were banished from the ward until they calmed down and were ready to "act like ladies" and promised, again, not to make another ruckus.

Well, my mom and dad explained to the nurses who we were, and how far we had come to see Uncle Stefan. We promised to just sit quietly with him, so they let us go back into the ward. When Uncle looked up and saw my mom and dad and me and my little brother Gussie, his face lit up. He was speaking so softly that I couldn't hear what he was saying, but he seemed really glad to see us. Every once in a while, we'd hear a commotion out in the hallway, and we could see Luba and Laraine and the other banty hens taking turns to look in through the little round windows on the doors that opened into the ward.

Uncle Stefan actually propped himself up in bed to have some of the food we had brought, to talk, and tell us how he wound up in the hospital with chest pains. I sat there, finally settling in enough to try to read from one of the books I had brought along. Gussie tried to crawl up onto Uncle Stefan's bed, but Uncle reached over and started rubbing Gussie's head, and my brother seemed happy enough with the attention.

Uncle Stefan was talking quietly with my folks when I heard a noise outside. I looked up at the little window above Uncle's bed, and I saw a face appear, disappear, appear, disappear, over and over. "Uncle Stefan, Uncle Stefan, don't die . . . until you . . . accept . . . Jesus . . . Uncle Stefan . . . ." It was my teenage cousin, Lettie, hopping up and down outside, trying to see her Uncle Stefan.

"What the hell is that damned racket," Uncle Stefan asked, upset by Lettie's yelling. He suddenly turned all gray, his eyes rolled up, and he fell back against the pillows. All of a sudden, a half-dozen or so of my female relatives rushed in, like ants pouring through a crack, and took turns grabbing Uncle Stefan by the shoulders, shaking him, screaming, "Uncle, Uncle, accept Jesus, accept Jesus as your savior! Do you accept Jesus? Just say it, Uncle." He finally stirred, half opened his eyes, started mumbling in Romani, then English. "Yessiree! I love my savior Jesus."

Hearing those magical words, the harpies pulled away from Uncle Stefan's bedside and flew out of the ward as quickly as they had come in.

"Uncle Stefan," my dad said, "are you ok?"

"Hell, yes," Uncle blurted out. "You know that I don't believe in all that religion bullshit! I just said what I had to, to get those crazy bitches outta my face!"

Finally, a nurse and two orderlies showed up, began checking out Uncle Stefan, and politely asked us to please wait outside. We went out to the lobby and ran into the noisy group of bushy-haired cousins who had "saved" Uncle Stefan, talking excitedly over one another in a fog of cigarette smoke.

"Danny," Cousin Luba screeched, flicking her cigarette ash vigorously in my direction, "Uncle Stefan is saved now, so . . . ."

"So?" I said loudly, almost like a challenge.

"So, he can go ahead and die now, and he'll be met at heaven's gate by our Lord Jesus," she said, as if she was explaining something to a little kid. "I mean, I hope he *don't* die this time around, but if he does, he'll be with Jesus for all eternity. Yesiree. Praise Jesus!"

Fuckin' bitch, I thought. *She's probably already figuring out how to get that heavy mirror and her lard-ass through the trailer doorway at the same time.*

I had never liked Luba. She smelled like an ashtray, or onions, or burnt garlic. Sometimes she just smelled, period. Luba was probably one of the first bigots I ever met. Most Gypsy folks have a live-and-let-live attitude. We do kinda divide everyone into Gypsy and gadjo, probably because dealing with gadje through the centuries has often been a painful experience. Still, most Gypsies like to get to know a non-Gypsy as an individual and not judge him or her based on some stereotype.

Luba stood out from most other Gypsies. She was a loud bigot, often using the n-word to refer to anyone—white or black, Gypsy or gadjo—that she didn't like. And, she practiced an equal-opportunity bigotry: If you dared to disagree with something she'd said, she would be on you, pointing a pudgy finger in your face, screeching, "You Jew!" Nice, huh?

Luba was vain, selfish, and self-centered, always talking about someday joining the Grand Ole Opry and being a big star. What money she didn't spend on cheap cosmetics or illegal drugs, she squandered on voice lessons. I still cringe when I remember the time her dad played back a wire recording of her screeching her way through "Pistol Packin' Momma."

My dislike for Luba became outright hatred about three months after this particular trip to Columbus. Luba's nana Vadoma was visiting Luba's folks at the time. Luba needed to get high, and she needed to get her hands on some money real quick. Well, her folks were out when she got home, so Luba asked her nana for some money. The old lady said no. Luba asked again, screaming at her nana. Again, Nana Vadoma said no and started to turn away. Luba grabbed her nana's jewelry box off of the chest of drawers, hit the old lady in the face with it, pulled her by her hair into the entryway, then pushed her backwards—hard—out the trailer's open front door. Nana Vadoma tumbled down the long run of steps and onto the cement pavement far below.

Folks said that every bone in her body was broke, but truth be known, Nana Vadoma had been knocked out, broke an arm, a hip, and both legs in the fall and would never sit up or walk again. After the few surgeries Nana Vadoma could have at her advanced age, she wound up back at her own trailer home, unable to talk, with a nurse and grandkids to do for her until she passed away quietly in her sleep just a few months after the "accident."

Luba's lover, Timbo Stanley, told me and my folks exactly what Luba had done to poor Nana Vadoma, how Luba had hit her and pushed her out the trailer door. When Luba got high on drugs with Timbo, she told him about what she had done, and how much money she got from the "Jew pawnbroker" for her nana's jewelry. Timbo told the story to some of his buddies, who told their wives and girlfriends. That got the trailer camp rumor-mill going. Now, that pawnbroker was an honest and decent old guy. He called the sheriff and told the deputies that he suspected the jewelry was stolen. So Luba had her fat ass thrown in jail, charged with grand theft.

It's a sad fact that we Gypsies will say or do almost anything to keep our kids out of jail or get them back home. In this case, Luba's folks swore to the sheriff that Nana Vadoma had given the jewelry to Luba as an engagement gift. The old lady had surprised a thief in the trailer, cried out for help, and Luba came into the trailer's front room just in time to see the would-be burglar push Nana Vadoma out the front door. Nana Vadoma, of course, never recovered enough for the police to question her.

Luba getting off scot-free is an example of what can happen when honest and upright folks don't let their kids face the consequences of their bad actions. I know that there were occasions when I was growing up when a son or daughter would do something illegal, like let's say steal a truck, and the family would have a meeting to decide which of the older Gypsies would take the rap so that the young person charged with the crime could continue working and making money for the family.

Back to my story: Over the next few years, Uncle Stefan was hospitalized half a dozen times, and family groups would show up from all over whenever they thought that it might be the last chance to get on Uncle Stefan's good side. Finally, one terrible hot summer, Uncle Stefan took real sick real fast. His housekeeper called the doctor, but Uncle Stefan passed away before old Doc Campbell got there.

A week or so before the funeral, the early birds had already started preparing for the hundreds of people that were expected to come and pay their respects to Uncle Stefan. The clans pretty much took over the grounds of the capital's largest funeral home, set up camp in the large lounge areas inside, and pitched tents and parked their trucks and trailers on the beautifully landscaped grounds.

Family groups took turns holding vigil next to Uncle Stefan's open coffin. Gypsies trickled in from all over the U.S. and Canada to pay their respects. The local family members put on a feast that lasted over a week. Pigs were roasted in open pits that the men dug on the front lawn of the funeral parlor. Soon, wonderful and exotic aromas filled the air and the interior of the funeral home as well. We heard later from one of the maintenance men there that the owners had to pay to have the premises fumigated after the last pig carcass had been hauled away.

Just before Uncle Stefan was buried, some of the old-school Gypsies dropped paper money and loaves of bread into his coffin, along with cartons of cigarettes and bottles of Canadian whiskey that some cousins from Canada had brought down with them. Uncle Stefan had developed a taste for Canadian whiskey during Prohibition, and he still preferred it to U.S. whiskey, which he called "hillbilly hooch."

Uncle Stefan's gravesite was overflowing with flowers, fancy floral tributes of all shapes and sizes, and big and small wood-crafted items, everything from brightly painted wooden toys to heirloom furniture and beautifully carved artwork. The handmade items had been brought to Uncle Stefan's gravesite by his wood-crafting students from the local youth center. Not a lot of the younger guys in his own family appreciated his skills, so he had taken some local kids under his wing.

As Uncle Stefan's coffin was about to be lowered into the grave, a gratingly familiar female voice in the rear of the huddle of close family members cried out, "No, no, no! Jeezus, don't take my uncle!" Cousin Luba pushed through the mourners and threw herself on top of the coffin. "Take *me*, take *me*, take *me*!" Well, we pried her off of the coffin three or four times, trying to avoid her flailing arms and wild kicking.

On the final attempt to pull and push Luba off of the coffin, someone with a deep, resonant voice shouted from the middle of the crowd of mourners: "By God, leave the bitch! Bury her with my cousin and let's get in out of the heat!" Grand-Uncle Remo had no patience for fools and their mischief. Cousin Luba was finally dragged—sobbing and wailing and dabbing at her melting makeup—back into the crowd of mourners, and Uncle Stefan was at last lowered into his final resting place, next to his beloved Irene.

A Gypsy funeral isn't the final event to honor the deceased

and mourn his or her passing. It marks the beginning of a period of mourning observed according to each Gypsy clan's particular customs. My family always holds a *pomana*, a last supper (funeral feast or memorial meal) right after the funeral, also on the anniversary of the deceased's death, and on the first Saturday of November. Other Gypsy clans do a pomana for the deceased every so many weeks or months for a year or so after his or her death and then hold a last supper every early November. How often, how, and when each family celebrates the pomana depends on where in the Old Country the family is from. Weather permitting, the pomana is usually held outdoors and features food of every description: roasted meats, vegetables, fruits, nuts, all kinds of fancy breads, pastries, and desserts.

Some superstitious folks believe that if the deceased's spirit sees any leftover food lying around, he or she might think that not enough people showed up and might just hang around long enough to put a curse on whoever planned the last supper. So any leftover food is quickly wrapped up and later taken home by the family members and friends who have gathered to honor the deceased.

In our family, someone—usually the surviving spouse or oldest daughter—buys and brings to the funeral feast a complete outfit in the deceased's size. Like maybe a nice suit, belt, shirt, socks, and shoes for a man; dressy dress, coat, shoes, and accessories if the deceased is a woman. At the end of the pomana, the immediate family chooses by lot the person of the same sex as the deceased who they feel was most loved, respected, and admired by their dearly departed. Then, that person is presented with the outfit.

A few weeks after we buried Uncle Stefan, the cops were called to the cemetery when workers there discovered that Uncle's coffin had been dug up, and the money, booze, and cigarettes had been taken. Local family members were called to the scene and they were feeling munca that somebody would do such a thing.

My folks and I figured that the prime suspects were some young English Gypsies that traveled around the U.S. and Canada attending Gypsy funerals, weddings, and other special community events. They had been caught more than a few times picking pockets and stealing money, smokes, and booze from unsealed coffins. I'd seen some of these good-for-nothings lurking in the back of the crowd at Uncle Stefan's funeral, smirking and poking at one another, laughing their broken little airplane-glue-fueled laughs until they were chased away.

Turns out that the bad guys were closer to home! After receiving some anonymous tips, delivered over the phone in heavily-accented English, the local sheriff, who was a good friend and former student of Uncle Stefan's, chased down and arrested the true culprits. They were local Romanian Gypsy guys, our very own cousins, who had already spent a lot of the stolen money on dope and hookers. As far as we were concerned, they were grave robbers, plain and simple, just like in the olden days in the Land of the Pharaohs!

4

Lena

I had lived in Chicago on and off since I was eight years old, when my mom's parents, Rosa and Manfri Vano, retired from their traveling theater, and my parents took us kids back home to Chicago. I lived there longer than anywhere else, and when we were on the road, Chicago was usually the place we went home to.

My life was about to go off in a whole new direction. My mom and dad announced over dinner one evening that they were thinking of leaving Chicago and going on the road again for a while with the Sherman Bros. Carnival. My cousin John's wife, Mabel, had written to my folks and asked if they would be willing to go back on the road one last time to help her and her daughter, Lena, deal with a difficult family situation.

My cousin John had developed a serious drinking problem and was going to lose his job if he didn't quit boozing. He had been verbally and physically abusive to Mabel and Lena, and Mabel said that she was at her wits' end. My dad and John had once been so close that they were more like father and son, so we weren't surprised that Mabel would ask my dad for help.

This came at a time when my dad had been getting itchy feet and was talking about taking the family back on the road for a spell. We had returned to Chicago from Oak Ridge, Tennessee, right after the war, and already my dad was unhappy living in the big city. He really missed the close-knit extended-family life we had in Oak Ridge, and the camaraderie, changing surroundings, and unique experiences of life on the road.

We lived in a trailer park inside the Oak Ridge compound, made some good friends there and reconnected with some of my dad's cousins who I had never met. And that was where my sister Edie met her fiancé, Pete Foad. Dad was getting up there in years, but he was still strong as an ox, and he thought that this might be his last chance to live a traditional traveling-show life.

My dad called his old pal Johnny Anderson, who was a top Sherman Bros. talent recruiter. Dad told Johnny that he just couldn't adjust to settled life such as it was in a big noisy and dirty city like Chicago, and that he was hoping to go back on the road for awhile to help his cousin John through a rough period.

Dad had a good reputation with the Sherman Bros. organization as a master carpenter, woodworker, mechanic, rigger, and canvas maintenance guy. Rumor was that there was nothing broke that he couldn't fix. He was respected for his hard work and ability to take charge of just about any job.

Johnny said that Dad's carpentry and mechanical skills were more in demand than ever, and he offered Dad a job on the spot. Johnny told my dad that since my brothers and I were now older, we could work with Dad, gain experience in a trade, and be paid to boot! Everything was official and settled real tidy-like with the Sherman Bros. by the end of that same day.

Me and my brothers and my younger sisters, Rosie and Edie, were sitting around the table after finishing dinner, listening to what our folks had to say about going back on the road for a spell. Dad asked if we were ok with the plan. It sounded like a no-brainer to me and my brothers and sisters! We all said that we missed life on the road and were looking forward to helping Cousin John and his family. It would be no big deal for Uncle

Gheorghe and Aunt Ina to run the family awning and outdoor furniture business by themselves.

Traveling shows were nothing new to me. I had spent the first eight years of my life crisscrossing America with my family in *Nonna* (Grandmother) and *Nonno* (Grandfather) Vano's traveling theater company. When my grandparents retired, my uncle Benno took over managing the show.

When I was almost thirteen, I went back on the road with the family's traveling theater, which now had a "bonnyfied" traveling teacher to keep kids up to speed with their studies while they were on the road. Uncle Benno remembered how good I was at making flowers even as a little kid, and right away he put me to work making flowers and decorating willow trees to be used in whatever kind of production we were putting on. Later on, he put me to work building sets, a skill that came in handy later on in my career as a display guy when I had the opportunity to branch out into broadcast and theatrical set design.

The only downside to working for my uncle was that I got a crush on Peggy Weco, an older *Rumneechel* (*Romanichal,* English Romani) girl who taught me how to smoke cigarettes and how to make out. She was pretty advanced for a fourteen-year-old girl! I guess the whole thing was kinda one-sided, because when I was getting ready to ask Peggy to be my gal, she up and eloped with a twenty-five-year-old guy. Anyway, I was so discouraged and upset that I screwed up my work a lot, and Uncle Benno sent me packing back to my family in Chicago.

This time around, we were all counting on enjoying our time on the road. Now that my brothers and sisters and I were older and had already graduated from the eighth grade, my folks would no longer have to worry like last time about our schooling while we were on the road.

Boy, it sure was a different story when I was younger and we were on the road with my Nonna and Nonno's theater company! The states we traveled through had different laws about when kids had to start school and how old they had to be before dropping out. School districts trying to impose their regulations on Gypsy folks was a big deal and was one of the biggest sources of friction between Gypsies on the road and the gadje. All of the paperwork and rigmarole really upset my grandparents and was one reason they decided to retire when they did.

Some carnivals and circuses subscribed to correspondence courses that were taught by carny volunteers. Some outfits employed full-time traveling teachers. The largest traveling shows though were like cities on the move and had their own schools, just like they had stores, restaurants, and post and telegraph offices. Our outfit was pretty small, and it was often difficult to find a qualified teacher willing to spend more than a half-year or so on the road for not a lot of money.

School districts got paid for every student they enrolled, and the school-age kids in the traveling shows were easy pickins. The gadje couldn't have cared less about educating Gypsy kids; they just wanted the bucks. In some places, especially in the South, a little money changing hands would get rid of the school district inspectors or truant officers who showed up where we were setting up.

Sometimes, the inspectors wanted to know the qualifications of whoever was teaching. But more often, they were interested in where any school age kids had been born, what schools we had attended, and for how long. They asked for our birth certificates, report cards, and other documentation that a lot of Gypsies just didn't have, at least with them on the road. I guess the paperwork was on file somewhere, but my folks didn't know where or how to get their hands on it. I was the first of my siblings to be born in a hospital—in Columbus, Ohio—but I had never even seen my birth certificate. My oldest sister, Kezia, had a baptismal certificate signed by a priest, and at one point she had to sign a declaration that she had seen me being baptized.

Gypsies have always had a hard time dealing with outside authority and laws that just don't seem to make sense to us. *Nebun* (Romani word meaning crazy or crazy person) is a word I heard often as a kid after someone had an unpleasant encounter with an authority figure from the gadjo world.

When Nonna and Nonno retired, my parents weren't interested in taking on all of the hassles involved in managing a traveling theater. They decided to leave the road, go back to Chicago and live a settled life there with my grandparents. My dad went back into the awning and lawn furniture business with his brother Gheorghe, putting to good use the many skills he brought from his years on the road.

Now we were finishing up loading everything onto our brand-spanking-new Ford truck and into Uncle Gheorghe's big van. We got a late start, but were finally on our way, heading out to meet the traveling show in Wichita, Kansas, where there was a snazzy new trailer waiting to become our new home on the road.

When we finally arrived in Wichita, we checked out our new digs and immediately started to unpack. My dad especially was real anxious to get settled in and was ordering everyone around. Uncle Gheorghe was outside unloading his van when we heard a knock on the front door. "Hey, Brother," my dad yelled out, "why'd you let the door close? I told you that I gotta fix the lock!" Suddenly a woman's voice rang out, "Well, next time I got an armload of home-baked goodies for youse, I'll send youse a telegram!" It was Mabel, my cousin John's wife, carrying a thermos bottle and a basket of what looked to be a loaf of bread, muffins, and little cakes.

Mabel half-tripped into the trailer's front room, helped inside by a young woman standing in the shadow cast by the bright light streaming through the doorway. She stepped into the light—and my God—the young woman was Mabel's daughter, Lena! She had matured so much since the last time I had seen her. I stood there staring at her, unable to move. Wow, Lena was all grown up: real pretty, slimmer, her long hair pulled back in a bun. She glanced over at me, her face all skewed, like she was looking at a picture hung crooked on the wall. "Well, Danny Miller," Lena said real blunt-like, "you'd make a better closed door than an open one. You're blocking our way!" She brushed by, and gave me the first of many disapproving schoolmarm looks that she would send my way in the years to come.

Mabel sidled up to me, pinched my cheek, handed me a pastry, and grabbed Lena around the waist. "Not bad, huh? My little girl has become a real *chi shugra* (pretty Romani girl). Lena came in a few weeks ago from my ex's place in Norfolk, Virginia, and she's going to be traveling with us for a while. John is still a real handful, and all we can do for him is to try and calm him down and keep his belly full so he don't wander off to tie one on. The manager says we've got one last chance to fix John, git him sober, or he's gonna have to let him go. Right now, John is pretty much useless, and the manager needs every able-bodied man and woman to help get the carnival to Covington."

Lena smiled and said, "And you, Mr. Danny Miller, can close your mouth and stop gawking at me. Then, I might even say that I'm glad to see you! You sure are a hit with my mom! She's told me over and over about your mom and dad bragging how handy you've become doing carpentry and fixing things, and she can't wait for you to get started here. I just remember how good you are at making flowers and all."

"Glad to see you again, Lena," I stuttered out. Lena rolled her eyes and turned back to the kitchen counter, cutting what looked to be garlic bread into thick chunks.

Mabel plopped down in a kitchen chair, nervously lit a cigarette, and sighed real loud, "Thank the good Lord you folks are here! Lena and I have had our hands full with the twins and trying to keep an eye on John. He's having a horrible bad time coming down off of the booze. I don't know what we would've done if you folks hadn't dropped everything and offered to come along and help us."

"Well, Mabel," my dad said in his relaxed way, "we're glad to be here with you. We're looking forward to leaving city life behind for a spell. Never could get used to all the noise, the traffic, and the rude gadje. Carnies are so different. We've been missing the kinship and the road. We just thought it was about time to get back into things."

My mom managed to give a little smile when she heard that. She was probably going to miss the city a lot. She had quite a few non-Gypsy lady friends and had seemed at home in the city. "Oh, Mabel," she added, leaning over and giving Mabel a big hug, "we're all family, and me and Tom and Danny are here to help youse. John and Tom used to be so close; they'll get close again, and we'll help John find his way."

"The twins will be wanting their bottles when they wake up," Lena announced impatiently. "So I'm heading home. Nice seeing you again, Danny. Drop by sometime for some of my mom's delicious home cooking! You can come tonight with your folks, if you promise not to stare at me with your mouth open like I'm a Martian or something."

Lena hurried by me, dropping another pastry into my hand. And that was that: my first encounter with the newly-beautiful and still-sassy Miss Lena Boswell!

Well, this was our last venue before heading out to Covington, Louisiana, for winter quartering. Because of the rain, not all of the carnies liked the idea of spending the winter in Louisiana. But a bunch of people had a lot of work to do on their concession stands and on the carnival rides, and Covington was the best place to do the repair work. There were huge barns on the fairgrounds where we could pull our rigs right into the work area. At one time, in the 1930s, it was a circus grounds. That's why all these huge buildings were built. They could actually set up the big tops inside these buildings to repair the canvas, and there were heat flues for the trailer heaters and sewer drains leading outside to the sewer system. So most of the trailer homes were parked in these barns. There were about six of these big buildings especially for the trailer homes. The remaining barns housed workspaces.

In Covington, it rained more than it didn't! My cousin John's trailer was in a barn several buildings away, so I didn't really get to see my buddies too often. Buddy is what Mabel would call me, as in "Hey, buddy, come with your folks in the morning and have breakfast with us." My folks spent a lot of time over at Mabel and John's: cooking, talking, playing with the twins, keeping an eye on John. Usually, the only time I saw Mabel was when we ran into each other at a food market in town, at dances or parties, or at family gatherings.

We'd been in Covington for about three weeks or so, and I felt that I was finally making real progress on the *pan joint* (gambling booth) that I had been working on. One morning, Lena showed up out of the blue at my workshop. "Hey, Danny! My mother wants you to come over tonight at about six o'clock and help her carry a couple of planks of food over to your place. She's making old-fashioned lasagna the way your mom taught her. She'll have a big old heavy iron pot for you to carry. Don't eat no supper today! It's a surprise for your mom, so don't say nothing and don't drop the pot with your dinner in it. Hahahahaha! You know you're kinda clumsy!" With that, she grinned, turned, and walked quickly away from the work area.

I headed over to Mabel and John's a little before six. When I was leaving our trailer, my mom was just starting to sort through some potatoes, so I thought for a moment that maybe I should say something about the surprise dinner. But then I decided that I didn't need Lena on my back again, this time for ruining Mabel's surprise of an authentic old-fashioned Italian lasagna dinner.

About a quarter after six o'clock, Mabel and I made our way into my mom's kitchen, arms overflowing with food gifts. "Here, Aunt. You don't have to cook tonight," Mabel said with a big smile. "I hope that you'll enjoy the old-fashioned lasagna that you showed me how to make a while back. I had to go to three food markets to find everything!"

My mom had a big toothy grin on her face as she watched us plop the food containers down on the counter top. She had a knife in her hand, ready to chop up some green peppers. "Oh, thank you, Mabel! You saved the day! I'm just so tired! I went shopping today with Cousin Sylvia to buy some bridesmaids' gowns for Edie's wedding. We started hitting the shops at ten o'clock and we didn't get home until after three-thirty. We still didn't find everything that the girls wanted. Ready-made was hard to find. One shop had two dresses that the girls liked, so they'll have two more coming in a few days from New York City."

"Does Edie have her bride's gown yet?" Mabel asked.

"Cousin Florence is making her gown and the matron's gown," my mom said, and added, "Flo's the best at what she does."

Then my mom and Mabel started talking a mile a minute about my sister Edie's upcoming wedding, which is about all they had talked about since my family had gone back on the road. Yikes! That's when I got up to leave, and Mabel said, "Hey, buddy, don't wander too far away and lose track of time! We're gonna be eatin' in half an hour or so. Well, I gotta git on home and help Lena git the twins ready to come over." Then she turned to my mom and said with a big smile, "Auntie, I'm gonna adopt your son. He's already done so much for me and John. Danny and John are already more like brothers than cousins. I don't see him much, but he's been helping John rehab a new joint. Oh, I almost forgot, Auntie Elena! I got you some dried olives too!"

"Well, you know they're my favorites, Mabel dear," my mom said. "Thank you so much!"

I was excited about dinner and seeing Lena again, so I hurried back over to my workshop to find some sketches I'd forgotten to take home. I closed up and started home after just a quarter hour or so. When I was almost home, I saw Mabel and Lena coming into our barn. Mabel was carrying what looked like even more food. Lena was pulling a big red wagon behind her that was carrying the twins and their high chairs. They didn't see me, so I scooted up our back steps. I had just closed the back door when my mom said, "That Mabel sure likes you, Danny! She said that she wishes you would get sweet on her Lena."

Then I shot back, "Oh, Ma! Lena's my cousin!"

"She's not your cousin. She's Mabel's daughter. Mabel is married to your cousin John, but she ain't your cousin, and Lena ain't either. Remember that, Danny."

I nodded, paused for a few seconds, then added, "Well, I take her for my cousin."

My mom did her famous "I give up!" routine: sad-sack face, flailing arms and all, and said real impatient like, "She's a nice girl, Danny. She speaks her mind. You always know what she's thinking, not like some girls. Well, hurry up and change out of them dirty clothes. Mabel and Lena will be here any minute with the twins!"

I finished washing up, put on some dress slacks and a nice shirt, and headed back to the kitchen. "Danny, you're late," Mabel announced as she was helping my mom set the table.

"John's working on somebody's joint with your dad. He'll eat later tonight. Your dad should be on his way home to eat with us though. John really don't stop to eat. That's one bad habit he still has. But better working late than out drinking. So far, so good. He's doing fine, thanks mainly to your dad. What's important is that he's stopped drinking." Mabel put some plates of food down in front of the twins, turned to me and said, "Boy, these guys are really growing fast. Seein' them out like this, they look like they're ready to go to school! I don't want them to grow up that fast. I want them to stay toddlers for quite a spell!"

Then Lena came in, turned to me, and said, "Danny, we sure do miss you! We just don't see you all that much." I looked at her. She had her hair up in a bun. How beautiful and mature she looked! How strange I felt all of a sudden. I stood there staring at her, and I saw her notice and turn away.

During dinner, I tried to make eye contact with Lena. Sometimes she returned my gaze; other times she would suddenly break eye contact to get up from her chair to go around the table to sort out whatever the twins were up to instead of eating. As we ate, Mabel said that she and Lena and John were so fortunate that my family had come to help straighten John out. "Life's been such a pleasure since youse has come back to us," Mabel said, and continued, "What booze can do outta some folks! John's as he used to be years and years ago. I feel so blessed!"

The twins had finished eating. Their highchair trays looked like little war zones, with pieces of food all over. Lena showed me how to put the twins back into the cribs that Uncle Gheorghe had brought on his last trip from Chicago, and she told me to always make sure that the sides were latched and secure.

Mabel fired up the coffee maker and served some spumoni.

Every once in a while, I caught Lena looking over at me. Our eyes would meet, and she'd smile and look back down at her plate. I finished the spumoni, downed the last of my little cup of coffee, and excused myself to head off to bed early. I said my adoos and thanked Lena and Mabel for the wonderful dinner and homemade dessert.

As I crawled under the covers that night, I kept visualizing Lena's beautiful face and her classy, grownup hairdo. Gosh, what was going on? I had never thought about my former girlfriend, Peggy, this way. Could I possibly be falling for Lena? As I slept, images of Lena's beautiful face and that hairdo popped up over and over in my dreams.

I guess it was about 5 a.m. when I woke up from a dream of Lena wearing one of the bridesmaid dresses that my mom had brought home. Well, not a real dream, I guess. It was more like a series of little flash pictures. Lena's face and hair were so beautiful as she walked toward me, reaching out for my hand. I tried to fall back asleep to find out what that dream was all about. I know for a fact that I did fall back asleep, because my dad woke me up. "Hey!" he said real loud. "Get out of bed *now*! We gotta go into New Orleans this morning. Son, it's not like you to be getting up so late!"

No, it wasn't like me at all. I usually got up around seven, sometimes at the crack of dawn, other times around six o'clock. But this time around, I really slept. Boy, did I sleep, almost like Lena was pulling me back to sleep and back into those dreams of her wearing what was now a wedding gown, her glistening hair pulled back into a bun. Well, those were just glimpses I had of Lena, outlines of her figure and face and hair, more like unfinished sketches. I knew that the bridesmaid dress had become a wedding gown, but I couldn't even remember what color it was. All I remembered from these dreams was that Lena looked so lovely, so mature.

All the way to New Orleans, I kept thinking about this dream. Finally, my dad said, "Son, you're not saying much. You look like you're daydreaming." Little did he know that I really was. I was thinking to myself: *Could I be falling in love? Do I really know the difference between love and a crush? Do I know what love is? I think I can feel it.* I'd been around a lot of different girls at family gatherings and carnival events. But after getting burned by Peggy Weco, I hadn't focused on any one girl or even thought about girls that much. I was much happier just working with my dad and brothers, doing carpentry, painting, and refitting concession stands.

When I did go out, it was always in a group with my male cousins. None of us ever tried to take advantage of the girls we were with. Sometimes, when there weren't any girls around, the conversations got a little scorchy. When the other guys started talking about sex and masturbation, I just threw it to the wind.

One evening, while we were just goofing around, an older guy took me aside and said, "You don't talk about girls or sex or things like jerking off. I noticed one time when I saw you at the urinal that you're not circumcised. Maybe that's what's wrong with you, why you don't get no sexual feelings." Well, I just brushed that aside at the time, but now and then, I would think about what he said.

Whenever I had urges and got an erection, I really didn't understand what was going on. I didn't have the nerve to ask my dad, my brothers or cousins. My uncle Yanko, one of my dad's younger cousins, used to answer all of my sex questions patiently and matter of factly, but he died suddenly just before the war.

My very first orgasm happened just three days before my fifteenth birthday, in 1943, when we were doing construction work for the United States government in Oak Ridge, Tennessee. One morning when I got an erection, it was a lot larger and harder than ever before. It stayed real big and hard for so long that I was afraid it might damage my penis. I just started playing with the erection as I had seen other guys do in the showers, when they would talk dirty and get hard and masturbate.

It didn't take long for something to happen. My erection was pulsating when I put my hand on it. I felt my testicles swell up, and all of a sudden, this sticky fluid shot out of my penis. It felt so strange, and it felt really good. I was hoping that everything was still ok down there, and that I hadn't done nothing to hurt myself. On the other hand, maybe keeping that stuff inside when it needs to come out could cause problems too. Again, other than the older guys, who a lot of times just made stuff up, I didn't have no one to talk to about all this.

I found out later that—at almost fifteen years old—I was a late bloomer, and a lot of boys reach puberty before they are even twelve years old. I also found out later that I had very low testosterone. A lot of guys who used to brag about their sexual adventures were amazed that I was still a virgin. "Man," my friend Willy said once, "dat ain't good. So many *gadja* (non-Romani girls or women) out there are just givin' it away. We gotta git you some o' dat!"

As Dad and I were returning from New Orleans, I was getting aroused more than ever before. I was really glad when my dad pulled into a service station to get gas. I ran to the outhouse and relieved myself, masturbating like never before, with even more semen than before. Now, I can't even remember what made me get all aroused.

We got home kinda late, but I still had some work to finish up in my workshop. I was tired from the long day and couldn't focus on what I was doing. So I closed up early and started dragging my sore body home. As I was heading out, Cousin John came over to me. We talked a bit about this and that, and Cousin John grinned when I said, "Cousin, your wife can really do lasagna! I knew it would be good; that's why I took off from work early yesterday!"

"Hey, kid, I see your handsome mug every day, but Lena and Mabel don't see you around much. Come over for breakfast sometime. Mabel cooks some mean French toast!"

"Thanks, Cousin! That's a deal," I said, as I picked up my pace to get home and sit by the furnace as soon as possible.

Later that night, some of the young carnies brought out a portable record player and put it on a picnic table near a blazing fire that a couple of boys were poking at with long sticks. There was going to be a carny wedding the next day, and as soon as the music started, more folks showed up. Pretty soon we were shoulder to shoulder around the fire, roasting marshmallows and trying to keep warm.

Lena was already there. So were the groom-to-be and his pretty fiancée. They were kissing on each other a whole bunch, and I noticed right away that the groom-to-be had a bulge around his pant zipper. I saw his fiancée reach over and actually touch the bulge. As they started dancing and twirling around to the music, she reached over again and touched his big bulge.

Yikes! Just seeing the bride-to-be touch her fiancé that way sent something to my brain, and I too got a hard-on. I looked over at Lena. She was looking right at me, and I just knew that she had seen the bulge in my pants. I didn't say nothing, but left right away, went home, and jumped under the covers. Just thinking about the bride-to-be touching her beau, and thinking about what they were going to be up to on their wedding night really got me going!

When I saw Lena the next day, I still felt embarrassed, and I just tried to steer clear of her. A little bit later, she came over to me and asked me why I had left the party the night before so early, just when a lot of people were getting there. I told her that I had been really tired from working all day and had started to get sleepy. So I went home and went right to bed. Lena seemed as though she wanted to talk. She had her hair down again and looked younger. I wanted to tell her that I liked it better when she had her hair scooped up in a bun. But why would I even say that? Why was I so interested all of a sudden in whether her hair was down or up in a bun? And why was I watching her so intently as she walked away? So many *whys*!

I had had an awful time falling asleep the night before, so I added another *why* to my list: Why was it so difficult to fall asleep when I was so tired? This time around, I still hadn't fallen asleep by 5 a.m. I drifted off for a bit, but couldn't stay asleep, so I finally just got out of bed and got ready to go to work. I had a lot to do. I liked working on several projects at once, and I hated it when a project got all complicated and I had to spend a lot of time sorting things out. It became like real work, getting bogged down like that.

As I was returning to the workshop that day after lunch, I heard heavy footsteps right behind me. A familiar voice called out, "Hey, Danny, how are you, pal?" I stopped in my tracks and turned around. It was H.P. Orr, carrying a couple of suitcases.

"Hey, H.P., I'm doing just fine, but if Uncle Bosco sees you here, you're a dead pigeon!" Uncle Bosco didn't approve of his daughter Diana seeing H.P., and he did everything he could to keep the two of them apart. H.P. was a Rumneechel, and Uncle Bosco considered him unsuitable to marry Diana. He didn't like H.P. as a person—he called him Sneaky Pete—but he was also afraid that Diana would get caught up in having to follow the Rumneechel customs, which, even today, are a lot stricter than what we *Ludad* (*Ludari, Romanian Roma*) observe.

Rumneechels follow strict rules about cleanliness that affect how they interact with one another, with gadje, and their surroundings. They wash their hands before handling food or dishes, after getting dressed in the morning, and before going to the kitchen. They don't use the same cleaning rags for counters and tables that they use to scrub floors. They might even use different washcloths for their upper bodies than they do to clean their *bad places* (private parts) and lower body and feet.

I've known English Gypsy families that use an outhouse rather than making the bathroom "dirty." Some ladies cover their clean couches and upholstered chairs with plastic, and go so far as not to let anyone wear outdoor and work shoes inside the vardo. Anyway, Uncle Bosco would go on and on about how he wanted his girls to make good marriages and not have to work so hard. A lot of Gypsies keep to the old ways, and in traditional Gypsy households, the women still do all of the housework: cooking, cleaning, shopping, taking care of the older folks, raising the kids, etc.

Most Ludad marry within the Ludad community, and when they marry outside, most of the time they wind up marrying Russian

Gypsies because they have similar customs. Anyway, a Romanian Gypsy marrying an English Gypsy is pretty rare and discouraged.

H.P. seemed nervous about running into Diana's dad and asked me if I would be a pal and go fetch Diana for him. I said ok and walked to the other end of the barn where my cousin's trailer was parked. I didn't see Diana anywhere, so I asked my aunt Zina if she knew where I could find her. Aunt Zina said that Diana was cleaning out the car to take it to the car wash at the Texaco station to get it washed and waxed for my sister Edie's wedding.

As I was leaving the barn, I saw Diana pulling away and couldn't catch her, so I went back to H.P. and told him, "Diana went to the car wash behind the Texaco station. That's where you'll find her."

"Well, pal, I don't have wheels. Can you take me there?"

"Sure, let me go get the truck."

On our way to the Texaco station, H.P. told me that his mom had had a heart attack and he had to get back to Blytheville, Arkansas. He wanted to see Diana before he left. We found Diana, and she and H.P. kissed and got into the car while the crew started to wash and wax it. Gosh, it seemed like forever before they finished the car. Diana got out of the car first and asked me if I would drive H.P. to the Greyhound station to catch his bus back home. Diana and H.P. kissed and hugged, both with tears in their eyes. It was a real sad situation, and I could see right off that they really cared for each other.

We got to the Greyhound station, and H.P. hopped out of the truck, grabbed one of his bags, and ran for the station. "I think I'm late for the bus," he turned and shouted at me. I took his heavy bag and followed him into the station. The station agent said that we'd missed the bus by about ten minutes, and there wasn't another bus to Blytheville until eight o'clock the next morning. But he said that the bus H.P. had missed had a big shipment waiting for it at Hayes Corner, just eighteen miles north. "If you folks chug on along, you can board the bus there. I'll call ahead and tell the driver to expect you."

So off we went. H.P. didn't say much; he just sat there next to me, chain smoking, with tears in his eyes. He was older than me, maybe twenty-four or so, and I'd never seen a grown man tear up like that. He finally said, "Danny, please tell Diana to be at the phone Wednesday night around nine o'clock."

"You guys really care for each other, don't you?"

"Sure, pal, more than you'll ever know. Maybe someday you'll find a gal that you'll love as much as I love my Diana. She told me that the gal you was sweet on got hitched on you because you wasn't fast enough to tell her how you felt about her."

"That's true, H.P. I had a big crush on Peggy Weco for quite a while, but I just took it for granted that she was going to be my gal."

"Don't take a good thing for granted ever again, kid—a good gal or anything else you really want in life—go all out for it."

All of a sudden, H.P. jerked forward in the seat and said, "Hey, pal, there's my bus!"

I pulled directly in front of the bus so it wouldn't take off. H.P. put his bags next to the big pile of luggage and boxes being loaded into the bus's undercarriage and hopped on the bus. I backed the truck out of the way, got out and waited until the bus was ready to pull out, just about ten minutes. H.P. sat with the window open and had a smoke while we watched the workers load the bus's undercarriage and finally close the door and lock it. It had just started to pour, and H.P. leaned out the bus window and said, "Hey, kid, you're super!"

I ran to the truck and headed back home. The next day while I was working on a joint, Diana came to see me, and I told her what had happened with H.P. She squeezed me tight and cried on my shoulder. Then I saw Aunt Zina heading our way, and I said, "Gosh! Your mom's coming!" Diana wiped away her tears real quick-like.

"Danny, I'm glad you're here," Aunt Zina said. "Go on and take Diana to the store. I need some milk and bread right away, and git one of them Entenmann's prune cakes that Aunt Bessie likes so much! She's on her way here with Marsh. They'll be here in a half-hour or so." So she wouldn't see Diana's tears, I held up my big bunch of keys and said, "Here, Cousin, go on and take the truck so I can finish up here."

"You know I can't drive a stick shift, Danny, so take me to the store real quick and you'll still have time to finish." We headed out the side door of the barn, and as soon as we had left the fairgrounds, Diana burst into tears again. "Danny, I don't know how long H.P. and me can stand it, being apart for so long." I didn't want Diana to feel any sadder, so I didn't mention how H.P. had had tears in his eyes.

"Danny, could you go ahead and take me to the drive-in tonight for H.P.'s call so I can get there plenty early? I'm just so afraid that your sister won't be back from shopping in time to take me. Rosie is spending so much time out shopping and helping your mom get everything ready for Edie's wedding, and I don't want to miss H.P.'s call!"

"No problem, kiddo! I'll be glad to help you two lovebirds! Yeah, I know that my mom and the other gals on the planning committee are sorta in overdrive getting things ready for Edie and Pete's wedding. They booked two orchestras, and the carny band is gonna fill in on breaks. The last wedding my mom planned lasted four whole days, and I think she was in bed for a couple of days after, she was so tired. This wedding is going to be a biggie, for sure." I was on a roll and kept talking, because I thought that would cheer Diana up some. "There's going to be a bunch of people and family there that I haven't seen in quite a spell."

Diana seemed to perk up, and chimed in, "The weather's going to be super, Danny! Your sister's wedding is going to be so special, your mom being Italian and all. Italian weddings are always so huge, and there's always so much to eat and do! And I heard the parents pitched in and bought the bride and groom a television set! I sure wish that we had one! I know that in time everyone's gonna have one. They'll stop going to the drive-in and the indoor movie show!" It was good to see Diana her old self again, so excited about my sister Edie's wedding.

Finally, the big wedding weekend arrived! Everyone pitched in and cleaned out the dance pavilion and started painting, especially around the bandstand area and in the reception area where the bridal party would be. Some carnies carried in two big rolls of linoleum and started tacking them down on the rough floor to make a dance floor. It was about twenty-four by twenty-four feet square, but when my dad showed up, he took one look and said that wasn't going to be nearly enough room for dancing. Dad told me to go to the hardware store and pick up two more rolls of linoleum.

When I returned with the rolls, I got stuck supervising the carnies that were helping with the wedding set up. My dad announced he was leaving for a while to see if my mom needed help with anything, and that I would be in charge until he got back. After an hour or so, most of the carnies cut out to get something to eat, but a strong-looking young guy named Wilbur stayed to help me finish unrolling the linoleum. When it was all finished, we stood back and checked it out. It looked really great! Wilbur and I both made sure that everything was straight and all matched up before we tacked it down. Now the dance floor was forty-eight by forty-eight feet, plenty big for a crowd of dancers, just like in a big dance hall.

About ten o'clock, everyone started to decorate and got busy putting streamers along the ceiling and hanging balloons and round glitter balls. I had made several bunches of crepe-paper flowers that I tacked every few feet along the streamers. By three o'clock, the pavilion looked like something out of a Hollywood production! While we were finishing up, the lighting guys showed up and lit the place up like crazy. Early the next morning—the wedding day—the band-setup crew was supposed to come in and set up two bandstands, one for the alternating hired orchestras and a smaller one for the carny musicians who would play during the orchestra breaks. The plan was for dinner to start at about 3 p.m., an hour or so after the wedding church service was over. Dancing would begin a couple of hours into the dinner, probably around five o'clock.

Most of the out-of-town guests had arrived by the night before the wedding. Some came with trailers, and others filled up the little town's motels and guest houses. There were only about four small motels and a couple of cabin courts. A lot of out-of-towners would be staying with friends and relatives on the carnival grounds. By early evening, there were about fifteen or so camp fires blazing throughout the carnival grounds. There were so many groups of people milling around: talking, singing, telling jokes, dancing around the campfires. Some folks had brought portable record players, and the young people were organizing dance-offs, with each group competing to come up with the best routines and moves. Around three of the fires there were groups of girls singing all of the popular songs. Young and old were having a great time!

Then, all at once, I saw Lena, and someone had his arms around her waist and was holding her real close. I felt my blood boiling, so I hurried to get closer to see what in the hell was going on! The closer I got, the angrier I got. I hadn't felt this angry and mean since I missed a fly ball in a district-wide baseball game in middle school. I wanted to see who in the hell had his arms around Lena! Grrr!

Finally, when we were close enough to each other, I saw to my great relief that the guy was Howard, Lena's brother, in town from Norfolk for Edie's wedding! As soon as he saw me, he reached out to me with a big hug. He would never ever know how pleased I was to see his face and how deliriously happy I was that it wasn't anybody else holding Lena!

It was at that moment that I actually knew in my heart that I was really hooked on Lena. Lena smiled at me, I guess to let me know how happy she was that her brother was there with her. "My dad is here too, Danny," Howard said, pointing out a group of men and women I'd never seen before. They looked like real swells. One of the men looked so dapper and elegant standing there smoking a long thin cigar.

Howard asked me where the restroom was, so I took him to the one closest to my work area. I waited outside the door, and when he came out, he slapped me on the back and told me how happy he was to see me. "You owe me a letter, Danny, from about six months back. The last time we got together, you promised that you would write to me"

Lena said excitedly, "Dad and Howard drove here from Norfolk with my two uncles and an auntie who's related somehow to Edie's matron of honor. Boy, Danny, wait until you see my gown and, boy oh boy, just wait until you see my mom in her bright electric green gown and her new red hair. She just dyed it a few hours ago."

"Wow, I blurted out, "I just can't picture your mom with red hair!"

"I almost let her dye my hair too."

"Gosh, Lena," I said, "I can't see you with red hair!"

Lena was all smiles. "So you like it just the way it is?"

I was sorta surprised at her talking so much, but I jumped right in, "Yes, I like your hair just the way it is! When you wear your hair pulled back in a bun, you look so much more mature and classy!"

Lena laughed, "I do? Is that a good thing? Well, then, I'll wear it that way forever!" Howard laughed real hard too. "Come on, Howard. I told mom that I wouldn't smother you tonight. She wants to spend as much time as she can with you. If you only knew how much she worries about us, and how sorry she is that things turned out the way they have."

Howard slapped me on the shoulder and said, "See you, pal!" Then he and Lena took off toward the food concessions. I was hoping that Lena would look back at some point, but she just grabbed Howard's arm and kept talking. Gosh, it would've been nice if she'd said good night or something.

I went home and got into bed, still irritated that Lena had been all friendly and joking, then just took off without even saying goodbye. "Hot and cold:" I guess that's what folks mean by that. But anyway, I was all excited about seeing Howard again.

The next morning, Edie's wedding day, my brother Tony shook me awake. "Hey, Ace, you gonna go to the church with us?"

"No," I answered, more than a little pissed off. "I don't like going to church weddings! Too much standing, then sitting, then kneeling, then standing again. I've been once, and it was so long and nerve-wracking, and there were so many "tears of happiness" that I promised myself right then and there, that was it for me!"

"Well," Tony said, "I ain't never been to a fancy wedding, so I'm goin'! Probly gonna be some purty girls there! So Danny, you want to use the bathroom first, so I can shower up and get dressed?"

"No," I groaned, turning back over for a few extra minutes of sleep. "Take your time; I'll just use the bathroom outside." Well, it seemed that I was wide awake now, so I dragged out to the outside bathroom, showered and shaved, and got into the clothes and shoes I had brought with me. I was heading back to the trailer when Howard showed up and asked if I wanted to ride with him and Lena to the church.

"I wasn't planning on even going to the church service." I didn't know where to start explaining. It was too bad I didn't have a recording of what I'd told my brother earlier!

"Well, you sure are all dressed up to not go to the church! Ain't you just a Mister Fancy Pants! Is that a suit you got on?" Howard stood back and gawked at me, with a big goofy smile on his face.

"Yes, I bought it for another wedding, the wedding that convinced me never to go to another church wedding!"

"Oh come on, Danny, be a sport. Jeez Louise, it's your own sister's wedding. Think how that will look if you don't even show up! Come with us. I asked my dad if we could go in his new Cadillac, and I told him that you'd be driving! Besides, Lena's looking forward to riding with you. You know, most of the time, she actually likes you!"

Most of the time? Anyways, I didn't want Howard to get in trouble with his dad, so, all reluctant, I agreed to go.

Howard smiled and said, almost like he'd memorized it, "Everyone is gonna show up right at ten o'clock, just outside the fairgrounds. Then we're gonna form a line of cars: bride and groom in the forward car, then cars with the close family, then the photographers, then everyone else, and head over to the church. See that cream-colored Caddy over there? That's my dad's, the one that you'll be driving."

That sounded a little squirrely, organizing the line of cars like that. But at 9:45 a.m., I headed over to the Caddy. Howard, accompanied by a smiling man wearing a handsome gray suit, met me on the way. He was the same man that I had seen earlier looking so dapper as he stood with his friends, smoking a cigar. The smiling man reached over to shake my hand, "How are you doing, son? I'm Tommy Boswell, Howard and Lena's dad. So you're Danny! Howard here thinks that you're one super guy." Tommy grinned as he pumped my hand, then handed me the keys to the car, a gorgeous Cadillac Sedan de Ville.

We stopped in front of Mabel and John's trailer and waited for Lena and Mabel to come out. Boy, did Mabel ever look gorgeous! She was wearing a bright green gown that really set off her flame-red hair. Lena had been right about that! Mabel looked like a Hollywood movie star, which is what I would call her from then on whenever I saw her wearing that beautiful gown! Another car pulled up behind us, and Mabel got in. Howard said that just Lena and another couple he didn't know very well were coming with us. The other folks finally came out of the trailer, followed by Lena in a beautiful peacock-blue ball gown, with her hair in a bun. It was my sister's wedding, but as far as I was concerned, Lena was gonna be the belle of the ball!

"Gosh, Lena," I said, all excited. "Is that really you?"

"Oh, come on," Lena said, frowning like I'd never seen her frown before. "Don't I usually look good?"

"Hey, buddy," Howard interrupted, "my sister always looks beautiful, because she *is* beautiful, inside and out! She can't hide that!"

The guys rode up front with me, the girls in the rear seat. Lena was sitting right in full view of the rear-view mirror. As I gazed at her face in the mirror, she looked even more beautiful as we rode along. My heart was doing a tango—or maybe a jitterbug. I really was feeling proud as a peacock and was getting more excited and apprehensive about the wedding as we pulled into our place in the line of cars in front of the very quaint Roman Catholic church just outside of town. That's one thing this little town had, a bunch of churches, just like most small Southern towns have, even today.

As we entered, I looked around the packed church and was impressed with how beautiful the interior was. It looked like the inside of one of them churches on View Master reels. Wow! The photographers were sure to get some really good shots of the wedding and of the inside of the church. Lena, Howard, and I sat near my folks and my aunties. My mom and my aunties looked so grand! My dad was wearing his best fancy Italian silk suit and looked like he had just arrived at a movie premiere.

The girls entered the pews first, followed by us boys. It was a wonderful sight! The groom and the bride looked like something out of a painting. Pete didn't look a bit nervous. My sister Edie was just so animated and smiling, turning every which way. I had never seen such a happy, smiling bride; even her eyes seemed to be smiling! After a long wait, the ceremony finally got underway. Then, all of a sudden, it just stopped. People were whispering that Pete had left the wedding ring at home, and his brothers had gone to find it and bring it back to the church. In the meantime, while we were waiting, it was getting hot in the church. Edie and Pete went outside with everyone else to wait for Pete's brothers to get back. Finally, after quite a while, the brothers returned with the ring, and the service continued and was over in what seemed like just a few minutes.

Everyone filed out of the church and scattered here and there. Back at the wedding hall, the buffet tables filled up real quick with food. Almost everyone had brought a dinner table for their own group: round tables, picnic tables, breakfast tables, dining room tables, every size and shape of table imaginable. So many tables would be needed to accommodate the big crowd expected to show up over the next few hours. The only tables already set up in the wedding hall were for the food and drink and the wedding party.

The wedding party's table was beautifully decorated and set with sterling silver flatware and fine china. I had made a lot of the silk flowers myself, in shades of cream, purple, or violet. As folks arrived after the church service, they set up their tables, and the decorating crew quickly and beautifully decorated each table.

Outside the wedding hall, there were already six pigs

roasting in pits, plus there were plenty of fish dishes and Italian meat entrées and salads, so many that they took up two whole tables. Finally, the wedding party and the guests took their places at the beautifully decorated tables.

The first course was served from large decorated carts. There was plenty of roast pig, thick steaks, fish dishes, slabs of ham, all kinds of sandwiches, piles of mixed vegetables, baked potatoes, spaghetti, lasagnas, stuffed meatballs, and so much more. Desserts on the side tables included Italian favorites: gelato, cakes, pies, gelatin mounds, puddings, even ice cream and Italian ices, sitting on beds of crushed ice.

After a few hours, the wedding guests started piling cash onto the donation table in the middle of the wedding hall. We found out later that close to twelve thousand dollars was gifted to the bride and groom. What a wonderful start in married life! My mom and dad had bought Edie and Pete a 1949 Ford convertible, complete with a wiring harness and towing braking system, fully rigged and reinforced to pull a heavy travel trailer. Everyone stood and applauded my folks' generosity. The groom's parents had bought the happy couple a forty-five-foot-long by eight-foot-wide travel trailer, complete with two push-out rooms. Again, another standing ovation, this time for the groom's parents! The travel trailer had cost over ninety-six hundred dollars and was completely furnished. Bedding, linens, kitchen appliances, pots, pans, and tableware were piled high on tables off to the side of the room.

I was wondering how they were going to fit all of that stuff inside a forty-five by eight-foot trailer! The groom had his own flatbed Ford truck that was only about six months old. All this plus the twelve thousand dollars in cash! Even now, all these years later, I don't think I've met another young couple who deserved a better start in married life than Edie and Pete!

What an exciting day! But things were getting even better! At about six o'clock, the first orchestra started playing, and the giant linoleum dance floor quickly filled up. The orchestra played for a couple of hours. Then, after the carny band played for an hour, the second orchestra took over the bandstand and played for another good two hours. After that set, the young folks in the crowd set up some record players and held a sort of dance contest to see which couple could dance the most complicated routine to different popular songs. This went on for a little over an hour, then the first orchestra took the stand again and the whole revolving orchestra routine was repeated. The dance floor was always packed, whether there was live music or just the record player.

Most of the girls there danced with each other because no girl wanted to get teased by the boy she was dancing with, or by his friends on the sidelines. Some girls did dance a few sets with boys, but only boys they were related to, because both the Romani-speaking Ludad and the *Boyash* (Romanian-speaking Roma) frown on unrelated young people mingling and socializing with the opposite sex.

I danced a lot with all of my cousins and with Lena, who just looked so beautiful and so radiant in her peacock blue gown. Her hair was pulled back in the elegant bun that was my favorite way for her to wear her hair. I danced with her every chance I got, holding her tight and enjoying the feeling of being so close to her. But after an hour or so, Lena's brother Howard showed up, and she and I didn't get a chance to spend time alone or talk much for quite a while.

Lena spent most of her time on the dance floor for an hour or so—with or without me—with her brother Howard. She was trying, to no avail, to teach him how to dance without him clobbering her dainty feet with his big ol' clown shoes. I patiently tried to show him some simple moves, but he had two right feet and kept going to his right.

Finally, Howard just gave up, but he did go up to the bandstand and sing a couple of really beautiful country songs, to a standing ovation. His dad was so proud and walked around grinning ear to ear, having a wonderful time.

In between the sets, folks headed over to the buffet tables to get another plate of food or something to drink. The booze was really flowing, and no one was checking to make sure that everyone drinking was of age. The last orchestra finished at about 1 a.m., and a large record player was brought to the front of the wedding hall. I'd guess that way over half of the wedding guests were still there, and the dancing continued until after 3 a.m.

At 9 a.m. a mega breakfast was served, and at 11 a.m. or so, someone fired up the record player again. It went full blast for hours. By now, about a quarter of the wedding guests took to the dance floor again. A large luncheon was served while the carny musicians took over the band stand and had their own jam session. They encouraged everyone to sing along. A lot of folks joined in the singing, from little kids to folks in their eighties. This was by far the best wedding I'd ever been to, and the most fun ever!

After dinner at around 7 p.m., the first orchestra and carny band from the night before took turns playing again. It was just as lively as the night before but with fewer people dancing. A lot of folks had come quite a ways to attend the wedding, and some of them had left and were on their way home. But there were enough folks left to eat all of the food that was served, including two more pit-roasted pigs, crabs, shrimp, more seafood, more lasagna, even liver and onions. Someone even brought take-out Chinese food. And some local folks showed up with Southern dishes: greens, cornbread, sweet potatoes, Cajun food, even pigs in a blanket.

It was like a royal affair. The newly-weds slept in their new trailer on their wedding night. The next evening, they left for their honeymoon in Puerto Rico, paid for by my folks. As the happy couple left the wedding hall, the orchestra was playing the wedding song from the movie *The Jolson Story,* which I guess almost everyone had seen. Everyone sang along as the young newlyweds danced for the last time that evening before departing on their honeymoon. They had on matching outfits and were just beaming, they were so happy. Pete's brother Richie drove them to New Orleans to catch their flight to Puerto

Rico, which Richie kept mispronouncing as *puerco rico*, which someone later told me means "rich pig" or "tasty pig" in Spanish. Hahaha!

The festivities came to a close at about midnight. The wedding guests sat down to enjoy one more dinner before they headed home. The ladies in charge of the food preparation had done such a fantastic job, and my mom and aunties were involved from the earliest planning. I was so proud of my mom for all of the work that she had done, and how she managed to get the volunteers to all work together with no bruised egos or other problems that might crop up.

Howard and his dad left to go back to Norfolk about 1 p.m. the next day. I didn't get to say my adoos to Howard because I was busy ferrying people to the Greyhound station both times that he came by the trailer to say goodbye to my folks and me. Besides the small talk on the dance floor the night before, the only time I actually spoke to Lena was when she came up to me between my trips to the bus station.

"Howard was really disappointed that he couldn't find you to say goodbye before they left to go home. They heard that you was driving folks down to the bus station, so they was going to head down there to see if they could find you. But I guess you was already on your way back here."

"Yeah, I was going back and forth for a few hours. I wish me and him could have spent more time together, but he'll be back for sure to see you and your mom. I know youse both miss him a whole bunch."

"Well, I'm not sure when we'll see him again. He's real busy helping Dad with the taxi service. Howard and my dad do a lot of the driving and engine work and repairs themselves. Dad thinks that you're a very nice young man, and he was real pleased with you because you hunted him down to return his car keys. And Howard likes you so much that he told me that I should marry you because that would make you his brother! He really feels close to you, Danny, and he's hoping that you'll answer a letter that he sent you a while back. He's really disappointed that you didn't take the time to answer yet, and he told me to tell you to write to him. That kid really likes you, Danny. It wouldn't break your back to answer that letter!"

"I like him a lot too. He's all grown up but still a lot of fun to joke around with. Look, kiddo, I'll go ahead and write Howard. Maybe to make him real happy, we ought to get married like he says." Lena turned her neck sideways and gave me the strangest look.

To get past that awkward moment, I quickly added, "You sure looked swell in your new gown, with your hair pulled back in a bun!"

"That dress wasn't mine. I borrowed it from your cousin Maya. You sure got some great cousins!"

"They're your cousins too."

"I know. They all told me that they take me close like a relation."

"Wow!" I said, "That's great! They're always saying how sweet you are, and how smart.

"But let me say one more thing about Howard, ok? He seems really torn between helping out your dad and spending more time with you and your mom here."

"I know, Danny," Lena said, with hurt in her voice. "And it's so sad, not just for Howard and me, but for my mom and my dad too, because he knows how much my brother misses our mom."

I gave Lena a hug, said goodbye, and watched her head home, bouncing along the wide path leading from the pavilion. I stood there, remembering how beautiful she had looked in her peacock-blue gown the night before. And now—I couldn't believe my eyes—Lena stopped, turned around, smiled at me, and waved goodbye. I was one happy guy!

I headed back into the pavilion to to help with the cleanup and to see if anyone else needed a ride somewhere. The carnies had been so great. They volunteered to help and had really pitched in to make my sister's wedding celebration a great success. I wanted to help clean up and take down and save the decorations to give to my mom and Edie. Some folks were still hung over, but most were just tired—a good tired from having enjoyed a wonderful wedding celebration with a lot of fun, dancing, and great food! The carny volunteers in charge of the cleanup played records and danced on their breaks. I had never seen such happy workers, true to the carny tradition of friendship and good hospitality. I saw what my dad had missed so much in city life: the camaraderie and the sense of belonging. The carnies were so generous, sharing the good times in their lives with others.

I saw Lena again that night at one of the bonfires where everyone was singing and toasting marshmallows. She toasted two for me, and one gal said, "Ain't that sweet of Lena to roast marshmallows for Danny?" Some of the other kids made ooh la la sounds and laughed and made Lena blush. I moved off to the side and gulped down the marshmallows. We talked for a while with several of her dad's cousins, but I didn't want her to feel embarrassed again, so I said goodnight and headed to the next bonfire. They were roasting hot dogs, and I had one with tomatoes and onion and mustard. I washed everything down with a Coke, then said goodnight to everyone and headed home.

As I lay there remembering all the pleasures of the wedding and how much I really enjoyed myself, even at the wedding ceremony at the church, I thought that, all in all, my sister's wedding was grand. The most outstanding thing was that Howard told Lena that she should marry me. What could have topped that?

At Edie's wedding celebration, I reached a goal that I had been dreaming and fantasizing about for so long: I held Lena in my arms so good and tight that I actually sensed that she must have felt it too. I was in a world of my own. It may have been wrong for me to be holding her at all, and I may have overdone it by dancing with her so many times. Now I was spoiled. I was just so happy, and holding Lena in my arms made me feel close to her in my head too, closer than I had ever felt to anyone in my whole life. It wasn't like I was standing next to Lena, making plans and fantasizing about our future together; it was more like I was open to this good feeling lasting as long as possible.

So many times, I had tried to start a dream about Lena,

deciding what would happen and when, even deciding that she'd be wearing her hair up in a bun and would have on that fancy peacock-blue gown that I loved seeing her in. But none of that ever happened; those staged dreams just never took hold in those long nights spent trying to find sleep. If I *did* manage to dream about Lena, when I woke up the next morning, I couldn't remember a damn thing. That is until the morning after my sister Edie's wedding.

After spending so many hours with Lena at Edie's wedding celebration, when I woke up the next morning, I actually remembered a dream I had about her. But it had nothing to do with the wonderful time we had spent together. This dream was about visiting a zoo together. Not the zoo in Indianapolis and not the zoos in Chicago or New York City. This was a generic zoo; over the entrance, there was a big sign with the word *Zoo* written on it in large, plain letters. In the dream, both Lena and I were playing with—of all things—a baby tiger. As each of us leaned over to pet the little tiger, we would look at each other, smiling and talking, but I couldn't hear what we were saying. We were as quiet talking as we were smiling. We looked at each other tenderly as if we had already been together for a long time. All of a sudden, as I started to hand the tiger cub to Lena, it jumped down to the ground and bounced away from us. We had just started to run after the tiger when I woke up.

Boy, was I ever confused! Why had I been dreaming about a tiger? Lena and I had never even talked about tigers. I just couldn't figure out why I had been dreaming about a tiger cub. Maybe it was the coloring, the big clumsy paws, or the fuzzy, furry feeling of stroking the tiger cub's body. Well, all that next day I was walking around, trying to figure out why I had dreamed about a fuzzy baby tiger and what the dream meant. What was with all that smiling and silent-movie talking and passing the tiger back and forth, only to have it jump to the ground and run off? And why was the zoo a made-up zoo, not anything like the ones that I had actually been to?

When I ran into Lena the next afternoon as she was hurrying

home with some groceries, I tried to make small talk, and I finally just blurted out, "Lena, how do you feel about tigers?"

"Tigers?" she said, shrugging her shoulders and looking around like she was afraid that someone had overheard my stupid question. "I don't know! They're beautiful and dangerous, I guess. Why?"

"I just wondered . . . "

Lena shook her bag of groceries. "Strange question!" she muttered, walking away with a puzzled look and a frown on her face.

Then another crazy thought came into my brain: *Why not find a stuffed toy tiger to give Lena as a gift, not for any special occasion, just a spontaneous gift?* I was thinking that some of the concessions in the traveling show must have stuffed toy tigers in different sizes. Problem was, as I asked around, it seemed like all of the stands were already packed up in preparation for our trip to the next stop. A couple of days later, when I had to go into town for some supplies that my dad needed, I searched all of the toy stores, trying to find a stuffed toy tiger to give Lena. Well, no way. But the next day, I found a tiny toy tiger, not gift-size exactly, but it looked really cool hanging from my rear-view mirror.

The next few times I drove Lena home or out on errands, it seemed strange that she didn't notice the tiger on my mirror and say something about it. Finally, about a week later, we were driving into town, and with her left hand Lena batted at the little tiger dangling from the rear-view mirror. "So Danny, what was that crack about what I thought of tigers? Did you mean this one?" She poked at the little tiger one last time, setting it spinning.

"Nope. I had a dream about a tiger in a zoo somewhere, and you were in the dream!"

"Don't tell me that I'm in your dreams now!"

"Well, so far just the one with the tiger in it. I couldn't even hear what we were saying to each other, but you were smiling the whole time, until the tiger got away."

"Tell me about it."

"Well, there's not much to tell, except that we were petting a tiger cub."

"A tiger cub? How strange! Was that all?"

"Yes, we . . . "

"You mean you and me?"

"Yes. You and me."

"Boy, you sure dream screwy!"

"Well, when I dream, it just happens."

"Was the dream in color or in black and white?"

"I don't remember. If I have that zoo dream again, I'll let you know." As she walked away, I called after her, "What about you, Lena? Do you dream in color or black and white?"

She turned and stopped, frowned, looked me up and down, and—sounding very much like a primary school teacher determined to make herself understood—said, "I most definitely will tell you if my dream is in color or black and white!" I think I heard her giggle to herself as she turned and continued on her way.

Boy, what a conversation that was, if you could call it a conversation. It was more like a quiz! At first, I thought it was kind of delightful. I was so happy to see Lena, to hear her voice, to engage in a bit of friendly banter. That encounter made me feel ten feet tall! I headed home with a smile as wide as my whole face.

Looking back on our conversation the next day—mulling it over and over in my mind—I wondered what Lena's impression had been. To be honest, I guess our conversation was mostly me going on and on about my dream. Why had she frowned so much and talked down to me like I was a little kid? She had seemed kinda defensive, sarcastic even. In fact, maybe thinking that she had feelings for me—really liked me in the way that I liked her—was just a dream or a fantasy.

I laid there trying to go to sleep, but I was so hyper that all I could think about were my feelings for Lena. I went over and over in my mind the first time I had seen Lena and how much she had irritated me and how bratty she had been. But then she seemed to change and act more mature. I had always treated her real decent, so her change in attitude had nothing to do with me. Then falling asleep, I could hear Mabel and my mom telling me that worse things could happen than me getting all sweet on Lena. The more I thought about her, the more I would get all excited and have an erection. This was happening more and more. Boy, what a night that was! So many thoughts about Lena, all jumbled together, with me falling asleep before anything became clear in my mind.

The upshot of all this thinking and talking about dreams was that over time, I realized that I was trying too hard to plot out my dreams about Lena: When I just relaxed and let sleep come, the dreams came too.

The next morning, after I had been in the outdoor work area for a bit, I felt someone put their hands over my eyes and say, "Guess who!" I couldn't recognize the voice, but it turned out to be my cousin Buddy, who I hadn't seen for over five years. What a surprise! "Danny, our transmission went out just after leaving home, so we took a bus back to Detroit until the car was ready. We was just out of Chicago when we broke down about two hundred and fifty miles from here. I came with your old flame Peggy and Hal here. Danny, I know that you was sweet on Peggy. How come you love birds didn't get married?"

Boy, I was really irritated with Buddy, so I snapped, "Knock it off!" His face kinda went dark and he stood there all quiet and embarrassed-looking.

It was good to see Peggy's husband, Hal. Well, Hal and Buddy and I were standing there, chatting about this and that, when Buddy leaned into Hal and said, "Did you know that Danny here and Peggy had a thing going on?"

"Oh, come on, Buddy, that was years ago," Hal said. "That was puppy love, like we all go through. Danny was so young, he was still reading them comic books! Stop trying to embarrass Danny!" Buddy put his head down and walked away like a sick puppy. "I'm sorry he embarrassed you like that, Danny. That guy has a lot of growing up to do! Well, anyway, folks say Edie had a slam-bam wedding!"

"It was super," I said. We found a bench to sit on, and I entertained Hal with details of the wedding, from start to finish.

"Wow, kid, you could be one of them *Movietone News* guys," Hal finally said, laughing. "I feel like I was there!"

I asked Hal how he and Peggy were doing. "Well, we're doing just fine! We quit the traveling show, and now we're doing blacktop. I do miss the road, but we're making so much more with the blacktop and asphalt jobs. We do honest work, not like some of them fly-by-night outfits that give us Gypsies a bad name."

I kept looking over my shoulder, really hoping not to see Peggy at all. I just felt uneasy because I knew that I'd be teased later by anybody who saw Peggy and me together. I said goodbye to Hal, went to my work area to putter around for a bit, then went home and changed into my work clothes. I felt like I had been on some kind of vacation, and now I needed to really focus on my work for a while.

I went back to the work area, and was just starting to take apart a juice harness when in walked Hal and Peggy! "Boy, you look a lot older, Danny," Peggy said as she gave me a peck on the cheek. "I just wanted to say hi before we head home. Hal, you know that Danny and I used to be sweethearts when we was just kids."

"I've been reminded of that by all of Danny's cousins, seems like," Hal said with a big grin, and then the three of us had a good laugh. We talked about this and that for half an hour or so, then said our adoos. I tried to get back to work. I thought about Peggy and how she looked and how I didn't have no feelings for her anymore: none, nothing at all, not one iota. And, I had no more reservations about pursuing my feelings for Lena. The wedding, seeing Buddy, Hal, and Peggy again, my dreams about Lena: All these things just made my feelings for Lena stronger. I realized, finally, that what I had felt for Peggy had been puppy love, and what I felt for Lena was so much more. I thought about the feelings I used to have for Peggy and felt really stupid for thinking that she was my gal. Well, that was just water under the bridge, I thought.

What I had to do now was concentrate on how to proceed with

my feelings for Lena. How should I handle what I felt for Lena? I wondered at what point I should confess to Lena the feelings that I had for her. I was still confused about my feelings, or rather how to tell her how I felt. It went back to that time her brother Howard told Lena that he wished that she would marry me so that he and I would be brothers. I remembered the way Lena looked at me when I had said that maybe we should get married. I got a real mixed message with that look! Did she mean "Knock it off!" or "Why?" or "Look at you; how can you even think that?" I didn't take the look she gave me as meaning "I'd like that!" The message I got from the look Lena had given me was more negative than not, but then we didn't follow up with more conversation.

I knew that her mom and dad both really liked me, her brother was crazy about me, and my mom and dad both liked Lena a lot. After we finished breakfast, I decided on the spot to help my mom wash the dishes. I put dish soap in the sink, and my mom came over and said, "Do you really want to wash the dishes, or are you just nervous about something, Son? Go on, git outta here. You ain't washed no dishes in ages. By the way, what I spoke to you about Lena Boswell, I gather that you've put it to mind, 'cause I saw that your eyes was following her around at the wedding. I saw what I saw. Mothers can see things that other people can't, you know. I watched those eyes, because those eyes belong to me too. Don't be embarrassed, Danny! I'm your mother, the very closest friend that you'll ever have. If you need to talk about something, just go ahead."

"Oh, Mom . . . ."

"Well, if you feel uncomfortable talking about it, just know that I'll always be here for you, Son. Right now, you just seem confused or upset about something."

"Confused?"

"Yes, confused! I know you like I know the back of my hand, which I'm proud to say I've never had to use on you; same goes for your dad. We're so proud of you; it's just pitiful! Remember, Big Man, I'm here for you. You can always tell me your feelings. Am I wrong, Danny?"

"No, Mom, you're not wrong!" I felt like she had finally worn me down with all of her concern. "You and Dad are the best mom and dad anyone has or will ever have. If I need any advice, I promise that you'll be the first person I'll turn to!"

"I'd better be! Folks say that I'm a pretty good listener and give darn good advice!"

I was anxious to change the subject: "Hey, Mom, you sure looked pretty at Edie's wedding! I'm so proud of how youse all handled the planning and choosing the food, like coming up with that menu."

"Well, everything worked out, and you was such a big help." My mom looked at me with such emotion on her face, I felt that she was sincere in wanting to help me, if I could just figure out how to express my feelings for Lena. That was the problem, I guess—figuring out just what my feelings were before I asked Mom to help me sort things out.

After that conversation with my mom, I had a brighter, more optimistic outlook. Maybe that was because I knew that I had Mom to help me out whenever I got too overwhelmed or confused. Part of that confusion, of course, was from Lena herself, who seemed to give me mixed signals, or even totally different signals to things I said, I guess depending on what kind of mood she was in when we spoke. Sometimes, I thought our conversations were little contests, each of us trying to take the upper hand. If she felt that she wasn't getting her way, she backed away, making a face or saying something that made me feel like I was a dopey, clueless little kid again.

In the weeks following Edie's wedding, the picnic tables in the pavilion were dragged back onto what had been the wedding dance floor, and many of the families ate their meals there. Most of the travel trailers were too small to seat more than a few people at a time for a meal. Most couples just ate their meals on TV trays or sitting at the kitchen counter in their trailers, but even that was kinda crowded. And, it was hard to wash more than a few dishes at a time in the trailers' small kitchen sinks.

After a lot of pushing and dragging tables around and rearranging, what had been a wedding hall became a place for larger groups of folks to come together to share meals. There was plenty of room for picnic tables, and there was a large sink area for cleaning up and washing pots and pans and dishes. The extra space for folks to socialize and to eat meals and clean up was the big thing left over from Edie's wedding.

It wasn't long after my conversation with my mom that I went over to see Mabel. She was washing dishes and talking with my cousins Betty and Rula. I said hi to everybody and told Mabel that I just had to come over and tell her how beautiful she looked at Edie's wedding. "So I looked pretty good for an old married lady? And what did you think about how our little Miss Lena Boswell looked in that beautiful powder-blue dress?"

There was a noise outside, and Mabel looked over at the open front door just as Lena bounded up the steps and came straightway into the kitchen.

Mabel said real loud, "Danny's here to tell you how beautiful you looked at his sister's wedding!"

Lena looked annoyed and fired back, "He's already told me that!" She just stood there frowning.

Mabel continued, "Did you see how handsome my son Howard looked? Danny, did you enjoy the wedding? Someone told me that you drove the kids to the church and later ferried folks to the bus station when they was ready to go home." Mabel was on a roll, and just kept rattling on and on. "I've been to a lot of weddings, but this one takes the cake. It was like a prince and princess wedding! Them photos the newspaper guys took was beautiful, but they couldn't capture what the folks was saying, or the music, or the beautiful colors. I sure wish that someone had rented one of them movie cameras and made a movie of the whole thing. I'd never seen so many beautiful dresses and gowns in my life, and so many handsome gents, dressed up so smart. Even the carnies was dressed up! I guess that wedding was the highlight of the year!

"When Lena gets married," Mabel continued, "I hope that we'll be able to make a nice wedding. Will you help out, Danny?"

"Sure," I said. "You bet!"

Lena was frowning again, and Mabel said, "Why the big frown, Lena? Don't you think that Danny will help make a nice wedding for you?"

Lena responded in the most sour and caustic tone that I'd ever heard, "Well, that's what he says *now*!" It was almost as if she suspected I was already thinking of a way to get out of it.

Mabel drew her head back and said, "Well, Daughter, I don't think Danny's a liar! Certainly not!" She nodded at my cousin Betty, who said, "Oh, not Danny! Good Lord, he's like a preacher's son!"

Cousin Rula joined the chorus. "He's Mr. Goody Two Shoes! I've known him since he was four or five years old, and I've never heard him say one cuss word. Danny here is a good guy!"

Well, that made me blush! "Look, Danny's blushing!" Mabel laughed, giving me the sweetest smile. She reached over, like she was gonna try to muss my hair.

I stepped back, just in time, "No ma'am, I ain't blushing!"

"Well, you turned all red!"

"Anyways, Aunt Mabel," Cousin Betty said, "I just came by to tell you that *The Jolson Story* is gonna be at the outside theater on Monday. A whole carload of folks gits in for five bucks. Can't beat that! Maybe Diana can take us with their Cadillac."

I turned to ask, "What's *The Jolson Story*?"

"Just the greatest movie *ever*," Cousin Betty shot back. "Al Jolson is the blackface guy who made the first talkie. It's the story of his life in show business, and he sings that beautiful song that Edie and Pete danced to at the very end of the wedding reception."

"Gosh," I sighed, "That was a beautiful song, but so sad!"

Cousin Rula was quick to correct me. "It wasn't sad at all, Danny. It was just real romantic. That's something that you wouldn't know nothin' about, 'cause you've not experienced it yet."

Cousin Betty added her two cents' worth. "Oh no? Listen, Danny, I met your old girlfriend, Peggy. She sure is pretty, and her husband is quite a looker himself."

Mabel looked up from the sink and asked, "Betty, which girl was Peggy? What did she look like?"

Lena just had to get a word in: "Oh, Mom! She was that blonde in the beautiful yellow dress. Remember? I pointed to Peggy and told you that I wanted a dress just like the one she was wearing."

Mabel turned and looked at me over her glasses, "Danny, I'm guessing that pretty thing was your first-ever girlfriend."

I stood there like I was facing a firing squad, or like one of them deers caught in a car's headlights. My open mouth was real dry, and I couldn't say a word.

Betty said: "Well, anyway, she *was* Danny's girlfriend. She's done married now, and whatever happened way back when was a long time ago. What about now, Cousin? You got a steady girl?"

All eyes were on me.

Betty pushed on. "I noticed how all the girls on the midway go after you and want to run their fingers through your hair! Are you so busy getting rich that you haven't noticed all the attention?"

"Well," I finally answered, "You can't have enough money, especially if you want to get married and have a family."

"Why, Danny Miller," Rula said, all excited, "don't be a big dope! You'd better get a move on, and start lookin' around before the pickens gets real scarce."

"Pickens is already scarce," I shot back. "Most of the girls around here are my cousins anyway."

Cousin Betty just couldn't help herself. "Oh come on, Danny! You can tell us who you're sweet on!"

"No, Betty, I ain't sweet on nobody. Ain't got time for all that."

Betty's big mouth just didn't show me any mercy: "Well, Danny Miller, you better make some time! You ain't gettin' any younger."

"Oh, I still got plenty of time. I ain't in no hurry to settle down," I blurted out, mad as hell. "I still got time, lots of time." I glanced over at Lena, and I actually saw her try to catch my eye. I tried not to look in her direction for long, but Mabel may have caught that brief eye contact, because she started in.

"Danny, did you know that my son Howard told Lena that you should marry my girl so that you'd become his brother?"

Then Betty jumped in, "Why don't you, Danny, and we can make Lena our full-fledged cousin!"

"Well, I'll do that, Cousin," I said sarcastically, "just to make you happy."

"When?" Mabel asked. "Aunt Florence will need a week or so to make my Lena a wedding dress."

"Ok, Mabel, I'll be sure to give you a week's notice," I said in my deepest voice, like I was playing a part onstage. Lena was looking at me, looking at Mabel—back and forth—and frowning again, like maybe she thought we were ignoring what she thought about all this.

"I give you my solemn word." I made an exaggerated bow toward Mabel, who was standing real straight, all regal-like, as she reached for a clean dish towel.

"I'll just hold you to it, Milord," Mabel said in a fake British accent, making a snobby face and giving me a deep curtsy.

"Yikes," I said, almost losing my balance and turning toward the door, "that's enough of that!" I wiped my sweaty palms on my trousers and hurried down the stairs to cries of "fraidy cat, fraidy cat!" Poor Lena; I felt like I had abandoned her to the wolves, but I just had to get outta there!

The next morning, when I was visiting Mabel and scarfing down some of her famous pan dowdy, she got a telephone call that would give Lena and me several weeks to think about, or forget, all the nonsense talk from the night before. Mabel's ex, Tommy Boswell, called to tell her that he had to go to California to check out some taxicab repos that were up for sale. These were real fancy Chrysler taxi cabs, and he was hoping they would be a good investment for his taxi service there in Norfolk. The taxis wouldn't be available for another week or so, and he'd be away from Norfolk for maybe a good two weeks. "I'd sure appreciate it if you could send our girl over this way to keep an eye on her brother and minimize the damage while I'm out of town!"

"I don't see a problem with that, Tommy," Mabel said, looking around to see if Lena was in earshot. "She was real busy here taking care of John. He's doin' a lot better now, and a visit with Howard and a change of scene would do that girl a heap of good. I'll call you back if there's a problem." Lena came into the kitchen a few minutes later, spilling part of a bag of groceries on the counter top.

"Golly, Danny, if I'd known you was here taste-testing my mom's apple pan dowdy, I would have called and asked you to pick me up at the store and help me home with all these groceries. Could you have managed that?" Jeez, I hated it when she sounded more like a scolding school marm than my gal. So maybe that settled things for now: I guess in her mind, she wasn't my gal after all.

Mabel told Lena about the phone call from her dad, and Lena continued putting away the groceries, mumbling something like "Why not? No one here will miss me."

"That's not true, Lena, and you know it!" Mabel shot back. "You know very well that I couldn't have handled John without your help!"

"That's not what I meant, Mom!" Lena whined, giving me a dark look that made me feel guilty for not doing something that was news to me.

The very next morning, I took Lena and Mabel to the airport in New Orleans. We made it just in time for Lena's flight. She kissed her mom goodbye and gave me a peck on the cheek and a tight hug. She was blushing, but she didn't try to make eye contact, looking toward the loading gate as I grabbed her bag.

On the way back home, I was surprised that Mabel never once brought up the conversation from the previous night. We just talked about this and that: about Edie's wedding, about how my dad was really enjoying being back on the road, about how someone could make a good living on the road, good enough for two families to splurge on a grand wedding for their children.

Mabel told me how she just adored my mom, how my mom had been so wonderful to her, had taken to her like a real aunt. Mabel went on to say that she'd had a nice conversation with my mom, and wondered if my mom had mentioned it. I didn't answer, and Mabel didn't pursue it.

Two weeks went by, two weeks that were the loneliest two weeks that I'd ever been through. One evening, Cousin John came by my workshop, pulled a stool up next to me and said, "Danny, I need to go to Philly to see about some joints. I'm going to check out three different joints, and I'd like you to drive the target-game trailer back here. Your dad said that it was for you to decide if you want to come along. But I'm telling you, you sure would be good company and a big help. Plus, you'll get to meet all of my family that lives in Philly. When I told my dad that you might tag along, he said that he'd be so happy to see you again, 'cause you're his favorite nephew of all, serious."

I had to chuckle some. "Gosh, Cousin, no need to butter me up; I'd be glad to come along. I've never been to Philly, at least not that I can remember. And it would be great to see my cousins and Uncle Boyko."

"Well, on the way back, we're going to make a stop in Norfolk and pick up Lena and bring her back to New Orleans."

We left the next morning and got to Philly the following night. We drove straight through. I drove all day and John drove all night; then the following day, I drove all day until about dusk. We pulled into the fairgrounds just outside Philly at about eight o'clock. It was nothing short of grand to see my aunt and uncle and cousins, and it took a lot off of my mind. I had two relaxing days, but I still had my old sleeplessness. I was still all anxious about where Lena and I stood with each other, beause we'd kidded around but never had or took a chance to talk seriously about our feelings.

At dinner on our second evening in Philly, John leaned over my shoulder and said, "Danny, I spoke with your dad on the telephone today to tell him that the one joint I'm really interested in won't be ready for another week or so. They're gonna put electric brakes on it. You're gonna leave the pickup with me, and your cousin Mackie and his wife will take you home. Don't know if you remember her, but their daughter, Ib, will be going too. And, youse can stop in Norfolk and pick up Lena."

Hearing all that made my heart jump, I was so happy that I'd soon be seeing Lena again! Maybe by now she was missing me too. Mackie, Lucille, and Ib came by to pick me up around 7 a.m. the next morning. We sat around for a while and shared family news and gossip. We left Philly about 8 a.m. and got to Norfolk a little after 7 p.m.

Wow, what a beautiful house Tommy Boswell had, all nestled among trees and shrubs and gardens at the end of a road lined with guest cabins. Off to one side was a large car barn with fancy Tudor woodwork all around the doors and windows. There were a couple of shiny black Chrysler taxicabs and three long and elegant-looking white DeSoto taxicabs with large tires parked in the barn's driveway. Lena's dad's taxi service was doing real well in the touristy Norfolk area.

As soon as we came in, Lena's dad hopped up off the sofa, welcomed us and said that he hoped that we were all real hungry because he was going to take us out to dinner. Howard, Lena, and Tommy seemed relaxed and extra friendly. Howard ran over to me and grabbed me around the neck so hard that he almost knocked me over. I introduced Lena to Mackie and Lucille as Mabel's daughter and John's stepdaughter. I introduced Tommy Boswell as Lena and Howard's dad. "Mr. Boswell here is related to the singing Boswell Sisters and he plays a real mean guitar himself."

"I'm *Tommy* Boswell, folks. *Mr. Boswell* makes me sound like I'm a school teacher or something! Glad to meet you!" We all piled into one of Tommy's larger Chrysler cabs, and we were on our way. It was about a twenty-minute drive to this classy-looking seafood restaurant just outside the beautiful resort city of Virginia Beach. Mackie and Lucille were real impressed with the setting and the restaurant. As we got out of the cab, the sea air smelled different from the polluted city air we were used to.

Lena looked so beautiful, sitting so straight and regal at the table, like a princess with her court. Howard explained to Mackie and Lucille that his dad ran a taxi service there in the Norfolk area. They had nine cabs of different sizes, plus they owned the cabins around their own beautiful home.

Dinner was pretty delicious, I had to admit. I'm generally not too wild about fish, but I love shrimp, so I ordered a shrimp platter and a salad. Howard and Lena shared a large lobster. Cousin Lucille had shrimp; Tommy and Mackie had fried oysters, and both of them also had bluefish. Lucille ordered some clam chowder for Ib. We were all real hungry, and the food was fantastic!

Tommy was working his way through a pile of fried oysters, and I asked if I could try a couple. He was eating them with such gusto and enthusiasm, alternating with suddenly becoming all quiet, with closed eyes and a strange smile, like the look you see on a hillbilly's face at a revival! I just had to try some. I was sitting right next to Tommy, so he just slid a couple over onto my plate. Then Howard wanted to try the oysters, so Tommy asked the waiter to bring over another platter for us all to share. Like I said, fish was never one of my favorites, but the shrimp was delicious, and I really enjoyed my first fried oysters!

We left the restaurant around 9:30 p.m. As we pulled up to the last cabin at Tommy's place, he turned to Mackie and said, "You and Lucille can stay here, and Ib can stay with Lena in her old room. There's two twin beds in Howard's room, Danny, so you can bunk in there. Plus, you two will have your own television set."

We all settled in for what was for us a late night. We were all pretty much early risers. As soon as Howard and I were alone, he asked me a whole bunch of questions—starting, of course, with why I hadn't yet answered his last letter to me. "It's just waiting for a stamp and an envelope!" I shot back.

Howard seemed so happy and pretty much on top of things. We talked about the evening, missing Lena when she was away, how much he'd like to go on the road with his mom and stepdad's family. Howard asked me all about road life, running concessions, and moving from place to place in a trailer home. When I mentioned that there were new trailers up to forty-five feet long, with three bedrooms, two baths, plus air conditioning, that threw Howard for a loop, and boy did he laugh! "Gosh, Danny, that air conditioning sounds like a good deal! We're getting by with ceiling fans for now, and we get some real muggy weather in these parts."

We finally wound up back where the conversation had started: "I'll be expecting that letter you promised to send, Danny." With that, he finally fell into a deep and noisy sleep.

We awoke to the bellow of a nearby foghorn and the sounds of chatter and loud laughter and cooking utensils hitting countertops and stovetops. The moist coastal air was filled with the aroma of French toast, bacon, ham, sausage, pancakes, sourdough toast, and strong Italian coffee. The breakfast was just as delicious and at least as filling as the dinner we had enjoyed the previous evening.

Tommy had to leave before breakfast was over. "And by the way, folks, John is back early from his trip. He'll be happy to host what might just turn into a family reunion!" Lena and Howard were beaming. Tommy stood up from the table and exited so gallantly that we felt that we were front row center at a play or at the movies. Tommy had been a wonderful host and had made quite an impression during our visit. I had to wonder again what had happened all those years ago that caused the split between Mabel and Tommy Boswell.

After Tommy had left, Mackie turned to Lena and said, "Gosh, your dad's quite a charmer, just like your brother. Like father, like son—so I guess what they say about that is true after all. Howard's already starting to favor your dad, and what a handsome young man he already is!" Lena smiled and said, "Well, Uncle Mackie, now that your brother John's going to be home after all, I just know that you're looking forward to seeing him again when you drop me off."

It seemed like in no time at all we were pulling up in front of Mabel and John's place. They were waiting at the door. Mackie hopped out of the car and ran up the stairs to give his brother John a big hug. John was beaming, grabbed his brother again, and said, "Wow, it's been three years, Mackie, but it seems even longer than that!"

"You're right about that, Brother! Now, I'm anxious to meet this Mabel of yours that Howard and Lena have told me so much about! Mabel walked over, grabbed Mackie's hand and stood back, giving him and John the once over, "Well, if you two don't look like twins, I don't know who does!"

Mackie stood there grinning as Lucille headed up the steps. "And this is my new bride, Lucille. Best wife on God's green earth, and the best mom a widower's daughter could ever have. Right, Ib?" Ib hopped up the steps and grabbed Lucille's hand and leaned against her.

Mabel was just gushing. "Well, Lucille, I guess it's a little late, but welcome to the family! Gosh, if you ain't a purty little thing! No wonder Mackie is always bragging on you!"

John leaned over, gave Ib's hand a little shake and said, "So this is the baby! Boy did you grow, Princess! How old are you now?"

"Eleven years old, Uncle John. I 'member you. You took us to school sometimes when we'd miss the bus, 'member?"

"Of course I remember. How could I possibly forget? You've still got the freckles I remember so well!"

"I tried to pluck them out, but I couldn't."

"Forget about plucking them out. They look good on you! Oh, you're just so grown up already! I'm so happy to see you again!" John went back into the trailer, holding the door open for Lena and me. But I was feeling so tired that I said good night to everybody and turned and walked back down the steps.

When I came in our door, Mom was making spaghetti. "Mackie called about four o'clock and said youse would be in around seven or so. I hope that youse are all hungry! I'm dying to see Lucy; I haven't seen her since before they got hitched. I'll bet their little girl is big now."

"Yeah," I said, "with freckles."

"Oh, I forgot that she's a freckle-face. How she hated them things—always trying to wash them off!"

"Well, she still hates 'em, and last I heard, she tries to pluck 'em whenever she gets her hands on a pair of tweezers!"

My mom turned to my dad and said, "Mackie's here! Take these boxes and pack up the dinner so's we can git it over to John and Mabel's before somebody drops. Everybody is tired but nobody's too tired to have a good spaghetti dinner. Danny, don't be a party pooper. Go freshen up and help us tote all this food over to your cousin's."

I was tired and sleepy, but when I joined the others at the table, the food and conversation made me forget how tired I was. It was really wonderful to be with my family that night. My dad was talking about old times with Mackie, asking how married life was going, etc. Mom was talking Lucille's ear off asking about how married life was treating her, how Ib was adjusting to her new situation, etc. Ib fell asleep on the sofa just as my mom shoved a pillow under her head.

My mom finally asked me to go out and get Mackie and his family a quiet room somewhere. About seven blocks or so from the fairgrounds, I came across some nice secluded cabins in a little wooded area. They were set far enough back from the street to offer a quiet setting and a good night's rest. I got Mackie and Lucille a nice cabin with two beds, went home and handed Mackie the keys, giving him directions to the cabin.

After Mackie and Lucille left, scooping up Ib on the way out, I dragged myself off to bed. For the first time in weeks, I went to sleep as soon as I had crawled under the covers. Mackie and his family stayed a couple of days. I was busy doing my own thing, working on some new joints and trying to catch up with the work that I had already. Lena spent most of her free time with Ib, making up stories that made Ib laugh. I guess Lena was sorta the unofficial babysitter, entertaining Ib while my folks showed Mackie and Lucille around the carnival and introduced them to all of the family members who were on the road with us or lived in the area.

The day Mackie and his family were leaving, Lena came up to me with Ib and whispered, "Ib just wanted to say goodbye before she and her folks leave. I think this little charmer has a crush on you, Danny."

"Really? Hahaha! Jealous?"

"I can't believe you said that!"

"Neither can I, but I'm not sorry!"

It was getting late, but after everyone said their adoos—and Mackie, Lucille, and Ib were on their way back to Philly—I decided to head out to my workshop and get some work done on all the projects that had been put on the back burner for the past few weeks. At about 7 p.m., just as I was about to wash up and head home, Lena burst through the doorway and announced, "John and Mabel want you to come over for supper. And what was that crack you made about me being jealous of a little girl and you? What was that all about? Are you going bonkers? That's all I need: another nutcase to take care of!" Lena stormed out, and I washed up and headed over to John and Mabel's for dinner.

While we were still eating, John leaned over and said, "Thanks, Danny, for your time. I'm sorry that I took you away from your work, and I probably shouldn't ask this of you, but would you help me set up the new joint? You're pretty damn smart about putting these things together. Look, I'm a good carpenter and painter, but I'd like you to feel free to add a creative touch to the joint, maybe do some figures or palm trees or—it's up to you—whatever might make my joint stand out and draw in more customers."

"Sure, Cousin. I'm busy, but always up to a new challenge. And this sounds like something I could actually have fun doing!"

I felt tuckered out after supper and went to bed early. I was sleepy enough, but just lay there wide-eyed for quite a while, thinking about life and wondering if I would ever be able to open up to someone about my feelings for Lena.

I was finally at the point where I realized that I was in love with Lena, but I didn't have a clue how to act on it. She could be so bratty sometimes, making fun of me or putting me down. Imagine what kind of shape I'd be in if I told Lena how I felt about her, and she treated it like a big joke? I'd be humiliated for life, and there I would be, that one Gypsy in a million who never married, who lived the life of a hermit in a cave somewhere.

I knew that Lena had not had an easy life, as loved as she was. Her parents' divorce had to have had a huge impact on her, and now dealing with John's alcoholism must have taken its toll. It was wonderful seeing her talking with her friends at Edie's wedding, having some time to be a young woman without a lot of worries or cares, to be a normal teenager doing normal teenage stuff. She seemed pretty mature and well-adjusted, though. She was beginning to have a strong personality and assertiveness like her mom and dad. She didn't seem to be shy anymore about letting me or anyone else know what she thought about this or that.

In the meantime, Mabel and I had become pretty good buddies, as she called us. She'd mentioned to me more than once that she'd like to have me get interested in Lena *in that way,* and even told my mom as much. I would get really embarrassed when my mom would bring the subject up. Mom seemed to like the idea, which is probably one reason I felt so good thinking that I was falling in love with Lena, thinking about a future with her, and dreaming about what our life together might be like. Knowing how I felt about Lena would thrill my folks and all of my cousins.

I'd been really busy in the weeks since we got back from Norfolk, rebuilding some concession stands and rewiring some of the juice harnesses. I really enjoyed my projects and the feelings of camaraderie I felt toward everyone I worked with. A lot of my time was spent making short trips to pick up concession stands and bring them back to refurbish. The time away, mostly by myself, gave me time to think about my feelings for Lena away from the context of our daily dealing with each other. But more often than not, instead of making any progress, I'd decide that, yes, I was in love with Lena; but then, no, I guess I wasn't; yes, I was definitely in love—around and around in a goofy circle.

But however I decided, I really didn't have a very clear idea about Lena's feelings for me. Did she love me or not? Sometimes she was warm and affectionate. Other times she seemed intent on pointing out my faults. We needed to have a heart-to-heart conversation and talk about our feelings. The more I took this one-sided approach to our relationship, without hearing Lena's take on it, the more my frustration grew. If ever there was a mind in a muddle, mine certainly was. But whenever I was on my way back to the carnival with another real find to work on, I tried to put all of the *does-she-or-doesn't-she* thinking on hold. Then I could hardly wait to see Lena.

One time, I pulled into the barn right next to John's hot

dog trailer. John came out and was almost drooling over the concession that I had returned with from Philly. All it really needed was some pretty minor cosmetic work. I heard some voices and laughter, turned around and saw Mabel and the twins. I unhooked the trailer and headed home. Lena, Diana, and Betty were talking out front and looked up as I parked my truck and got out. Diana ran over. "Hey, Danny! We're on our way to see *The Jolson Story*. I know that you missed it last time, so why don't you go change and come with us? It'll be fun! It's playing at the inside movie show. Peter and Sally are going too. We gotta leave pretty soon, 'cause the show starts at eight o'clock."

I said sure and turned to go in to put on some clean clothes. After I finished getting dressed, I ran back down the steps to where the girls were waiting. I glanced over at Lena, and she didn't even look at me, or in my direction. I felt a little strange. Maybe I had built up something in my head that wasn't real after all.

I was the last one to squeeze into Diana's car. There were seven of us all together, including three girls—my cousins Sally, Diana, and Betty—but no Lena. At the inside movie show, I sat between Sally and Diana. Just before the movie started, Diana whispered to me that H.P.'s mom was really sick and his aunt had died. "H.P. was pretty darn tore up when he called me, but he wanted me to say hi to you for him and tell you how much he appreciated you being so kind the last time he was here to see me. He was so happy that you drove him to the bus station and was so nice to him."

"Well, I was glad to help out, and I'm real sorry that his auntie passed away. I—" Someone tried to get past me in the aisle and wound up knocking the box of popcorn out of my hand. So I went to get some more. Cousin Sally joined me, and when we got to the refreshment counter, Lena and Cousin Betty were already in line.

Lena looked over in my direction, then she put both hands on top of the refreshment counter and looked real intently at the rows of candy displayed in the shiny glass case. Betty saw me and actually said hi first. "Danny, I thought you saw this movie with the girls at the drive-in last month or so."

"No, but I've sure been looking forward to seeing it." I was so excited to see Lena, and if she wasn't in the mood to talk, Betty surely was.

"Oh, it's worth seeing three or four times," Betty gushed. "It's a great true story, and the acting and music are really wonderful. I really love those old songs. My mosha used to play Al Jolson records all the time when we was on the traveling show circuit. I never really cared for them when I was little, but now I just love them, especially "The Anniversary Song."

I asked, "Isn't that the song that Edie and Pete danced the last dance to, the song that was so dramatic, so beautiful?"

"Yes," Betty said, "but I love all of the music. This is the third time that I've seen the movie!" Betty called Lena over, and I was so happy that we spoke a few words at least.

While Sally and I were walking back inside, she leaned into me and said very slowly, "You know, Danny, Lena is sweet on you!" I just glanced at her with a puzzled look. "Oh come on, Danny," she said, "don't look so surprised. Everyone knows that Lena's mom and your mom want you two to be an item!"

"Wow," I said with a little gasp. "This is the first time I've heard that!"

"That girl's sweet on you, and it's not just your mom and hers that want you two to hook up. She's definitely interested, but until now she's been frustrated because you two kid around so much. She doesn't know how you really feel about her."

We sat down just as the movie theater lights dimmed. The curtains on the stage swished open, and *Movietone News* started. My brief conversation with Sally left me more confused than ever, as I thought about what she had just told me. Well, I'd take the time to mull that over later! I watched the news fly by on the screen, and before I knew it, the movie started.

The movie was as wonderful as everyone said it was, and to top it off, it was a true story about the career of the singer Al

Jolson, which made it an even better story! "The Anniversary Song" was pretty incredible. All these years later, I still can hear the music and see the dancing as it was on the movie screen and at my sister Edie's wedding. We were all humming and singing it on the way home. Diana dropped Cousin Sally off first, then Cousin Betty and the boys, then finally me. "That really was great, wasn't it, Danny?" Diana asked as we pulled up to my trailer.

"Sure was! Would you go see it again?"

Diana turned to me and laughed, "Hmm, maybe. But H.P. would probably really like it! Musicals aren't really my thing, but it did take my mind off of H.P. for a spell. Can't see as how thinking about it all the time is going to help; it hasn't so far. But the movie helped me relax and enjoy myself, I guess. Would *you* go see it again?"

"Well, I'd like to dance with Lena to "The Anniversary Song," that's for sure!"

"Danny, do you know that my sister Connie is trying to fix Lena up with my brother Orville? I don't know how that idea got planted in her head, but that's all she's been talking about. Orville is kinda sweet on Lena, and Connie would like to see Orville follow through and go ahead and ask Lena if she'd like to be his gal. She's offered Lena a complete *outfit* (a trailer and a car or truck), household stuff, furniture, money in the bank, etc., but, so far, Lena just ain't interested. Everything that Connie has come up with hasn't turned Lena's head one bit, because, as I said before, I think that she's sorta sweet on you."

"What makes you say that, Diana?"

"Well, I've got my own problems to deal with, but I certainly can tell when a gal is sweet on a guy, because she keeps mentioning him in the middle of talking about something else. Lena was telling Betty that you're a good worker, the nicest guy ever, and very reliable and responsible. And she says that you don't have no attitude like almost any other guy, who might think that he would be doing his gal a big favor by marrying her!"

"Gosh, that's what Cousin Sally was telling me when we went to the refreshment counter before the movie started. Maybe we should talk, like really soon. What does Lena think about Orville?"

"Well, you know that Orville is at least ten years older than Lena, and that's the first thing she told Connie: that Orville is too old for her. But you know how headstrong Connie is. She figures that Lena doesn't like John all that much and might like to marry and start a new life away from the twins and John and his problems. But Lena told me that she likes John just fine and doesn't want to get married until the twins are older. She doesn't want her mom to get stuck taking care of the twins all by herself. As much as John loves the twins, Lena said that men are really pretty helpless when it comes to raising kids."

"What does Orville say about marrying Lena? Do you think that he's serious?"

"Well, Orville says he'd be like a slave to Lena. He'd even be willing to clean the house, cook, and do the wash, just to keep her happy."

I had a vague recollection of something I'd heard my folks talking about a few years back. "Didn't Orville elope with an older lady when he was real young?"

"Oh yeah, back when Orville was seventeen. And this lady named Deanna was twenty-seven. They was together about eight months when she started going with other guys, and not even behind his back. She'd just get all gussied up, tell Orville that she was going out with a friend, then flounce out and get in a car with some fancy man that Orville had never seen before. Deanna usually was gone all night and came draggin' in early the next morning."

"Wow!"

Diana continued, "All this went on for quite a while, and one day Orville just showed up on our front porch with a small bird in a cage, a five-and-dime cardboard suitcase, and a brand new overcoat. Orville said that he was back for good, or until he found a lady more to his liking, more settled and quietlike. I think that's what he was hoping to find with Lena. But he's too old for her, and way too crazy, so Lena's not interested. This whole thing with Orville just isn't going anywhere.

"Danny, the ball's in your court, as they say. Go ahead and try talking serious to Lena. Let her know that you're interested but willing to wait until she feels that she's ready to be with you."

I leaned over and gave Diana a little peck on the cheek. "Well, I'll just say goodnight on that one!"

The next morning, Cousin Sally came by the house to help my mom sew some curtains. While my mom went out to the storage shed to go through some sewing stuff, Sally made me a large, old-fashioned working man's breakfast: cereal, toast, biscuits, hotcakes, eggs, fruit, bacon, etc. I sat down, and in between bites, I asked Sally, "Hey, what's this thing you were telling me about Lena being sweet on me?"

"Well, we was talking about my boyfriend, and Lena confided in me that Cousin Connie wants to hook her up with Cousin Orville. But she says that she's not going for it, because she thinks that Cousin Orville is a nutcase. She really hasn't seen any boy here that she fancies, except for you, Danny. She thinks that you're kind and considerate, responsible, and awful smart about almost everything. Lena told me that if you don't get involved with anyone else in the next couple of years, maybe, just maybe . . . ."

"What's with the *maybe*, and why wait a couple of years?"

"Lena said that she'd have to wait a few years to get married because she couldn't leave her mom stuck with the twins. Well, that threw me for a loop, Danny, and I really laid into her. 'Stuck with the twins?' I says, 'What do you mean, Lena? They're your mom's babies, and she loves them. Don't worry about your mom. She has her own life, and you'll have your own life. How do you feel about Danny?'

" 'If I was to choose someone, it would be Danny! He's the cutest and smartest and most polite of all the cousins, and he has by far the best personality and no hang-ups whatsoever.' That's exactly what she said, and then my mom came in, and Lena and I changed the subject."

"Well," I said to Sally, "so I'm the cutest, the smartest guy in the whole united world, at least in our little part of it, and I have no hang-ups! My, my, my! I guess that I should feel good, hearing all this. I'm glad I don't have a hat on, because it might split as my head gets bigger." We both had a big laugh over that, but later that same day, I remember wondering if I would be able to calm down enough to go to the work area and get some work done on my projects.

That was the best feel-good morning that I'd had in quite some time, and I did manage to get some work done after all. Then, at about eleven o'clock, John came by to check on me and see how far I was on the projects and said that maybe if I was happy with my progress, I would have some time to help him remodel the hot dog joint that my dad had traded him.

"Cousin, maybe I can help you in a couple of days . . . ."

"Well, come over later today and give me some ideas about what you'd like to do, so's I can get the materials that you'll need to get started on it. All I know is mechanic's work."

"Gosh, Cousin. I don't know about that! You're a darn good painter too. I seen those three joints you painted last week. Pretty good job!"

"Aw, anybody can paint with a spray gun and a jar of paint all mixed up and ready to go. But not just anyone can repair an engine or do body work. I been repairin' cars since I was fourteen years old. I even played hooky from school and stayed home to work on cars with my pa."

I told John that I'd take a break later that day, and I got over to his work place just outside his trailer at about 4 p.m. I wasn't there any more than fifteen minutes when Mabel came out with a huge chunk of chocolate cake and a big cup of coffee. "Kiddo, you been doing a disappearin' act on us for the past few weeks. I'm goin' to adopt you to make sure you're around more, 'cause we need to see more of you."

John piped in, "Mabel, Danny ain't a kid no more! He's an adult now and should be thinkin' about settlin' down soon in a life all his own."

John looked over at me, and I said, "Well, Cousin, I'm actually not in any hurry to settle down anywhere but right here."

John barely looked up from the engine he was working on and said, "Do your thing, kid."

Mabel stood there, hovering, and said, "Well, John, a good start would be for us to just let our Danny finish his piece of cake!"

I had brought a small scratch pad with me and was making notes and little drawings as I jotted down my ideas. John told me to go ahead—any of my ideas and suggestions were welcome, because I was always full of them, and he could use all the help he could get. I stayed a bit and figured out what I needed, like some Masonite for a bunch of cut-out figures and some appliqué to go around the outside of the joint, just below the roof. I figured, given where we were going to be setting up, that some figures in bathing suits would look nice and add to an overall Coney Island look. All John would have to do is paint around the joint and finish the cut-out figures. Easy, peasy!

I took the cake plate and cup over to the front door. Mabel didn't answer the door when I knocked, so I just stacked the dishes by the door and scooted on home.

My mom made some Italian sausage sandwiches with bell peppers and onions. Normally, she would only use the Italian sausage for spaghetti while we were on the road. But this time around, New Orleans was just a short drive away, and there was an Italian deli village nearby, making it easy for Mom to splurge and cook up some of our favorite Italian recipes whenever she wanted to.

We were just finishing up our dinner when my cousin Betty came to the door and said that if anyone was interested in going to the second-run indoor movie show, this was the last night for *The Jolson Story.* Rosie piped up and said that she'd already seen it a couple of times, but then my mom asked me to take her and my dad. Well, I didn't mind seeing it again, so I told Mom that I'd be happy to take them. It was such a great movie! I was sure that they'd enjoy all the romance and beautiful music.

It was on a whim that when we were on our way, we stopped at John and Mabel's and invited them to join us. I thought that it would be neat to see their reaction to the movie. Lena and Diana were sitting on the couch. "Well, John," Mabel said, taking off her housecoat. "Would you care to go see the movie? Danny and the girls just can't stop talking about it!" Mabel was already slipping into her coat and sat down to put on some comfortable-looking shoes. John said that he could use a break after a hard day at work. So off we went, leaving the sleeping twins safe and sound with Lena and Diana to watch over them.

My parents enjoyed seeing the movie so much that they were singing and humming the tunes all the way home. John promised Mabel that they would go out like this more often. It would do them both good, he said, to get out and enjoy themselves and see what the different towns on the circuit had to offer. After such a busy day and a ton of good food, and with the movie songs going around in my head, I fell asleep right away.

The next morning, I got to work on the figures and art work that I needed for my project at John's. I already had almost everything in my work area, and it only took me a couple of hours to cut out all of the artwork. With help from some of the carnies, we pulled out the four sides of the joint, and John got to work doing the overall paint job. My dad helped us get the awnings on all four sides just right. I painted the figures various sea-tone colors. After I attached them around the perimeter of the joint, John came over, beaming. He walked all around the joint, looked inside and out, poked at the figures and the decorative treatment I'd put all around, and then he opened and closed the awnings.

When John had finished admiring my work, he thrust out a hand and tried to give me a fifty-dollar bill that he had all crumpled up. I told him no, he didn't owe me a thing. We were family, and he'd helped my dad and me so many times with car and truck repairs. Then John just reached over and shoved the fifty bucks deep down into one of my pockets. He was gone by the time I fished out the fifty dollar bill. I tried to give it back to Mabel later, but to no avail. She told me sternly that there was no way that she would take back money that was well spent on hard work well done. "Danny," Mabel said, drawing away from me. "John wants you to have that money, and he's hurt that you're making such a big deal out of it. You deserve that money for all of your hard work. Absolutely!

"Everyone loves what you did with that joint, and nobody was surprised to hear that it was you who did such a beautiful job. Danny, you're just so darn talented, creative, and smart, and always ready to help make any job look better. Those is words that so many folks here on the circuit use to describe you. That's why not just your family, but also a lot of other folks love and respect you. So many carnies have told me and John and your folks that they'd be happy if their own children grew up to be even one-half as good as you. You're a serious role model. Don't stop now!"

I walked away just glowing, feeling so proud. Mabel had given me so many compliments, and she was known as a pretty tough cookie when it came to pleasing her. I was happy with all the compliments, but also kinda nervous about being able to live up to them! I had so much of my own work to do that I refused a lot of projects that the carnies wanted me to work on for them. But I did check out what they needed done and gave them ideas and even sketches.

I am in no way an artist in my own right, but even when I was a kid making flowers and doing floral arrangements for the stage and restaurant in my grandparents' traveling show, ideas for new fantastic flowers would come to me. Without doing sketches, I would just make by hand the flowers I was imagining. As for helping out the carnies, who were always ready to pitch in for weddings, birthday celebrations, etc., I was more than happy to share my ideas, with maybe an extra tip or sketch to suggest how to complete the job.

I managed to see a lot of Lena. I would show her whatever I was working on, and sometimes she would work alongside me, helping me rehab and decorate a joint or whatnot. I often did the basics, and Lena would put the finishing touches on a project. She was pretty much my assistant, and often had some real good ideas of her own about how to finish a piece or what the next step should be in renovating or repurposing a joint. She didn't really need to do drawings or sketches; she just seemed to be able to work out everything in her head. I was pretty impressed that Lena knew as much as she did about my work—all, I guess, from just watching me and others work on so many projects.

I decided to give Lena a little gift to show her how much I appreciated her help, but nothing that would embarrass her in any way or cause the other girls to razz her. Some of the girls had real sharp tongues and loved to stir up trouble. My gift had to be something nice, but nothing that would stand out and maybe attract too much attention. I asked my sisters for advice and wound up buying Lena a really nice off-the-shoulder white blouse and black ballerina skirt, a combination that was all the rage with women and girls at the time. A lot of the girls were already wearing these outfits, so no Nosy Nancy would be asking Lena where she got hers.

I gave the gift-wrapped skirt and blouse to Mabel and told her to give my gift to Lena and tell her that it was for her being such a good assistant and making my work easier. Mabel relayed my message and later told me that all Lena said, even before opening the box, was that my gift was cute. I guess that she would have been too embarrassed to say anything more, like to make a big deal about the blouse and skirt in front of her parents and give them any ideas.

It was actually several days later when I was walking with Lena that she thanked me for the blouse and skirt: "You really didn't have to do that, you know," she said softly, looking down with a little smile.

"Lena, I just wanted to," I answered, in the same soft tone.

We continued our slow-paced walk, and all she said was, "I know that," real quick-like.

Lena was going skating with some of the carny girls one night, and she came to my sister Rosie and asked her for a little bit of the Tabu perfume that was so popular then. Rosie put a small amount in a makeup jar, and Lena left, smiling as she took a little whiff. I asked my mom what Tabu was, and she told me it was a fancy perfume that so many girls were buying. My mom winked and smiled at me and said, "You should buy Lena a bottle of that Tabu for helping you so much with your projects. It would mean a lot to her, 'cause she does so much for you, and sometimes I think that you take her for granted."

The next time I went into New Orleans, I bought a bottle of Tabu, had it wrapped up real nice, and wrote a little note thanking Lena for all of her help. "Wow," she said with a big smile. "Thanks, Danny, but you don't really have to buy me stuff to thank me."

"I know that, but I just wanted to give you a special gift to show you how much I appreciate all of your good ideas and suggestions on how to make my projects better. Folks have been saying how much they like the work that you've helped with. I think that you and I make a good team!"

Anyway, Lena seemed happy with all the attention. A few days later, Mabel asked me if I would take her to the store, and as we were leaving, Lena handed Mabel a couple of dollar bills and a tube of lipstick and asked her mom if she could bring her a tube of Revlon's fuchsia shade of lipstick. "Junie Weco gave me this, and I need a new tube. All the older girls are wearing it! I think it makes me look more grown up."

"Well, whatever, Missy!" Mabel said through pursed lips. "You're growing up too fast as it is, but that color does look nice on you."

We got to the store, and I grabbed a shopping cart for Mabel. She'd obviously been in there more than a few times, because pretty soon she was wheeling the cart around at a good clip, crisscrossing the store, retracing her steps to grab more stuff. I was getting frustrated trying to follow her around, so she finally told me to go sit up front and wait for her to finish. A half-hour later, I saw Mabel coming toward me, pushing the shopping cart even faster as she went right by the cosmetics counter and veered off toward the checkout.

"Mabel, stop!" I yelled, and I went over to her as she maneuvered the cart to the end of the shortest checkout line. "Did you remember to get the lipstick for Lena?"

"Oh, Danny, what a lifesaver you are! Could you go back to the cosmetics counter and grab the lipstick for me?" She dug around in her purse, then handed me the tube that Lena had given her.

I went back to the cosmetics counter, handed the tube to the saleslady and watched as she quickly gift wrapped the lipstick box. I got back to Mabel right when it was her turn to check out.

"Oh, good, Danny! Thank you for remembering! I'm glad one of us has a good head on his shoulders!" When we got back to Mabel and John's place, I was carrying in the shopping bags when Mabel handed Lena the tube of lipstick. "Here you go, Daughter! Danny here remembered you wanted this!" Lena blushed, and quickly unwrapped the little box. She turned to me with a big grin and said, "Gee thanks, Danny! You even had it gift wrapped! You're really super!"

The next day, Lena came over to my workspace and asked me if I knew how to ice skate. When I said no, she asked me if I'd like to go with a group of the young folks to the skating rink. That night was one of the free nights, with complimentary lessons for beginners. Well, I had to help my dad finish up a renovation that the show manager wanted ASAP, so I told Lena maybe some other night, when I was free.

The very next day when I was hurrying back to my work area, Lena popped up out of nowhere and asked if I was chicken and afraid to skate. "No way," I said. "It's just that I have to help my dad almost every night."

Lena wouldn't let up, "So, fraidy cat, maybe we could go this afternoon, before six o'clock." I went with Lena that afternoon and had so much fun that I snuck out for the free lessons every Tuesday night. I did real well, because I was a good dancer, and I guess that helped me learn real fast how to skate and manage to do some of the fancier steps and routines. That first afternoon, I did fall down about a dozen times, but everything was fine as soon as I learned how to keep my balance.

One regular skate night, when most of the young folks who were already good skaters liked to show off their moves, I snuck out after dinner and went skating with my sister Rosie and my brother Tony. When I got out on the rink, my skating really threw my sister for a loop because she didn't know that I had been going to the free lessons.

That night, I showed off all of my best routines. I skated backwards and side to side and wowed every girl I skated with. Just before the rink was going to close, Lena pulled me back onto the ice. As we skated, she laughed and said, "Well, I'm guessing that you took my advice and had some of them free lessons! And I'll just bet that them girls you was showing off with was taking the free lessons with you. You're really good, Danny. You're good at everything you set your mind to do."

"Hahaha," I laughed, "You're right. I took your advice! I had to be real careful, though, and not let Mom find out. She's a real worry wart!"

Lena and I were doing some push-and-pull moves, and she said, "I've been skating since I was nine, and when I was eleven, I won fifty dollars at a skating competition in Virginia Beach. For a while, I taught little kids and older folks how to skate, but I've been too busy with John and the twins to do much of anything else. All I can say, Danny Miller, is that you are a super smooth skater, and I'm impressed!"

I had enjoyed the lessons and the skating, but I just had too much work to do, and I felt that I was neglecting my livelihood by not keeping up with my projects.

My mom wasn't too happy either about my brother and sister and me going skating. She was afraid we'd fall and get hurt. She was worried about us, remembering how her younger sister, Lettie, developed a bad limp after a serious fall at age twelve while trying a fancy routine. Mom never did find out about Rosie and Tony going skating after I stopped. They'd just fib and say that they were going to the movies. I think that sneaking off to go skating was just about the only thing we kept from our mom, or our dad, when we were kids.

Well, the skating caper and Lena helping me on projects reinforced my feelings for her, and I guess that by then I'd pretty much decided that she was the gal for me. But I still didn't know where I stood with her. I knew that she'd told my gal cousins that I was the only boy she liked and respected, but maybe that was just so much girl talk.

When we were together, she still got annoyed with me sometimes and treated me like I was a little kid—scolding me, talking down to me, walking away all of a sudden.

"I'm not one of the twins, I'm not a baby! You can't talk to me that way!" How many times did I call that out to Lena whenever she turned and stormed off?

If we were in a group of young people, she often just ignored me or seemed to take the lead in teasing me. Even if we were alone, sometimes she made flippant little remarks that made me feel unsure whether she had the romantic feelings for me that I had for her. And were any romantic feelings she might have for me stronger than the sense of duty she felt to help her mom raise the twins?

I didn't know if my feelings for Lena were real, just wishful thinking on my part, or something from a dream—like that little tiger cub in the dream that I told Lena about, that had gotten away as I tried to hand it to her.

5

Auntie Ilona Meets Her Maker

It was just after my birthday in July of 1950 when we received an awkwardly hand-printed letter from my dad's cousin Meno, who lived near Columbus, Ohio. It was addressed to "the miller famlee," and right away, I recognized Cousin Meno's childish hand-printing. We were sitting around the dinner table, and I laughed as I watched my folks and brothers and sisters try to read the letter.

My youngest brother, Tony, held the letter every which way, pretending that he couldn't make heads or tails out of it. My dad grabbed it, laughing as he held it close, then at arm's length, trying to decipher his cousin's chicken-scratch writing. Finally, my dad made a "what-the-hell" face and passed the letter across the dinner table to me. I had become pretty good at reading the poor hand-printing of my parents' generation, even better than my mom and dad. Cousin Meno's letter turned out to be pretty easy to decipher after all.

Grand-Uncle Jake, Mosha Dragosh's youngest brother, had taken ill during a visit with Cousin Meno and his family and was in the county hospital over in Columbus. Uncle Jake had had chest pains and trouble breathing all of a sudden at Cousin Meno's, and from what the doctors were saying, he had suffered a heart attack. Uncle Jake was probably going to be in the hospital for quite a while.

My dad told the carnival manager what was going on and got a month's leave so that we could go visit and do for Uncle Jake and his family. Stewie Hearn, one of my dad's carny buddies, offered to get our trailer and car to the next stops. My folks threw some household stuff, clothing, and food into the new truck, packed in anybody who wanted to ride along with us, and off we headed to Ohio.

The plan was to drop off me and my nephew Nate at Grand-Uncle Jake and his sister Ilona's place near Marietta, Ohio, then head to Columbus. It turned out that everyone in the house except Auntie Ilona and her grandson Boban had already taken off to do for Uncle Jake. Auntie Ilona had stayed behind because she said that she was feeling poorly and didn't want to make her brother any sicker than he already was. Knowing Auntie Ilona as well as I did, I think that she was looking forward to having her large and noisy family out of the house for a while!

On the way to Uncle Jake and Auntie Ilona's place, my dad told us more about how they and other members of the newly-minted Miller clan left Chicago and wound up living in Ohio years ago. Chicago was where almost the entire clan settled when they arrived in the United States. There was already a large Romanian-Gypsy community there, and that would make settling in and learning the ropes of life in their new country a lot easier.

As it turned out, Auntie Ilona and some other Millers decided after just a short time in Chicago that they didn't care that much for big city life. The noise, crowded streets, traffic jams, cramped housing, skies filled with black smoke—everything seemed too different from the big sky, wide-open spaces and quiet life they had known in their little village back in Bosnia.

Auntie Ilona, Uncle Jake and his wife, Selma, the four Misho cousins, and Cousin Dervo and his family decided to explore their adopted country. The Misho cousins went on the road with a circus and crisscrossed the United States, traveling up and down both coasts and through the middle of the country. Uncle Jake and Aunt

Selma, Auntie Ilona, and Cousin Dervo and his family joined a carnival and traveled its various routes throughout the eastern half of the United States—from the East Coast to the Midwest and back, to the southern states, and as far north as the Canadian border.

After seeing so much of what America had to offer, Auntie Ilona, Uncle Jake and Aunt Selma, and Cousin Dervo and his family decided to put down roots and lead a settled life in Washington County, Ohio, a peaceful, green, and beautiful area about a two-hour drive from the West Virginia border. The Misho cousins soon followed, bringing with them some of the Miloradovitch clan from Chicago.

Washington County was a quiet place where the men could earn a living doing what they had done in rural Bosnia: training and selling horses; farming, blacksmithing, carpentry; building and repairing buggies, farm wagons and travel wagons. Over the years, as more people bought automobiles and trucks, the men of the Miloradovitch clan were pretty quick to take to auto repair and buying, selling, and trading cars, trucks, and trailers.

Auntie Ilona herself was awful smart, and had quickly learned how to read and write English. She taught herself just about everything she needed to know to go into business for herself, and she had a real knack for working with numbers and keeping track of money. She did the bookkeeping for the family's businesses and made some good investments through the years.

After years of hard work building up her bookkeeping business and managing to put away quite a bit of money, Auntie Ilona was ready to slow down and enjoy life. She turned over her bookkeeping business to two of her granddaughters, knowing that they were hard workers and would do just fine on their own.

Now Auntie Ilona had the means to pretty much do whatever she wanted. For many years—and through three marriages to men she usually described as "useless," men who were "a waste of good space"—what she had wanted most was to own land of her own. That was something that Gypsies weren't allowed to do back in many parts of the Old Country.

Aunt Selma passed away soon after Auntie Ilona decided

to retire, and Uncle Jake and Auntie Ilona started looking for property with a house big enough for the two of them and their extended families. They finally found an old disused farm with a huge ramshackle two-story main house that had a bunch of bedrooms, a large kitchen, a full attic, and a finished basement. There would be plenty of space for a wood-working shop for Uncle Jake and a quilting and sewing room for Auntie Ilona. Their master plan was to develop all of those fallow acres and open what eventually would become the county's largest trailer camp, complete with stables, riding trails, and a large man-made pond.

Auntie Ilona and Uncle Jake knew this dream was going to cost a lot of money, but they hadn't realized just how much. They thought that when they left Bosnia, they were also leaving behind the time-honored Bosnian custom of having to pay a meeta to get anything done. That didn't happen! Auntie Ilona and Uncle Jake wound up paying Washington County land surveyors and construction inspectors a small fortune to get the trailer camp up and going. The cost of doing business in Washington County, Ohio, was pretty damn high!

Their project took off, and soon they had one hundred permanent residents and plenty of room to accommodate folks passing through. Ilona and Jake decided early on to put in juice (electricity) and sewer hookups, which a lot of the smaller camps and trailer courts didn't have. They poured a lot of money into the trailer camp but never got around to doing much more to the old house than what was needed to keep it standing.

Besides Uncle Jake and his hard-working grandkids, Auntie Ilona lived with a "special" grandson, Boban, unmarried and childless. And then there were two older, pretty darn helpless grandsons, their wives and four rambunctious kids. I'm not sure why Auntie Ilona called her grandson Boban special. To me and just about everyone else who knew him, he just seemed work-shy, real slow upstairs, and crazy. He was always working on a scam or some outlandish scheme that he bragged was going to make him rich.

Lately, Boban was fixated on capturing a bear cub and training it to dance and prance around like the dancing bears in the Old Country that he had watched over and over in *Movietone News* at the local movie theater. Cousin Meno had told him that our grand-uncle Vadim had bear acts in his circus back in Bosnia. Well, we'd just have to take Cousin Meno's word for that, because Grand-Uncle Vadim disappeared the day he arrived in America, leaving behind his wife, his Belber travel trunk, a couple of trained bears, and four singing monkeys.

Boban's little pea brain just couldn't grasp the idea that a lot of people, including me, thought that it was wrong to take a bear cub away from its mother and train it to do tricks or to *dance*—hop around on its hind legs to music.

The very first time that Boban told me about his bear-training scheme, I really laid into him. "Geez Louise, Boban, the whole bear training thing is a terrible idea. You steal the little cub from its mom, put a ring in its nose, knock out a bunch of its teeth . . ."

"That just ain't true, Danny! Where'd you hear that sob story?"

"I read about it in a book at the liberry!"

"Well, I'm aimin' to do away with . . . "

I rambled on, "Like I said, tryin' to train little bear cubs is just wrong!" "Even putting bears and other animals in cages at the zoo is terrible awful!"

"Oh, come on, Danny, don't get all holier-than-thou with me! I saw them bears at the zoo, and they was fine. I even rode me one; he seemed happy enough to me. Right then, even after that short ride, I knew I had to get one of them bears for myself."

So much for my concerns! Boban had seen bears dancing and doing tricks in the newsreels and saw how the onlookers went crazy with applause and laughter while the bears were performing. He thought trained bears would be his ticket to fame and fortune, and he wanted one. Boban and his ne'er-do-well cousins had already gone bear hunting a few times, flying high on moonshine and model airplane glue.

The first time out as a big-game hunter, Boban came back with a snake bite. Second and last time they went hunting, Boban and Cousin Ned came back with buckshot wounds and the clap. I don't know how all that came about, but Ned told me that Auntie Ilona had made them eat by themselves and sleep out in the barn for quite a while.

I figured Auntie Ilona would be glad to have the place to herself for a week or so and have some peace and quiet while her family was gone. I planned to keep myself and Nate out of Auntie Ilona's way as much as possible but to do for her whenever she needed help with something. The second day we were there, Izzy Green, Auntie Ilona's gentleman friend, stopped by early in the morning and rapped gently on her front door. I knocked on Auntie Ilona's bedroom door and asked her if it was ok to go ahead and let Izzy come in.

"Danny, is that you, Danny? Where'd you come from? What are you doing here?" she hollered through the bedroom door. I tried to explain that Izzy Green had stopped by to see her and was at the front door.

"Good Lord, Danny, don't let Izzy stand out there in the cold! Let him in! Oh, never mind. Just clear a spot for us to sit, and I'll fetch Izzy. You could have just let him in. He won't bite!"

I scooped up Natie in one arm and tried to push his toys and clutter off to one side of the couch. I opened the door to let Izzy in and plopped Natie down in a chair on the enclosed porch.

Auntie Ilona finally came out of her bedroom, closing the door with a strong tug as she turned and shuffled through the living room and into the parlor. "It's just too damn quiet," she said in a half-whisper as her eyes adjusted to the soft early-morning window light. "I dunno, Danny, I woke up with a bad feeling. Something's not right, kiddo. What's going on?" She asked me again what I was doing there.

Auntie Ilona told me later that the first thing she noticed was that there was no smell of fresh coffee, no crackling sound of breakfast bacon sizzling on the griddle, no strained conversation between her granddaughters-in-law, trapped together in a shared living space, who had hated each other from the get-go.

"Sweet Baby Jesus, where *is* everyone?" Where were the grandsons, sitting around, always in the way—gulping food down, laughing and scheming, not good for much, except for making another brat. And those brats, noisy and dropping food all over the place: Where were the little bastards?

Maybe for a brief moment, Auntie Ilona thought that this was heaven, just as run-down and dreary as her earthly home. All at once, Ilona's face brightened. "Oh, hell's bells, Iz! When Danny woke me up, I wondered what in the hell he was doing here and why the place was so damn quiet. I remember now," she said, after breathing a big sigh of relief and getting a bear hug from Izzy.

"The whole sorry bunch drove to Columbus to do for Jake. He can hardly breathe, so this might be the last time he has to look at their ugly mugs! Take a seat, Iz. Here, let me get Natie's crap off of the couch! He's a good little tyke, just likes to take things apart to see what makes 'em work. Problem is, once they're took apart, they don't work no more."

Auntie Ilona pulled a ragged pack of Camel cigarettes from a pocket of her Sears and Roebuck dressing robe, nervously took one out, lit it, and inhaled deeply. She saw something through the gray smoke that confirmed that she had been right: Something *was* wrong—very, very wrong. There was a jumble of Camel cigarette packs on the little table by her well-worn reclining chair.

"Christ! Where's my Camel carton, my special carton with the see-through top?" Her face contracted as she stared angrily at the pile of cigarette packs. Who would have dumped the packs of cigarettes and made off with the empty carton? "Ah, of course! Who else?" Auntie wobbled up off of her favorite overstuffed chair. With two skinny, nicotine-stained fingers, Auntie Ilona pushed the lit cigarette between her thin, tight lips then grabbed the chair back to keep from falling.

"Natie!" Auntie Ilona screamed out, her eyes flashing. I grabbed an arm to help steady her as she headed out to the porch. As she lurched out onto the rough planks of the front porch, we saw Natie sitting in a chair next to the screen door, holding the cigarette carton, turning it every which way, finally setting it down on its side. He pushed his hand through a pile of Tinker Toys, grabbed a handful of round ones and waved them at

Auntie Ilona. "Look Auntie, these will make good wheels for the bear cage I invented. See, no iron bars or chicken wire, just thick glass. I just need to figure out how to attach the wheels!"

Auntie Ilona reached over, trying to grab the carton. "Give me that, you brat!" she squawked. "That's for my Camels, to keep 'em neat on the table." Nate laughed and waved the carton at Auntie Ilona, poking it at her, holding it just out of her reach. "You little hellion, let me have that, or your mosha Jake will give your hide a good strapping!" She grabbed Natie's free arm and pulled him back inside the house, kicking aside the scattered Tinker Toys.

"What you do outta me! You make me so munca," Auntie Ilona moaned, as she fell backwards onto the old couch under the parlor window. One by one, Natie took the little wooden bears out of the Camel carton, carefully wrapped each in a clean white handkerchief and put them back into their log cabin storage box. Nate put the see-through lid back on the carton and handed it to Auntie Ilona before plopping down beside her and Izzy on the couch.

"Iz," Auntie Ilona said, "I need your help! Ever since he rode that damn grizzly bear over at the zoo in Columbus, Boban's been talking non-stop about getting a bear, training the bear to do tricks and dance, maybe even taking the bear peddling. He's been bragging that after he makes his first million dollars, he's gonna buy more bears, start up a traveling bear circus, and go on the road across America! Lord knows that boy's slow, but you know, now he's got some of his half-wit cousins involved, and they's become just as bad as he is, scouting out places to build their bear village—complete with bear rides, bears performing plays and bears dancing all the latest dances. Yikes, Iz! They was out back again last weekend, digging around in that hard clay soil, trying to dig a fire pit."

"Well, Ilona," Izzy said in his deep, calm voice, "usually I'd say cooler heads would prevail, but from what you're telling me, there ain't no cooler heads in that bunch. They ain't going to find no bears in these woods, and even if they did, it wouldn't take Sheriff Stokes long to catch wind of it. And soon enough, Boban's gonna get fixated on a new lost cause and take his pals with him."

"See, Iz, I just knew that you'd put my mind at ease!"

"Well, Miss Ilona, thank you for that! I'll be takin' my leave now. I know I just got here, but I've got to git to the post office and pick up some packages that my kids sent me. Just wanted to stop by and see how you're doin'. Give me a holler when you want some company."

A couple of weeks after they'd left, the family returned from Columbus, Uncle Jake in tow. "Why, we told them doctors we could help Uncle Jake mend right here in his own home," Cousin Hedina chirped. "Nothing like family to heal what ails a body."

Uncle Jake tussled a bit with Natie, then came over to me and said, "I'd like for you and Natie to stick around for a while. Can you manage that? I'm fixin' to make willow lawn furniture to sell, and maybe introduce young Mr. Nate to the fine art of peddling! You'd sure be a big help, Danny."

"Sure, Uncle! You'd be doing me a big favor too, letting me hang around for a while and take a break from some gal problems back home."

"Gal problems? You must be talkin' about your girl, Lena! Mabel tells me every time we talk that she and your mom sure wish that you'd pop the question. You're not gettin' any younger, Danny! Hell, all that gal's gotta do is stand back, take a good look at your handsome mug, see that twinkle in your eye, and think how special you treat her. Right then she'll know for sure that you're the one for her. Go on, stay awhile, and mebbe it's true what they say about absence makin' the heart grow fonder! Stick around, and we'll go in a few days to cut some willows and get started makin' the lawn furniture."

Well, that was just fine with me, because it was a chance for me to think about something else for a while besides where I stood with my gal, Lena—if she even was my gal. She ran hot and cold, sometimes so friendly and affectionate-like, other times treating me like I was a silly kid.

I would dream about her every night, and hump the bed thinking about how she was the prettiest girl in the world in her peacock-blue dress, with her hair up in a bun, dancing every dance with me at the last carny wedding we had gone to. All I knew at this point was that I hadn't liked anyone as much since my ex-girl, Peggy Weco, up and eloped with some other guy.

Late one afternoon, Auntie Ilona asked me if I'd take Natie with me and go look for Boban. She tended to worry when he was out of her sight for more than a few hours. So we went out back where I'd seen Boban and Spare Change and Besnik poking around with shovels, trying to find a spot just right for the centerpiece of the Marietta Bear Circus: the fire pit. We wandered around out in back of the house, whistling, calling out. No response. We were almost down to the old quarry when something landed with a big plop right in front of me. I stopped so hard, I almost fell over. I grabbed Natie, pulled him to me, and looked down to see what had just missed hitting me. Jeez! It was a way-long black rat snake, with its head all crushed in! Boban and Besnik jumped out from behind a big boulder, laughing and screaming. "Hahaha! Well, that's one that didn't git us before we got him! Watch out, Danny! He might rise from the dead for one last bite."

I just stood there, frozen, holding on to Natie, looking down at the snake brains splattered all over my brand-new Keds. "Hey, Danny," Besnik finally said between his hillbilly snorts of laughter, "if you're not doin' nothin' tonight, come out to the old covered bridge with me and Spare Change and Boban. We's goin' to git some supplies for our bear trainin' center."

As turned off as I was by Boban's bear-training scheme, I figured that I would be doing Uncle Jake and Auntie Ilona a favor by tagging along with Boban, Besnik, and Spare Change and seeing to it that they all stayed out of trouble. So I said to count me in.

"Well, alrighty dighty, Danny! We gotta git everything ready and in place before we can even think about goin' bear huntin' again," Boban said. "First things first. I was pickin' up Besnik over at where the county's workin' on the road, this side of Lafaber's Mill Bridge. I noticed that they was removin' the asphalt on the steel plates leadin' up the bridge. They gotta shore up the road on this side of the Little Muskingum 'cause the heavy rains have washed out the filler under the paving and around what they call the 'ay-but-ments.' Them's the same twelve-hundred-pound steel plates we put down when I was doin' road work for the WPA. All we gotta do is git a hold of a couple of Torque Master wrenches and loosen them bolts."

"Whoa," Cousin Spare Change blurted out, "how heavy did you say?"

"Twelve hundred pounds," Boban said matter-of-factly. "Piece of cake. We can ask Oil Can Harry to borry us one of his tow trucks. I got a bottle of whiskey here somewhere that should persuade him. He's lifted cars and trucks a lot heavier than a measly little twelve-hundred-pound steel plate."

"I must have missed something, Cousin," I said, "because I just don't get why we need to grab the steel plates."

"Well, never you mind, Danny Boy," Boban answered, "I'll explain all that later. All you need to know right now is that the steel plate is goin' to help us change the way bears is trained in these United States: Out with the old, in with the new!"

Boban, Besnik, Spare Change and I got over to Harry's garage just as he was locking up for the day. Boban started in with his spiel, "Harry, we need you to borry us your tow truck. I know this ain't much notice, but we's fixin' to go out to the Mill bridge and grab one of them steel plates the county is digging up."

"Jeezus, Boban, let me guess: This has something to do with trainin' bears, huh?"

"Yep, we's gonna put the plate over the fire pit so's the little fellas don't burn their paws and . . . "

Harry jumped right in: "Well, they gotta burn 'em some, else they won't be hoppin' 'round to your tunes. Heh heh heh!" He had a fine throaty laugh, primed with hooch and Lucky Strike cigarettes.

Boban went on like one of those holy-roller preachers. "Harry, you gotta finesse them bears into dancing, little by little. You don't need to make 'em walk through hot coals or nothin' like that. That's just mean! A steel plate over a fire pit is the way to go, just hot enough to where they's itchin' to hop around."

"How are you squirrels gonna git down in the pit to build the fire? That steel plate's pretty much gonna have to stay put."

"We's workin' on that, Harry. We don't gotta cover the whole fuckin' pit. If we make the pit wide enough, we can just put the plate across the middle so there's some room for the firewood and such. But first, we need to git the steel plate before the county carts it off. It's not like them plates grow on trees. We gotta strike while the fire's hot, so to speak." Boban choked back a laugh at his silly play on words while the others just stood there grinning from ear to ear.

"Well," Harry said, "the only way youse is gonna get to borry that tow truck is if you let me do the drivin'. The clutch needs to be coaxed in an out a special way when youse is changin' gears, or you'll strip 'em good."

"Fine. Have it your way, but let's git goin' before it gits any colder," Boban sputtered, shivering in the cold. "Hey Danny, you're good with tools an' such, so I'm glad you're comin' with us! Do Natie a big favor, and bring him with you. He needs to spend more time away from all them "fe-males." He can be our little Injun scout, mebbe whistle if he sees anybody headin' our way. I'm goin' to tell Aunt Ilona that we's takin' him out on a tow job, showin' him the ropes."

When we got back to the trailer camp, Auntie Ilona stared daggers at Boban as he sweated and stammered through his cock-and-bull story about taking Natie out on a tow truck run. Then she turned to me. "Well, Danny, Natie will be with you, so I suppose no harm can come. I'll fix you squirrels a basket of vittles and some hot chocolate and coffee. That should keep you from freezing." I thought at the time that she was probably so anxious for a few hours of peace and quiet, she would have said yes to whatever cockeyed scheme Boban might have come up with.

As we were leaving on our adventure that evening, Auntie

Ilona came out to see us off. "Harry Wooters," she yelled at Oil Can Harry as we drove off, "you keep them boys outta trouble, or you'll be prayin' that the Lord takes you before I can git to you!"

We headed out toward Parker junction with me, Natie, Spare Change and Besnik bumping around back in the winch well. It was a cool and clear night, with the smell of approaching rain hanging in the still air. All of a sudden, Boban stuck his head out of the passenger window and yelled out, "Thar she blows, mateys, there's the bridge. Let's check on our prize." So Natie and I hung back while the others hopped down from the truck and walked ahead and checked out the plate. "Hells bells," Boban said, "they done our work for us! They's just a couple of them bolts left to remove!"

Well, fifteen minutes later—and after Natie had learned a ton of new English and Romani cuss words—Boban and his pals were still at it. Boban was getting frustrated. "Damn! The bolt thread is stripped or somethin'! The fucker's turning but won't go up or down."

"Try using the Torque Master again," I suggested.

"Yeah, right, we already know that's not gonna work," Boban snarled. Besnik grabbed the wrench and went to work.

"Cousin Besnik, wait a minute, I have an idea," I said in my most manly voice. As he tightened the Torque Master wrench head against the bolt, I took two large screwdrivers, and placed their shanks between the metal plate and opposite sides of the bolt. As Besnik turned the wrench, I pulled up on the screwdriver handles with all my strength. The bolt finally popped off and rolled off of the plate.

"Well, shit! Good job, Danny!" Besnik said, poking at me with the wrench. "I guess somebody had his Wheaties this morning, boys!"

"So let's get moving," Harry called out, taking another swig of whiskey from his flask. Harry backed the truck up to the bridge. The others lowered the winch head and wrapped the heavy chains around and around the plate, feeding the smaller hooks through the bolt holes. Within minutes, we had it hoisted up into the winch bed and tied down with more chains. Oil Can Harry slapped me on the shoulder and let me have a swig of his whisky. "Jeez, kid, we was at that fucker for fifteen minutes! We shoulda brought you on board sooner."

We all climbed back into the truck: me and Natie up front with Harry, and the others riding shotgun in the equipment well behind the winch bed. We had brought blankets, and I pulled Natie into my torso and covered him with one blanket and then wrapped both of us together in another one. While we were getting settled in, I was trying to get the story straight in my mind that Boban had told Auntie Ilona about where we were all going.

Ashcan Harry put the truck in reverse; it sputtered and lurched backwards, slipping and sliding on the wet earth. The load shifted suddenly, and the truck shook and rocked back and forth and up and down and threw the men against one another. Harry's foot slipped off of the accelerator, and he frantically stomped back down, the quick movement causing the gears to make a grinding noise that echoed in the quiet night. The truck's wheels spun in the soft earth, spraying tar and mud and gravel in all directions.

"Shit, boys, git out and check them wheels!" Harry yelled out the cab window. "Come on, git out, dig them wheels out, find somethin' to stick under 'em. It's goin' to be fuckin' daylight soon!" Once they'd hopped off the truck, Boban and his sidekicks frantically dug under the wheels with their worn shovels, found a pile of lumber scraps and shoved the bigger scraps under the wheels.

The men stood off to one side as Harry manoevered the truck. To a chorus of profanity, the wheels finally caught. The truck flew backwards in the darkness, and slammed into one of the county's old WPA trucks—so hard that when Harry pulled forward again, the WPA truck was listing in the mud and gravel, like an old rusty tanker losing its battle with a stormy sea.

"Shit, git back in," Harry yelled, his big hands grasping at the gearshift lever. He threw the truck into drive, and we bumped down the road, sending roadside critters scurrying back into the underbrush.

The trees shook as birds flew off into the cool light of the new day. As we drove off, I looked back at the construction site just as daylight touched the old county truck. The tarp covering the back of the truck had slipped to the ground, revealing a stack of steel plates glistening in the early morning light.

We were definitely more than a little late getting back to Auntie Ilona and Uncle Jake's place. As we skidded up to the screened-in front porch, Ilona and Jake hurried out, both telling Harry what they would've done to him and his dead body if they weren't decent God-fearing Christians. Boy, Natie sure did pick up a lot of new words that night!

Auntie Ilona grabbed Natie and half ran back into the house before all hell broke loose. Uncle Jake pushed by Spare Change and Harry and moved quickly past the truck cab, slamming his metal cane against the side of the truck as he wobbled up and down on his way to the winch well. Uncle Jake was so angry, he was shaking, and he grabbed the side of the truck to steady himself. "What the hell is this doing here, Boban?" Jake said, lifting the canvas.

"Well, Uncle, as you can see, it's a steel plate."

"I can see that it's a steel plate, you moron! Just what in Christ's name is it doing hanging from the winch on Oil Can Harry's sorry-ass truck?"

"Now, Uncle, you know how I've been hankerin' to start me a bear trainin' business. It's pretty much all I been thinkin' about fer quite a while. There's a lot of greenbacks in trainin' them little bear cubs to hop around and dance for folks. Problem is, you gotta go with the modern ways of doin' these things. It's a science now: the way bear trainin' is done in America. So we gotta do away with makin' them little fellas walk through hot rocks and coals and such to git them hoppin' around. Well, Boban Stevens to the rescue! I figure by throwin' this here steel plate over the fire pit, the little fellas' feet won't get burned and it won't hurt so much."

"Jeezus, Boban!" Uncle was half-yelling now, and I was afraid maybe he'd have another heart attack or something. "Hot is fuckin' hot! You can get burned touchin' hot metal just like touchin' hot coals. One's as hot as the other!" Uncle Jake was holding on to the side of the truck bed again now, gasping for air like a fish out of water. "I'd ask you what you was thinkin', but thinkin's not your thing! How are you gonna make the metal hot enough to get the bears to hop around?"

"Well, we's going to dig a fire pit, light a big fire, then put the plate over the fire."

"And what are you geniuses gonna use for fuel, and how are you gonna keep the fire going?"

"Well, we's workin' on that, Uncle. Like I said, it's a science, and we gotta go about this whole thing the 'sci-en-ti-fic' way. "

"You're makin' me munca, boy. We'll talk later about gettin' this plate back to where you got it, but right now, you gotta hide it."

"Hide it?" Boban reached over and grabbed one of the chains wrapped around the steel plate, like he wanted to keep Jake from taking it.

"Well, I assume you didn't get the plate at Woolworth's! It's full daylight now, so any minute somebody's going to report it missing, and Sheriff Stokes will be around lookin' for it. He always hits the Gypsy camps first."

"It's one of them plates leading up to the 'ay-but-ment' out on the covered bridge over in Buelton. We can't keep totin' it around. It must weigh as much as the truck," Boban whined.

"Not even close," Uncle Jake said. "It ain't as thick as them plates they're using now. Even so, how you fools came up with this scheme is beyond me. You can't raise and a lower a heavy steel plate like it's a lid on a saucepan!"

"No, no, Uncle, we wasn't gonna try to cover the whole pit, jus' lay the plate down the middle. We . . . "

"Shut the fuck up, Boban, before I make you dig that damn pit right now, and throw your sorry ass into it."

Gosh, I'd never heard Uncle Jake use bad language before, not even words like damn or hell.

Boban looked really flustered, “Uncle Jake, you never did take to none of my ideas, so I won’t bother tryin’ to tell you about how I’m gonna . . . ”

“All I can say is get that damn plate up on the porch roof. Stokes ain’t gonna look up there. Too much work for his lazy ass. This looks like a right puny winch to me. If it’s not heavy-duty enough to carry all that weight up to the porch roof, go over to Lonnie’s and borrow that winch he uses to lift out them big truck engines. Just get the plate up on the porch roof. We’ll worry about taking it back later.”

“Well, this one’ll do just fine,” Harry squeaked out. “We’ll git her to work. She’s never failed me yet.” He was going hoarse, and his voice sounded raw from the cold air. He hunched over and busied himself making sure that the heavy steel plate was secure.

Well, it turned out that Uncle Jake was right. The steel plate was heavier than we remembered, and once it was up over the roof, the top part of the winch came loose, and the plate came crashing down onto the roof.

“Jesus!” Uncle Jake looked disgusted and sick to his stomach at the same time. I decided to make myself scarce and scooted into the house, planning to lay low for a few days.

Heavy rains came the next night and soaked the Gypsy camp over the next three days and nights. The roof of the old porch groaned and creaked as Auntie Ilona and I made our way to the porch on the last night of the storm to watch the rain pour down, so much and so fast that the rain bounced every which way off of the hard earth. Auntie Ilona settled into the comfortable old stuffed chair across from the screen door and lit yet another cigarette. Boy, was that roof ever heaving and creaking under the weight of the steel plate. The whole house was squeaking and settling in the heavy downpour.

“Danny, would you go and get my heavy robe? It’s in on the couch.”

“Anything else?”

“Well, maybe heat up some of that coffee. But be real quiet, Danny. We don’t want no company out here.”

I was busy in the kitchen when I heard a terrible crash. I ran back toward the porch so quickly that I still had the coffee spoon in my right hand. Lord! I looked through the doorway to the porch and all I could see was a big pile of wood and tar paper and wires and what looked like several big pieces of corrugated metal, all jumbled up together on top of where Auntie Ilona had been sitting. Well, by then the whole house was awake, and . . .

The coroner told Auntie Ilona's beau, Izzy, later that when his crew was peeling off everything that was covering poor Auntie Ilona, they got down to the metal plate and the pieces of roofing below it and saw Auntie's arms and legs sticking out from underneath, like she was a big gingerbread man cookie. God forgive me for repeating that, but that's what the man said. The coroner had to call for some extra manpower and a winch to lift the steel plate off of Auntie Ilona.

It sometimes seems like I grew up at funerals, but nothing had prepared me for all the hubbub over Auntie Ilona's funeral. Folks came into town from all across the country. Soon, the trailer camp was filled with trailers, trucks, cars, station wagons, and even a couple of horse-drawn carriages. The overflow visitors headed to the funeral home, and soon enough their parking lot and lawns and lobby and viewing rooms were filled with a great mass of Gypsies, old and young, all working at their assigned tasks: welcoming newcomers, digging pits to roast the pigs; setting up barbecues for chicken, sausages, and burgers; and Lord knows what else. Providing food to the hundreds of mourners was the first priority.

Everyone pretty much brought their own shelter or found it easily enough with relatives or in-laws, or at motels or hotels. First stop for close relatives was the funeral parlor. Even today, Ludad are real careful to keep a vigil by the body of the deceased. The heavy rains continued as more Gypsies arrived and crowded into the little town.

I heard later that Marietta, Ohio, had never seen such a ruckus, not even on the WWI Armistice or VE Day or VJ Day. Or even when the KKK used to take over the whole town for their rallies or whatever they called their gatherings. There were so many Gypsies that a couple of babies were born and a few older Gypsies died. The folks who had died had to be buried, so even more Gypsies made their way to Marietta.

Now, in our particular tradition, burial is supposed to take place three days after the person passes away. With all the hubbub and folks coming from all over Canada, the USA, and Mexico, the family decided to put off Auntie Ilona's burial until all of the clan elders had arrived. One of them, Jimmy Jenkins, "The King of Most of the Gypsies Everywhere," was in prison for fraud and wouldn't be paroled for another week or so.

Uncle Jake wasn't happy with all the ruckus, and he thought that Auntie Ilona might just come back and haunt him if he didn't follow tradition. But, his family nagged him until he reluctantly agreed to ask the owner of the funeral home handling Auntie Ilona's funeral to "put her on ice" until Jimmy Jenkins and other muckety-mucks of the various clans arrived. The preparations for the funeral continued, and even more stragglers crowded into the already congested little town.

Pretty soon, there were groups making lawn furniture under the tents and awnings that were set up against the rains. The new arrivals were busy selling the "genu-wine," hand-crafted willow and birch furniture they'd just made. Other folks were buying, selling, and trading trailers, cars, and trucks. There was music, a lot of music. The band that would be marching at the head of the funeral procession was practicing all of Auntie Ilona's favorite tunes. Izzy was there, of course, heading up the fiddle section.

Local radio and newspaper people arrived in droves to cover the preparations for Auntie Ilona's funeral and all the goings-on. One of the national radio networks sent a crew to cover the funeral and interview the family and others attending the funeral.

After Auntie Ilona's burial, a reporter showed up at the trailer camp to do a follow-up piece. I offered to take him around to talk to the townspeople he had on his contact list.

Our first stop was at the Mendez Funeral Home to have a chat with old Doc Mendez. I figured that was as good a place as any to start, especially since the funeral home was sort of the ground zero of everything that had been going on.

Doc Mendez said that he still couldn't figure out how so many people had showed up so quickly. "Hell, there was Gypsies here who didn't even know Miss Ilona! There was folks who wasn't even Gypsies, who just showed up and asked for directions to the big Gypsy barbecue—roamin' around, parkin' all over, peein' and poopin' everywhere, campin' out on folks' lawns. We was already full up with Miss Ilona's kinfolk and Gypsies coming out of the woodwork.

"The older folks seemed respectable enough, but some of the younger ones drove around hootin' and hollerin', carryin' on, drinkin' and carousin' with the locals and stayin' up all night. In the meantime, it seemed like all of 'em had a barbecue fired up or a pit blazin', stinkin' up the inside and outside with their damn roasted pigs!

"You know, I buried a couple of Miss Ilona's husbands and some of her men friends. I'm signed up to do a Hebrew funeral for her beau, Izzy. Miss Ilona was a nice, decent lady, not one of them Southern-belle fake-friendly types. She was always interested in what a person had to say. Good listener. *Hated* the sheriff. Said he put up signs just to confuse people and get money out of 'em to avoid going to court. Miss Ilona didn't like to be fussed over. She would have gotten up and walked away from this mayhem if she could have!"

Doc Mendez continued, dabbing at his face with a big white handkerchief, "Well, finally, I'd had it. Couldn't put up with the ruckus no longer. The Missus has a bad heart, and she was doin' poorly with all them strangers loiterin' around, peein' and poopin' in our garden, playin' that damn music all day and night.

"Miss Ilona had been pretty clear that she didn't want no fuss or ruckus when it was time to lay her to rest. If I had known who told all these folks from hell-knows-where about her dying and all, I'd have killed that son of a bitch with my bare hands and fed him to the pigs.

"Anyways, before the week was up, me and the Missus had had enough of all the visitors' shenanigans. So, I did it. I got rid of the lot of 'em!"

"How'd you manage to do that—get rid of 'em?" the reporter asked, his pen at the ready.

"Well, goin' on a week, we hurried things up a bit and just up and got ready to bury the lady. I finally grew some balls and just told her family that embalmin' or no embalmin', our coolin' system was cuttin' in and out and we just had to bury her then and there. We plopped her casket down next to the open grave, called the padre, got the immediate family together, and that was that.

"Once word got round that things was over and done with, most of the Gypsies paid their respects at the gravesite, then pretty much packed up and headed out right after the burial. I think that the older folks was just happy to be going home. The sheriff and his men got the stragglers to head out ASAP. Hell, we've still got an extra grounds crew and folks from the parks department cleaning up the mess that the out-of-towners left behind."

Writing about all this so many years later, I still think that Auntie Ilona would have approved of how old Doc Mendez handled things. She hated being fussed over. And she didn't like it when folks stopped by to visit and stayed too long.

6

Way-Too-Young Love

Within a few weeks after Auntie Ilona's funeral, Uncle Jake seemed to be doing pretty good. But not so good that he was ready to follow through with his plan to make a new batch of willow lawn furniture and take Natie peddling. There would be plenty of time for all that when we returned in a year for Auntie Ilona's pomana—her memorial dinner.

I decided that it was time for me and Natie to get back to the family and the carnival. We took a Greyhound bus from Marietta to hook up with the carnival in Indianapolis. After just a couple of days of Lena and me being back together, it seemed to me that things were finally beginning to fall into place romantically for us—in my head, anyway. I was more sure of myself now, and finally my uncertainty about how Lena felt about me was beginning to give way to me trying to imagine what our future life together might be like.

I felt that Lena was the only gal in the whole world for me, at least those parts of the world that the traveling shows had taken us through. Lena was so happy to see me and so affectionate and nice to me, that I no longer had any doubts. It was obvious to me, to her folks, and to mine, that she really did care for me. A few days after I got back from Ohio, Lena's brother Howard told me again, maybe for the third or fourth time, that Lena and I should get married so that he and I could be brothers.

But Lena and I still hadn't had any personal alone time together. We crossed paths now and then, stopped to chat, or I grabbed the groceries or whatever she had and carried them home for her. Sometimes, my mom or Mabel would ask me to give Lena a ride somewhere, or I'd see her walking and offer her a lift. But our banter never became a serious conversation about our feelings or what each of us hoped for in the future—stuff like that.

Mabel called my mom *Aunt.* Remember, Mabel's husband, John, was my cousin, but Lena's dad, Tommy Boswell, was Mabel's ex-husband. So Lena and I weren't family and we had to be careful when we were in public and at carnival events.

Back in the day, an unrelated young man and woman couldn't spend time alone together, so young people especially were watched real close. Even at dances, girls danced with one another or male family members, and the young men either danced with girls and women they were related to or stood in little groups, kidding one another about being sweet on whatever girls caught their eye.

Family time was different, as was the case when we were at carnival events, weddings, etc., with family members. Our parents seemed ready to break the rules and cut us a lot of slack. Even before I had gone to Ohio to visit Uncle Jake and Auntie Ilona, my folks, Mabel, Cousin John, and Lena's brother had hinted that they were hoping that something romantic would happen between Lena and me. They were more up front about that since I returned. They seemed pleased whenever they saw Lena and me talking or laughing together.

We were still bantering with each other, joking around, going back and forth, and kidding one another, but this time around, all of this seemed more affectionate and playful, a settled pattern of upbeat conversations, not a competition to prove which of us was just fine without the other.

Sometimes, the way that Lena looked at me revealed real affection for me, but again, we didn't spend enough time together alone to really talk about our feelings for each other. When we weren't on the road, we were setting up, then working the crowds, then having meals together or planning and participating in some kind of gathering. We talked, we danced, and we worked side by side—never alone—always with other folks around.

But the confidence was there inside me. So no more sleepless nights—nights spent humping the bed while thinking about Lena. After I returned from Ohio, I really wanted to show Lena how I felt about her. I wanted to hold her close to me. How I wanted to press my lips against hers! Some nights, I still had sexual urges, but at least now I eventually fell into a deep, restful sleep.

Lena and I were all excited when we heard that a carny family was planning a wedding. It probably wasn't going to be as elaborate as my sister Edie's wedding celebration, but still, it would be another chance to dress up, be together with friends, and show off our dance moves. There would be a lot of good live music, and food to last for days, including a couple of pit-roasted pigs! The groom's father was an experienced fisherman, so we knew that there would be plenty of fish dishes to share. The wedding itself and all the food and drink and socializing would help us forget for at least a couple of days all of the hard work involved in getting the carnival packed up and ready to leave for winter quarters in Sarasota, Florida.

Like almost all of the other young people, Lena and I both volunteered to get the wedding reception area ready. We were still at the fairgrounds in Indianapolis, so the juice, the lights, and the dance floor were ready. All we needed to do was set up a lot of tables and decorate. It was events like this that usually got my creative juices flowing. I had already come up with a lot of ideas about what I like to call my fantasy flowers, flowers that were smaller or larger, or different colors or had different foliage, than people were used to seeing. But folks were always happy with what I came up with. They knew that my flowers and greenery were unique.

Well, this time around, the bride-to-be decided on the really original idea of decorating with streamers. "They'se all rolled up and ready to go in them little round packages at the five-and-dime. Let's git movin' and git this show on the road!"

I guessed there would be no need for flowers, trees, or greenery—real or fantasy. Wow! But being a good sport, I volunteered to help put up the streamers. I went up and down that damn ladder so many times that I was ready to collapse onto my bed around 9 p.m. I had to quit early. I'm not known to be a quitter, but I was bushed. I let someone else finish.

The bridal party showed up early—about 1 p.m.—on the day of the wedding. I guess they were antsy or hungry and thirsty and decided to get things going on their own schedule. Yikes! The wedding table where the bride and groom and the bridesmaids and best men were going to sit wouldn't be ready for another couple of hours. Well, we couldn't tell the bridal party to come back later, so everybody who was busy decorating had to just stop what they were doing and concentrate on getting some snacks and food ready to serve before dinner time.

The folks setting up the seafood area turned up the burners under the dozen or so fish dishes. Soon, there were some fish snacks ready for the early arrivals, then some plated seafood entrées. There were no real complaints, but since a lot of the younger guests didn't like seafood, the planning committee called to have the band show up early. While we were waiting for them to arrive, the local carny musicians started playing some hot Latin dance music.

The wedding guests started dancing and drinking kinda early. By four-thirty in the afternoon, the wedding dinner was set out. We started dancing again at about six. Each set lasted about two hours. After each set, the band took a break, and the carny musicians would play for about an hour, then the hired band would play for another two hours. By the time the band had finished their first set, a lot of the wedding guests, especially the younger ones, had been drinking hard booze and mixed drinks for over six hours. While all this was going on, volunteers at the wedding table were taking cash donations for the happy couple. They raised over thirty-six hundred dollars—not so shabby—and everybody was having a really great time. We all drank and ate and danced a lot. The dancing probably kept some of the guests from getting drunker and sicker earlier.

I had never danced so much in my whole life. Before it got dark out, I had already danced seven dances with Lena. I was so happy with my time on the dance floor with her that if the busybodies were going to razz us and gossip, I didn't really care. I danced with all of my cousins and a few carny girls, but when the slow ones came around, I'd search out Lena. She was soon following me real good, especially on the Latin numbers. Oh, how she loved the fast-paced Latin numbers, which were my favorites too! I felt at times that I was holding her too tight during our last dance that night. I was in all of my dancing glory as we glided across the dance floor. As we passed my brother Tony, he called out, "Hey, Brother! Could you hold Lena any tighter?" We just danced away from him to the other side of the dance floor and stopped to take a little breather.

As soon as we had grabbed another drink, Mabel walked up, grabbed my hand, and dragged me out onto the dance floor for a jitterbug. As we finished and walked back to where Lena was waiting, Mabel said to me, "The next time that you dance with my girl, don't crush her so much that she can't breathe. Look how tired and out of breath she looks. You kids have fun tonight, but remember, John and I want Lena back alive!" Well, Lena did look a little pale, but she said that she wasn't tired and wasn't complaining.

The bride and groom had left about nine o'clock, driving to Miami for a week-long honeymoon. Duke was twenty-one years old, and his lovely bride, Letty, was nineteen. Their dads had been business partners years ago. Even as a little kid, the groom used to watch Letty and follow her around, and she seemed to really enjoy all of the attention. I wonder if the parents thought all those years ago that their children would wind up married to each other. Letty's parents had just joined the traveling show the spring before the wedding, and met up with Duke's folks who had been traveling with the show for over ten years.

For a couple of weeks, I barely saw Lena. We were both busy with our families and didn't have much free time to spend together. Whenever I did run into her, our encounters were brief but smiling and affectionate. We always touched or hugged each other now, and once in a while she would surprise me with a kiss on the cheek.

When I finally had some free time, I went to call on Lena. Mabel met me at the door, all sad-eyed. Lena's brother Howard had been in a bad accident in Norfolk and had to go to the emergency room. The doctors said that he had a serious concussion and would need to take off work for a while and get a lot of rest at home. So her dad had asked Lena to go help take care of her brother.

Every day that she was gone was agony for me. One week, two weeks, three long weeks without seeing Lena. I was climbing the walls during the long days and humping my bed at night just thinking about her.

I'd call her dad's place to see how Howard was doing, hoping that at some point Lena would be the one to answer the phone. Every single time I called, the housekeeper would pick up the phone and tell me that Lena wasn't home. She was at the store or at the doctor's office with Howard. He was having a real tough time recovering from the accident.

Finally, after Lena had been gone about a month or so, Mabel knocked on our door and asked if I could go to the airport and bring Lena home. I got to the airport and waited and waited for her plane to land. It had been re-routed to Kansas City because of the stormy weather. Finally, two hours late, the old airplane dropped down out of the storm clouds, landed—sputtering and bouncing around—and squeaked to a stop. I had made several calls to Mabel and John to let them know what had happened and when the airplane might finally land.

When I saw Lena drag herself into the terminal, she looked so tired and forlorn, like one of those war refugees we used to see in the newsreels at the movie shows. I hugged her and pressed my lips to hers as I squeezed her tight and whispered, "Oh, how I missed you, my girl!" She was in such a daze that she probably didn't realize that I had just kissed her—our first real kiss! She didn't smile or respond or even look right at me; that's how tired and out of it she was. She finally mumbled that we had to go to the luggage area to grab her bags. We hurried over to the baggage claim area. When we got there, Lena was so exhausted that she kinda staggered over to a bench and actually laid down and fell asleep. Or had she fainted? Yikes! I ran over to one of the baggage guys and told him that I needed a doctor right away!

A doctor and nurse came and hovered over Lena, taking her pulse and checking her breathing. Lena looked even paler now. I tried to explain to the doctor and nurse that Lena wasn't used to flying, that the flight had been delayed, etc. Then the doc put some smelling salts under Lena's nose to see if he could revive her. Lena coughed, opened her eyes real wide, and moved her head from side to side.

The doc lit a cigarette and said, "Look, pal, there's nothing to worry about. Your little lady's going to be just fine. She just had too much to drink. All you can do is let her sleep it off. Make sure that she gets plenty of rest when you get her home. And give her these, the first one as soon as you get home." The doctor handed me a couple of little packets containing a white powder.

Too much to drink!? What the hell? Jeez! My head was spinning, trying to take in everything that had happened and what the doctor had said. The doctor and nurse stayed with Lena while I grabbed her baggage claim tickets and picked up her bags. I had the Red Cap guy carry the bags while I slowly walked Lena to my truck. It took both the Red Cap and me to get Lena into the cab of the truck. She was limp and flopping around, like a big drunken rag doll.

"These things happen, Mister," the Red Cap guy said, shaking my hand. "Kids drink too much now and then, like kids has always drank too much sometimes. I know I sure did, 'til the war straightened me out." He smiled and patted me on the shoulder. "Just take care of the little lady."

When we got home, I pulled right up to the trailer. Then Lena's folks came out. I was so tired and disappointed, I guess, seeing Lena barely able to sit up in her seat. John just stood there, holding the truck door half open, like he was trying to decide how to handle the situation. "She's real exhausted," I finally muttered, sounding kinda tired myself. "The airport doc told me to give Lena these powders to help her sleep." John took the little packets and held them up and shook them before handing them to Mabel. I reached over to steady Lena as she swung a leg toward the truck door. "The doc said to put her to bed and let her sleep as long as she can," I said quietly. "I guess that the flight took a lot outta her, poor kid. But the doc said that she should be fine in the morning."

I took Lena's luggage down from the truck and then helped John maneuver Lena out of the front seat. As John helped Lena into the trailer, Mabel started to follow them in, then turned around and gave me a hug and a peck on the check. "Oh, Danny!" she said, sounding as tired as could be. "Thank goodness you're in our lives. Sometimes I just don't know how we'd manage without you here. Even Miss Independent Woman in there has said as much."

Man, I had a terrible time trying to get to sleep. I tossed and turned and almost rolled off the bed a few times before I drifted off to sleep. The next morning I got up real early and went over with my mom and sisters to see Lena. She still seemed out of it, but at least she made sense when she talked. Mabel was trying to get her to drink some tea, but Lena pushed the cup away and got up from the kitchen table, saying that she just wanted to get more sleep. Mabel took Lena to her bedroom, then came back and made some coffee. My mom said that she was going to stay for a while, so me and my sisters went on home.

Mom came home in the early afternoon and said that Lena finally woke up about eleven o'clock and was so hungry that

Mabel couldn't cook fast enough to keep her happy. Lena told my mom that she didn't remember coming home at all. She remembered falling asleep at the airport in Kansas City and someone gently shaking her awake so that she could get back on the plane to Indianapolis. She said that she sorta remembered me holding her up as we walked to the truck. So she had already forgotten our first real kiss; at least it seemed that way!

I went back over to Mabel and John's place later and asked Lena if she'd like to take a short walk. We were barely underway when she turned to me and asked if I had kissed her at the airport.

"You kissed me right on the lips?"

"Yes, I did."

"You was that glad to see me?"

"Yes, I was."

I left it at that, because I didn't want to confuse her any more than I already had. I couldn't tell her why I had been so glad to see her, that I had thought about her all day every day that she had been away, that I had humped my bed every night thinking about her before falling asleep, wondering when I would see her again. And certainly, no way could I tell Lena that I thought she was the brightest, prettiest girl in the whole united world, that I loved her and wanted to spend the rest of my life with her. But wow! Lena asking me if I had really kissed her on the lips made me think that all of my plans for our life together weren't so crazy after all.

I stuck to my story, that I had kissed Lena because I was so glad to see her. I gave her a hug and walked away toward home, feeling pretty confused and stupid. I stopped at the work area where my brother Luca and I were repairing a couple of pan joints. I told Luca and the other guys about my strange conversation with Lena. We chatted back and forth, finally settled back down into the repair work, and I did my thing as if nothing had happened earlier with Lena.

Luca and I finally headed home, tired and hungry. As soon as we were in the front door, Mabel showed up with a tray piled high with pigs in a blanket, bacon, ham, and toast—enough for the whole family. Mabel was a really good country cook, almost as good as our own mom. Mabel came back a little while later for the dishes and brought Luca and me Good Humor bars and some snacks for later. She leaned into my brother and said, "Luca, you know, I might just adopt your brother! He just does so much for Lena and John and me."

After Mabel left, I was tired and ready to hit the sack when my brothers started teasing me nonstop: "Oh, I might just adopt you, I might just adopt you, Danny!" I told them to knock it off and headed off to bed. After all of the emotions I had experienced with Lena, I fell asleep in nothing flat. My mom mentioned to me at breakfast the next morning that there was going to be a surprise birthday party for my favorite girl cousin, Diana.

When I was on the road with my uncle Benno, Diana calmed me down and helped me keep going when Peggy Weco (who I think of as my first serious girlfriend) broke my heart. Peggy had called me just before we were supposed to go out on a date and told me that she couldn't keep our date because she had eloped with Ashcan Harry's oldest boy, Hal. Things were all patched up between Peggy and me now, largely because of Diana's efforts. Cousin Diana had been so good to me and my folks over the years, and I was looking forward to seeing her again. I finished the huge breakfast and headed on over to the wedding reception area to help decorate for the party.

It was supposed to be a pretty small event, just the immediate family and folks on the same work crews as me and my dad and Diana's dad and brothers. Ashcan Harry and his family were there too, and that was about it, at least at first. As soon as they put some records on, other carnies started streaming in. Pretty soon there was quite a crowd, and then someone showed up with a car trunk full of booze: all kinds of different already-mixed cocktails and the straight stuff. And there was plenty of beer for the folks who weren't big hard-liquor drinkers. Someone had brought along a bartender's guide, and they were putting together all kinds of mixed drinks.

Lena went along the bar tables and sampled a lot of the different drinks, most of which were some kind of fruit juice with the hard stuff mixed in. I don't think she could taste the booze, because she was downing the cocktails like they were Kool Aid!

Diana had way too much to drink and was wobbling around and staggering from table to table. All of the guys and a few girls danced with her to sober her up and keep her from getting sick all over the place, like she did at the last big wedding. Most folks were still enjoying themselves and drinking more and more. The pizza and chicken and desserts disappeared pretty much as quick as they were put out, so I guess almost everyone just figured there was nothing else to do but keep dancing and drinking.

Even I started to feel a little tipsy after tasting so many of the fancy drinks the hosts were lining up along the bar table. My voice sounded kinda muffled, and I was really enjoying how I was beginning to feel. I don't think that I had ever drank so much in my entire life. Some drinks were real sweet; others tasted like regular pop and soft drinks, especially the sloe gin. Someone handed me a drink called a zombie, which I downed right away and really enjoyed. But then I saw Lena heading toward the side door, getting sick to her stomach before she made it that far. I went out after her and held her head as she tried to throw up some more. At first she just got up a little bit. I took some tissues and wiped her face, and then she threw up real good.

I looked around and saw that we were standing right by Drake the Snake Man's little trailer that he was rehabbing to sleep in. I went ahead and opened the door. I knew that there was a couch in there, and it had already been opened up to make a bed. I just maneuvered Lena over onto it and closed the trailer door because I heard somebody peeing outside. I pulled myself up and over to the other side of the bed against the wall and laid down beside Lena, feeling really tipsy and cold. There was a blanket there, and somehow, I managed to cover us as we both drifted off to sleep.

Oh, Lord, I can't explain even now, all these years later, what happened, or how it happened. I found myself with my arms wrapped around Lena and my hands on her breasts, first on top of her dress, then right on her breasts. Of course, I later blamed it on the booze, but would a decent person—a person who really loved someone—do what I did no matter how drunk? I was squeezing and fondling her breasts, and finally, Lena woke up. She saw my face in the moonlight streaming through the little window next to the sofa bed and kept repeating, "Hey, hey, hey! What are you doing?"

I wasn't thinking about what I was doing, about what I was about to do, about anything. My body was like it was on automatic: I started kissing Lena, and she started to struggle and tried to pull away from me. But I was holding her so tight that she couldn't get out of the bed. I was kissing her roughly, and finally she pulled her mouth away from mine long enough to blurt out, "Do you want me to scream?" But I just kept kissing her, and telling her that I loved her, and wanted to marry her. The more I kissed her, the more I fondled her, and soon my hand was down rubbing her in her bad place, all moist and warm.

Well, it just happened. And ever since, I've regretted how it happened. But it happened. Before I knew it, I had pulled down Lena's panties, crawled up on top of her, and slipped inside her as she struggled and cried out in anger and pain. I fell back onto the side of the bed. Lena tumbled out of bed, trying to straighten out her clothes. She was sobbing and cried out, "You bastard! I'll never, ever forgive you for this. I'm going to tell my folks and Howard what you did to me, and you'll be sorry, Danny Miller!" Shaking with anger, Lena clutched at the blanket, turned, opened the trailer door, and hurried out.

Daylight was just coming as I sat up in the bed and started thinking about what I had just done, wondering how my life could even go on, how I could ever forgive myself. I gathered up the bloody sheet and headed home, thinking that maybe John and Mabel and my folks would be outside waiting for me, to tell me to go away, that I was dead to them. I went through the back door and slipped into bed.

I couldn't sleep. Oh my God, what had I done, and why? I finally crawled out of bed and showered, then showered again.

How is Lena, I wondered. *Has she told anybody about what I did? Is she ok?* There was so much blood on the sheets that I had tossed into the trash on my way home.

Well, my mom fixed one of her a-lot-of-everything breakfasts, but I couldn't eat even a bite. I just sat there, staring down at the plate. I was sure that Mabel and John would show up at any minute, John with a gun—his finger on the trigger—ready to execute me on the spot. Finally, my dad asked why I looked so glum, was I maybe hung over? I just mumbled that I had sampled too many drinks and felt really lousy.

About ten o'clock, Mabel came in. I pretended that I hadn't seen her. I finally managed to say, "I need some coffee." And right away, Mabel came over and said, "Don't tell me your young Danny has a hangover! Good God, Lena was up early, throwing up all over the place! On my way over here, I passed by Lucy's boy Lonnie getting sick outside of his truck. You young folks just can't handle your booze!"

Two days later, about 6 p.m., Lena came by, opened the front door and walked over to me, pushing her face right up into mine. I had to look away; I just couldn't look her in the eye.

"I just came here to tell you that you know what you did, Danny Miller! As much as I used to admire and respect you, and how much my folks love you, if I was to tell John or my mom, they would shoot you dead, you son of a bitch! But most probably, your own dad would beat them to it and blow your head off. Don't you ever dare talk to me again!"

All I could say was that I was so sorry, that I loved her so much, that I just didn't understand how I could have done what I did to someone I loved so much.

"Boy, what a way to show me how much you love me! Just don't even try to speak to me ever, ever again. You are dead to me, Danny Miller!"

I spent days wondering how I could ever make this right, still too upset with myself to get much done in the way of work. When I wasn't in the workshop, I just wandered around the carnival grounds like a zombie. I really didn't think that I could go on.

But I had to stop feeling sorry for myself; I had to go on. I couldn't let my family down. We were going to be really busy getting the carnival ready to go back on the road. It was like taking apart a little town, finding a place for everything and everyone, then arriving at our next stop and repeating the whole process in reverse motion. Like running film backwards in a movie projector.

I felt like I was a walking, undead zombie, and I acted like one. My folks knew something was very, very wrong, because I had just become a different person, a stranger who looked like the Danny Miller they had raised to be a good, decent person. I just worked, ate, and tried to sleep enough to keep up my energy. I certainly felt like I didn't deserve my wonderful, loving family. We had never had a bad or cross word between us all the time I was growing up.

My mom just knew that something was up with me. "Danny, I'm your mother. Son, I know that there's something terrible wrong with you. I feel that you need help with something, and it hurts me that you won't tell me what it is. You're not yourself at all, my love. Please, just tell me what's going on. I promise that I won't tell another living soul, not even your dad. He's so worried about you and so sad that you won't talk to him man-to-man about what's going on with you. Your brothers and sisters and Mabel and John, they're all concerned and want to help. One thing I do know, Son, is that something terrible happened to make you so standoffish and withdrawn. Come on, Danny, maybe I can help."

All I did was hold my head down. I couldn't let my eyes meet hers. If she had looked into my eyes, she would have known that the reason for my strange behavior was inside me, and no one else had done anything to make me feel this way. I was carrying around so much guilt and remorse, my mom would have sensed that right away. I felt so dirty, so guilty, that I couldn't even think straight.

Other than my dad and my brothers, the guys I worked with were just keeping themselves to themselves; they didn't even bother to ask me questions or my opinion any more. Days, weeks, and then months of working quietly in guilty silence went by. I no longer looked up to see someone glancing over at me with a sad or hurt look on their face. Now, when they looked in my direction, they looked right through me, like I wasn't even there.

One day, Lena came over to the workshop and—totally ignoring me—tried to make small talk and conversation with my dad and my brothers. She went on and on about how she'd like to try carpentry and painting and maybe when she got good enough, she could help rehab and paint the concession stands. She finally took a breath and said, "Well, maybe not the painting. I can't stand the smell of paint. If I breathe it in long enough, it makes me dizzy." Finally, she turned in my direction and said, "Mom really needs you to drive her to the store when you finish up here for the day." Then, she turned and walked away. My God, how was I going to face Mabel? Maybe this was a trap to lure me over to their place, where John would put me out of my misery with one of his hunting knives, maybe feed my sad ass to the pigs, and no one would ever be the wiser. But why had they waited so long?

I knocked on the door and called out, "Mabel, your chauffeur's here!" John opened the door wide, beamed, and said, "You don't have to be the chauffeur today after all, Danny. I came home early. But, I'm sure glad that you're here to pitch in and help out when I'm working in town. I've been doing some welding and painting so I can catch up on all of my bills. The payments on the trailer and new truck are awful, so I'm trying to get ahead as much as I can. I really do appreciate everything that you do for me, Danny. You're a good cousin. You've always been helpful, since you was a little tyke."

Jeez. John building me up and being so nice was like a hundred needles pricking me, reminding me what a louse I really was. "John, I gotta get home. I'll be seeing you later. And as I was on my way out, Mabel and Lena were coming in with laundry baskets. The twins were right behind, yelling and shoving each other. Both Lena and Mabel looked pretty grim. *Oh, great,* I thought. *Mabel knows; any minute now John will know too, and I'll be dead. They'll never find my body.*

Mabel finally looked up, smiled, and said, "Hey, Danny, you must be a busy beaver. I haven't seen you since I don't know when! You're like one of them hermits, off keeping yourself to yourself in a cave somewhere!" Her words were like more needles pricking my skin. So I headed home, feeling like the biggest phony in the whole world.

About a week later, I was sawing some wood in the covered work area when Cousin Diana pulled up to me, looking real serious. She leaned part way out of the truck window, and in a tinny, edgy voice, asked, "Danny, can we talk?"

"Sure," I said, waiting for the ground to open up under me.

"Lena told me the whole story about what happened in Drake's trailer at my surprise party. Can you meet me at about eight tonight at the diner?"

I hardly caught my breath after she pulled away. All day long, it seemed, I was making one mistake after another and wound up redoing a lot of the little projects entrusted to me. Finally, my brother Luca walked over and asked if he could help me. I said no but thanks. As he walked away, he looked back at me with such a sad face that I figured he was probably wondering what the hell was wrong with me.

After supper, I headed down to the diner. Diana was sitting by herself in one of the corner booths. Even before my butt hit the smooth leather bench, Diana blurted out, "Lena is pregnant!" I almost fell out of the booth. I started to shake and tremble, and Diana grabbed both of my hands in hers. A couple of carnies came in and asked if they could join us. But Diana quickly told them that we were waiting for Lena and Mabel, so the carnies found a table across the room. I felt really bad until Diana said that Mabel and Lena weren't really going to join us. Baby Jesus, I would've just fallen on a steak knife rather than face Mabel.

Diana leaned over the table. "Oh, Danny, how you looked when I mentioned their names! I'm going back to Arkansas as soon as my brother Buddy's wife has her baby, and I see that she and the baby are going to be fine. Rosie's due any day now.

"Lena is starting to show, so we need to come up with a plan pretty damn soon. I don't know how much longer she can hide the baby bump. Danny, I'm so disappointed in you! What the hell! Lena's way under age. You must have been so drunk that your thinking just shut down."

I sat there trying to hold back the sobs that I was afraid I couldn't keep inside any longer. I made a quick dash for the diner's door, made it to my truck, fumbled with the door handle before making it inside. I just sat there, arms and head on the steering wheel, crying like a baby. Diana opened the passenger door and climbed in beside me. I couldn't even speak, I was so devastated.

Diana reached over and pulled me to her. "Danny, like I was saying, I'm going back to Arkansas to be with H.P. just as soon as Rosie has her baby. Just listen to what I'm going to tell you, because Lena's in no shape to even begin to deal with the pregnancy. I took her to the doctor when I seen how awful sick she looked. She wasn't keeping no food down. When she came out of the doctor's exam room, she confided in me that the doctor had told her that she was pregnant. This all happened two weeks ago. Lena wants you to marry her, but she wants you and her to just go away together and not to get in touch with anyone for a while. You know that she's only sixteen, right?"

I looked up, dripping tears and sweat. "I thought she was seventeen, going on eighteen. That's what her brother Howard told me."

"Nope, barely sixteen; but she sure looks more mature, don't she? Well, anyway, my brother Buddy's wife is due any day now. They already ran her once to the hospital, but it was one of them false alarms. As soon as Rosie has her baby, I'll be going home to H.P. When I get home, I'll let Mabel and John and your folks know that once youse two get married, youse will be staying with me and H.P.

"Now all the Ludad—and I guess everybody else for that

matter—know that you only have to be sixteen to get married in Arkansas. Sixteen is what is called the "legal age" in Arkansas. You just have to get Lena a driver's license when youse get there."

"How can we leave our folks like this," I asked. "How can we just disappear on them? They won't know what's going on until you call them. I feel so munca. I've ruined Lena's life, and I'll never be able to make that up to her."

"Danny, you just need to focus on marrying Lena and being a good husband and father. She'll be fine. But there's a lot of steps to get to the point where you two are legal to be married. Just listen for now. Like I said, the first step is for Lena to get a driver's license. In Arkansas, they give them to folks right over the counter. All we have to do is go about twenty miles away from our place to the next county and get youse two married.

"But where do we stay until you finally go home?"

"Well, Rosie and I are so close, I can't leave until she has her baby. But youse two need to leave tonight or maybe tomorrow at the latest. Go to Springfield, get a motel room, and leave me a note at the Western Union Will Call. I'll get in touch, then we'll meet up and go to Blytheville and get youse two married! Lena is gonna leave her mother a note saying that she's in the family way with your baby, and youse two is too ashamed to face anyone. Just leave your folks a note telling them how ashamed you are, and it wouldn't hurt to say that you hope they can forgive you. You probably should also leave a note for Mabel and John, asking them to forgive you. Sound good to you?"

"Sure, I really appreciate you working all of this out for us, and I just hope our folks don't blame you for helping us."

"Well, you're gonna have to talk all this over with Lena, and the sooner the better. I'll tell her to meet you at your workshop, and youse two can decide on a good time to get on your way. Good luck! Remember, just stay in Springfield until I come to pick youse up."

I left the diner and went home a nervous wreck. I was so upset that I smoked three cigarettes on the way back home. At supper I looked at my happy family sitting around the table, and part of me felt that maybe this was the last time we'd all be together like this, like a real family. I felt like I couldn't keep from crying much longer, and I just wasn't hungry at all. I'm the kind of eater whose whole body gets real busy when I eat. We usually had a couple of conversations going at once, and now and then, one or two of us would just take up the other conversation. Our heads were bobbing around, our hands were moving around every which way, and my brother Tony would even get halfway up out of his seat just to get attention while he went on and on.

That day, I just sat there, all numb and quiet. My mom finally nudged me. "There's something real wrong with you, young man," she said. "Care to share your misery in exchange for a shoulder to cry on and some words of wisdom?" That was the first time she had ever called me young man, and everybody stopped eating and talking and just sat there looking at us. She reached over and felt my forehead. "Well, you don't got a fever, so what's going on, Son?"

"Sorry, Mom. I'm just kinda antsy tonight, I'm really behind on the popcorn joint wiring. I'm not going to be able to get any sleep until I finish the wiring." I excused myself from the table and headed out. When I got to the poorly lit work area just outside the workshop, I stopped to grab a kerosene lamp, and I put it on the workbench next to the popcorn joint I was working on. I lit it and waved it in the darkness around me. Good: There was nobody else around. I tried to get some work done, but I kept dropping tools and knocking over the little bins holding screws and nails.

All of a sudden, I looked up and saw Lena walking toward me out of the darkness. I was so upset, ashamed, and embarrassed, I couldn't even look her in the eye. She started to speak, so slowly and so low that I had to strain to hear what she was saying.

"Danny, I'm getting more and more paranoid about my bump showing. Can we go ahead and leave later tonight? Please."

"Sure, just tell me what you want me to do. How's this going to work?"

"Well, I think Diana had a good idea—that we should leave our folks notes. They might think the worst if we was to just disappear without saying nothing."

I grabbed some scratch paper and wrote a note to Mabel and John, sincerely expressing how sorry I was. I handed the note to Lena and looked down into her emotionless face. "Oh, Lena. I'm so terrible sorry. I know that doesn't begin to make up for the horrible thing I did to you. We both will never forget that. I'm so sorry."

She looked up at me, and all she said was, "So, about 2 a.m.? You'll meet me here again at 2 a.m., and we'll leave then?"

"Ok. Yes. But not here. I'll be parked outside the gate that's close to your place."

"Will you have some money, because I'm not packing any clothes. I figure that pretty soon I won't be able to fit in them."

"Well, I've been able to save up some money since I finished paying off my truck. So, yes, we'll have enough money to buy you some clothes, stop for food, and find a decent place to stay."

"Ok, 2 a.m. it is." Lena turned and walked back into the darkness with solid steps, her back and shoulders straight. She seemed to be in a lot better shape than I was. I couldn't walk more than a little ways before I started tripping over myself.

Jeez. The closer it got to 2 a.m., the longer the waiting seemed. Those last few minutes before Lena showed up just dragged. I had just packed a few things: some dress slacks and shirts for the marriage ceremony, then added some odds and ends we might need on the way. The hardest part was writing the note expressing my regrets, asking my folks' forgiveness, and hoping against hope that they would eventually do just that, forgive me. My truck was parked about halfway to the gate nearest Mabel and John's place. I parked just outside the gate at about 1:40 a.m. Talk about nervous: Those must have been the longest twenty minutes of my life!

Two o'clock came and went. There was still no sign of Lena. I was worried. What had happened? I started to freeze up again, afraid that maybe Mabel and John had stopped Lena as she left the trailer, and now John was on his way to take care of me with his trusty shotgun. Finally, the passenger door handle clicked and turned, and Lena was sitting beside me. I started the engine and drove down to the all-night service station, filled up, and asked the guy inside how far it was to Springfield, Missouri, and how long he thought it might take to get there.

We got to Springfield in just over two hours. The few motels that still had vacancies didn't have no twin beds, so we headed downtown. After more running around, we finally found a hotel that had a room with double beds. Years later, when I was thinking out loud about how hard it had been to find a room with double beds way back when, the lady I was with for a couple of hours—in a hotel room with just one bed—said something interesting: "Honey, like you and me today, most couples lookin' for a hotel room are happy with just one bed. Don't need more than that!" I guess she was right about that!

I paid for the room at the daily rate because we didn't know when Diana would come by to pick us up. I asked Lena if she was hungry and wanted me to go get something for us to eat. She just wanted a Coke and said that she was just too tired to eat anything. We both woke up at about 7 a.m. Lena went into the bathroom and washed up, and then it was my turn. We got dressed and went downstairs to the hotel restaurant. Lena said that she just wasn't hungry yet, so we had coffee and some toast. It was too early to go shopping, so we went to the hotel newsstand. Lena picked some movie magazines, and I got New York, Chicago, and St. Louis newspapers.

Back in our room, we didn't say anything for an hour or so, but finally, I asked Lena if she was hungry yet. She nodded yes, so we went back down to the hotel restaurant and had a nice big farm breakfast. I walked over to the Western Union office and left a note for Diana at their will call. They keep the messages for three days. No response, so I had to keep on renewing the message. It was like Diana had just dropped out of sight. What could have happened? Had she changed her mind?

There was a department store just across the street from the hotel, and we actually spent a lot of time there, not just buying what we needed for the wedding, but looking at all the modern things that might look good in our future home, wherever that would be. Lena would pick things up, check the price, then put them right back down. I gave her a hundred dollars and told her to buy whatever she needed. She said that she didn't need the whole amount, so she handed me back sixty dollars. I went over to the gift department and bought her a purse and put two hundred dollars in it for a rainy day. Lena peeked into the purse, then said that she didn't need that much money.

"Well, you'll have it if you're out by yourself and think of something you need or see a dress that you like. At least you'll have the money."

She sounded more than a little irritated. "What am I gonna need that's gonna cost two hundred dollars, Danny?"

"Gosh, I don't know, but any money that I have is your money too now, even though we're not married yet." She glanced up at me with an angry look, but poked the wad of bills back into her purse.

We walked across the street to the Western Union, and the clerk told us that no one had called for the messages I had been leaving. Over the next two weeks I left over a dozen messages, not even letting them sit there for the three whole days. Lena and I must have hit almost every restaurant in Springfield. We both ate all kinds of food that we'd never even heard of before. Then, we'd go take in a couple of movies.

Finally, we were running out of restaurants to try out and movies to see, so we decided to just head to Blytheville and try to locate H.P. All I knew was that H.P. worked at a lumber mill near the Arkansas-Missouri state line. At the time, there were still a lot of lumber mills in that area, so it would probably take a while to track him down.

All this rigmarole must seem strange to people accustomed to just picking up a phone—or pulling it out of their pocket—and making a phone call, or sending a card or letter to someone. But, back in the day, it was different. We didn't know how to contact Diana, because like a lot of folks, she didn't have her own telephone. I guess we shouldn't have stuck around for the two weeks or so, but the two of us weren't communicating very well, and we just let the time pass.

When we were on the way to Arkansas, we stopped along the way and checked for any messages at the Western Union. Nothing. We were really worried now. What had happened to Diana? We figured that maybe she couldn't get away, or something went wrong. Well, anyway, we were hoping that the mystery would be solved once we got to Blytheville. That was where we could get married if Lena was only sixteen years old.

It took us two days to get to Blytheville. We stopped at one mill after another without finding where H.P. worked. Climbing in and out of the truck was getting to be too much for Lena, so I hopped out and went into the last half dozen or so places that we stopped at. We were getting awful tired and discouraged and decided to try one more mill before finding a decent place to stop for a late country breakfast. We were driving along, and at about ten o'clock, we saw a sign for a mill called the Ark-Mo Mill. We turned into the long winding gravel driveway and pulled into the visitor parking area.

Lena was complaining about feeling all stiff and sore from being in the truck for so long, so this time, we both got out and went into the visitor reception area. I asked the pretty young receptionist if H.P. Orr worked there.

She smiled at us, and in a real thick Southern accent, said, "Well, matter of fact, H.P. does work here, but his shift don't start 'til later. May I ask who's calling for him, and how he can get in touch with you? He don't have no telephone, far as I know. But I'd be happy to leave H.P. a note and tell him you folks was looking for him. Ma'am, you look real tired. Won't you please have a seat?"

Lena thanked the receptionist and went over and sat down in a comfortable-looking chair. I smiled and said, "Well, we're family, trying to connect with H.P.'s wife, Diana."

"Family, huh? How 'bout I just tell you how to find H.P. and Diana's place?" The receptionist gave us directions and drew a little map for us to follow. She came out of the office with us and pointed us in the right direction. All in all, we were only going a couple of miles.

Pretty soon, on our right, we saw an older, well-kept wooden house, a genuine Southern farm house with nice woodworking and a deep porch as wide as the house itself. Nice tall, comfortable-looking chairs were scattered here and there on the porch, and the front door was half open. I yelled into the front room from the porch. Nothing. Figuring that they might be out back, I went back to the truck and laid on the horn.

Then we heard Diana call out, "Danny, Lena, is that youse?" We saw Diana coming around the corner from the rear of the house, her face half-hidden under a huge straw hat. A smiling, real fragile-looking older lady was holding onto Diana as they paused at the corner of the house. Diana slipped some kind of long trailing bag off of her shoulders before she and the older lady walked over to greet us.

"Youse two had us worried stiff! We was afraid that youse had an accident!" Diana gave Lena a hug and a peck on the cheek, then she hugged me and turned toward the smiling elderly lady. "Gladys, this here is my Cousin Danny, and this is Lena, who I was telling you about." Diana grinned and took Gladys's right hand. "Lena, Danny: This pretty lady is H.P.'s mom, the best mother-in-law a gal could ever have!

"I guess it's been almost a whole month now since we seen each other. I went into Springfield to the Western Union three days after youse two left Indianapolis, but they said that there was no messages for me."

"Well," I said quickly, "I checked for messages every day for weeks while we were in Springfield. We were staying just across the street at the Hotel Missouri."

"Hotel Missouri? Danny, where did you go?"

"Springfield, just like you told us to. We got a hotel room, and then I ran over to Western Union and left you a message at the will call to let you know that we had made it to Springfield. We didn't hear nothing from you, so we finally headed toward Blytheville to find the lumber mill where H.P. works.

Diana was staring at me right in the face when she asked, "And you left a message at will call telling me where youse two was staying?"

"That's exactly what we did. We wound up staying there three weeks, and I checked the will call every single day."

"How far across the street from the Western Union was this Hotel Missouri?" She sounded like she was onto something.

"Just kitty corner."

"How big was this hotel?"

"Hmm. Two stories high."

"You're sure about that?"

"Yessiree Bob!"

By now, it was Diana who was hanging onto Gladys to steady herself. "Danny, where in the hell was youse two?"

"Springfield, Missouri. We were staying at the Hotel Missouri right there in Springfield, Missouri."

"Oh my Gawd," Diana howled. "Youse two was supposed to go to Springfield, Illinois!"

"Springfield, Illinois? I did exactly what you told me. You said to go to Springfield and get a room and leave you a message at will call at the Western Union. You didn't say Springfield, Illinois."

"I didn't?"

"No, you didn't. You've known me since I was a baby. I don't lie; you know that."

"Oh my Gawd," Diana said, grabbing even tighter onto Gladys's arm. "I didn't even know that there *was* a Springfield, Missouri!"

As I went back to the truck to grab the map, a farm truck was coming up the dirt road like a bat outta hell, throwing dust and gravel every which way. The truck screeched to a stop just in front of my truck, and as I turned to look, H.P. jumped down from the passenger side with his arms out in front of him, his fists making boxer moves.

H.P. saw me and finally settled down and said, "Oh, it's you, Danny!" And turning to Lena, he added, "You must be Lena." He shook her hand, then lifted it up toward his face like in one of them foreign movies. He made a little bow, then ran over to me and gave me a quick hug. "Jeez, Danny, we was so worried about youse. What in the heck happened to youse two?"

Diana jumped in and said, "H.P., they went to Springfield, Missouri. That's where the mix up was."

"You mean they didn't even go to Springfield, Illinois?"

"No, they didn't. They left messages for me at the Western Union in Springfield, Missouri, for three weeks and never heard nothing back, so they decided to come to Blytheville and try to find you."

H.P. gave out a loud sigh, and hollered to the guys who had brought him home: "It's ok, guys. This is Diana's cousin we've been expecting for the past month. Go on back to work, and thanks for carrying me home!"

H.P. turned and gave me another hug, this one like he didn't want to let go. "Sorry about coming at you earlier, Danny! But when I got to work, there was a note in my mailbox sayin' that some of Diana's people had come by the reception desk and asked if I worked at Ark-Mo and where they could find me and Diana. The receptionist gave them directions here, and I went bonkers when I read that! I thought that it was Diana's bunch come all this way to grab her and take her back with them, like they tried to do right after she left the carnival."

We met H.P.'s dad, a very nice, charming gentleman with a good sense of humor. He was very welcoming and pleasant to Lena and myself, but since we weren't married yet, he didn't want us sleeping in the same bedroom, and Gladys didn't want us to either. Gladys especially was very religious, and she seemed more caught up than her husband was in what not to do if you wanted to be saved and make it through the pearly gates.

The next morning, after a real doozy of a huge and delicious Southern farm breakfast, Diana and H.P. gave us a tour of the place. As we walked from the front porch towards the back of the house, Diana pointed to a heap of canvas bags in a bin next to the house and said that those were the twenty-foot-long canvas bags that the cotton pickers put the cotton into that was left behind by the mechanical cotton-picking machines. So that's what Diana was trailing behind her as she came to greet us! What the heck!

Diana showed us the old wooden wagon with high sideboards that she would empty the bags of cotton into when they got filled up. H.P. got a fixed look on his face and said, "This ol' wagon and an outhouse behind the barn was about all that survived a raid by a company of Yankee soldiers during the War Between the States. They burned almost everything to the ground."

After the tour of what turned out to be the Orr family cotton plantation, Lena and I went into town to a drugstore that had a counter where folks could apply for several kinds of official licenses. I paid two dollars for a driver license for Lena and another five dollars for a marriage license. On the application, I put down that Lena was eighteen years old. Since Lena looked pretty mature, I didn't figure that anyone would question how old she was. For the marriage license to be valid though, it had to be published in the official notices section of the local newspaper. There was a three-day waiting period before we could actually get married.

When we went back to the drugstore to pick up our licenses, the lady on duty said that she needed to see some identification. I can't remember what Lena showed her, but anyway, the lady gave us the paperwork to fill out for the marriage ceremony.

We drove over to the First Methodist Church and were married by the Reverend Jebediah Bagley, a jovial older gentleman who gave a humorous little sermon on married life. Old Mr. Orr seemed to appreciate the sermon, but his straight-laced wife, Gladys, just sat there with a sour look on her face.

When Reverend Bagley said to go ahead and kiss the bride, I barely grazed Lena's cheek with my lips. Even with that, she kinda turned her head aside. "No, young man," Reverend Bagley said in his deep baritone voice, "go on, don't be embarrassed. Go on, give your pretty bride a nice kiss." So I did. Later Lena confessed that she thought that the peck was cute, and that when I gave her a real kiss, she was fine with that too.

When all was said and done, and we were officially man and wife, I turned to shake the good Reverend's hand and slipped him a ten-note gratuity. He was genuinely surprised, and thanked me over and over.

It was then about eleven thirty, so we headed back to the Orr house, where Diana and Gladys and a couple of neighbor ladies had prepared a real wedding feast for us. Everything but alcohol, because Gladys believed it was Satan's potion. The good Reverend—probably a local expert on Satan—apparently didn't share Gladys's opinion, though, because when the men were invited by old Mr. Orr to join him in his home office for whisky and cigars, Reverend Bagley was the first one through the door.

Even after the marriage ceremony, the wedding luncheon, and the pleasant company, I still felt a little out of it. And then, right before dessert was served, Diana leaned over toward me and asked if I knew how old Lena was.

"Well, you told me just before Lena and I eloped that she's sixteen," I said confidently.

"Hah, no way, Danny! Tell him, Lena; go ahead and tell your husband the big secret that you just told me!"

Lena smiled and said, "Actually, I'm only fourteen!"

"Jeezus!" I gasped loudly. Gladys gave me a sharp look, and I quickly lowered my voice. "You're not legal anywhere! If you tell anyone in the next so many years how old you really are, I could be locked up for rape at least."

"Oh come on, Danny. Calm down," Diana said, grazing both of my cheeks with her hands. "You'll be fine as long as you toe the line! Hey, I was only fifteen when I got together with my ex, and no thunderbolts hit us. Besides, I looked twenty-one when I met my ex, and no one ever questioned it."

I glanced over at Lena, thinking that never in a million billion years would anyone say she didn't look at least eighteen. Lena looked at me, smiled, and said, "When we moved to Indianapolis, I made myself sixteen 'cause that's how old you had to be to stay home from school or to drop out for good. No one ever said I looked younger when I told everybody I was sixteen. I thought I was caught once though, when I had stayed home for a week or so. A truant officer showed up at the door and asked mom and me both how old I was. He wanted to see real proof, like a birth certificate."

"What happened?" I asked, moving my chair closer to the table, all the while never taking my eyes off Lena. She just wouldn't make eye contact though. I was still nervous and upset to find out how young Lena was. I really felt like a terrible person, a child molester, the lowest of the low. I knew that there were guys in prison on the chain gang for doing what I had done to Lena that night in Drake's trailer. I was going to burn in hell, or, at the very least, never ever forget the horrible thing I had done to Lena.

"Wow, oh wow," I said in a loud whisper, interrupting Lena. As I rambled on and on, Lena, Diana, and H.P. just froze and sat there looking like deer caught in car headlights. "I mean, there's around eight years' difference in our ages. For a man and woman in their thirties or older, that's no big deal. But damn—fourteen and twenty-two! Yikes! There's a world of big difference there! A fourteen-year-old girl would be in the eighth or ninth grade, but a twenty-two-year-old guy could have been out of school for several years, maybe even be a teacher, or a soldier fighting in a war somewhere, or a cop chasing a bad guy—a bad guy like me."

I kept talking, thinking that maybe in all the words I was saying, I would somehow in the end convince myself and everyone listening that our situation was not so unusual or illegal after all.

Diana cleared her throat real loud and gave me a quick, nervous smile. Gosh! *What was I thinking,* I wondered, to keep going on like that? I shut up, and Lena continued with her story.

I have to admit all these years later that Lena was a good storyteller, all animated as she talked, and a damn good mimic. Growing up, our kids liked Lena's stories better than the ones they read in books. Lena described how Mabel had told the officer that Lena's birth certificate had been lost in one of their many moves, but he still wanted to see an official birth certificate and wouldn't budge.

Lena leaned forward, " 'Look, Missy,' the officer snarled, and grabbed my arm." She sounded like the Wicked Witch in *The Wizard of Oz* movie. Lena puffed up her face and continued, " 'You need to come back to school with me. In the meantime, Missus, if you want to keep your young'un home to help out, send for a copy of her birth certificate. That's one document that everyone needs to keep in a safe place.'

"Mom wrote to John's sister in Detroit and asked if she would send us a copy of her own daughter's birth certificate. Cousin Bina was sixteen at the time, and mom and I thought that was a good fake age for me. My cousin's last name is Western, and Western was Mom's maiden name. Anyway, I was staying home from school a lot, even when we wasn't on the road. One day the same truant officer knocked on the door again, and Mom showed him the birth certificate.

" 'Well, I'll be,' the officer said, shifting his feet, 'this little lady sure don't look sixteen. Say, Missus, it says here that your girl's name is Lucy. What's up with that?'

" 'Oh,' my mom said quickly, 'That's the name my ex and the in-laws chose for Lena. But after my ex and me got a divorce, Lena and me went to a judge and had her name changed to Lena, after my mother, Lena Western.'

" 'Do you have the paperwork for that, Missus?'

" 'No, again, all them papers was lost in the fire.'

" 'Fire? What fire, lady?' The officer sounded kinda cranky. 'I thought you said last time that the paperwork was lost during a move.' He was back to shifting his feet on the shallow trailer steps.

" 'Well, yes, that's true. The trailer caught fire when we was towing it here to Indianapolis.'

"The truant officer seemed eager to just complete the papers and not spend any more time on them tiny trailer steps. 'Ok, Missus,' he finally said. 'Your daughter just really fooled me. She looks so damn young.'

"The officer gave Mom the carbon copy of his report and was off. Hahahahaha! Mom could've won an Oscar if she'd had half a mind to!"

"Wow! Boy oh boy, Lena! I just realized that happened when you were only thirteen. Thirteen! And the truant officer and everybody at school thought you were at least sixteen. Wow!"

Lena just sat there squirming and looking around. I was really hoping that someone else would say something, like maybe how great the food tasted or how pretty the tables were decorated.

Diana and H.P. were whispering and laughing quietly about something, so I just cleared my throat and went on, still trying to make eye contact with Lena, "Your mom confided in me just last year that she was only fifteen when she eloped with your dad. But even so, I don't get why our folks were all encouraging us to get together. What were they thinking, you being so young, not even of age and all? This isn't Bosnia fifty years ago!

"I sure wish that you had said something to me about all this before we started going together to dances and the movie show, spending time alone together. I love and admire you, Lena, and respect you so much. I would have been willing to wait until you were ready. Not to mention that what happened that night in Drake the Snake Man's trailer would never have happened."

But it *did* happen. All these years later, as I'm writing this chapter of my life story, I'm thinking about the events of that awful night so long ago, which still fill me with so much guilt and anger with myself about what I did to Lena.

7

On the Road With the Sherman Bros.

One thing was certain: We had been spending a lot of money on the road. I had a little over four thousand dollars when we left to get married. Now I was down to about seven hundred dollars. I said—a little nervously—to Lena, "We're getting kinda low on cash."

"I was wondering when we'd come to that. Like how low?"

"Like seven hundred dollars low."

"Well, we've been spending money like it was going out of style! You know, I still got all of the money that you kept stuffin' into my pocketbook. I just never spent that much."

Lena grabbed her pocketbook and emptied it out on the bed. Twelve hundred and fifty dollars! If I hadn't thought that she might deck me, I would have grabbed her right then and there and given her a big kiss! All I said was that we were rich. Lena carefully folded up the bills and said that she was going to hold onto fifty bucks.

The next morning, I approached Lena and said, "What if we buy a nice little trailer and go hit the carny circuit? After a while on the road, maybe we'll have a better idea of what we really want to do. I can be a concession agent until I have enough money to build my own joint."

It took Lena and me four days to find a cute little travel trailer for eleven hundred and fifty dollars. The inside was real nice, clean and in good shape. But it was pretty obvious from the shabby-looking exterior that the previous owner had spent a lot of time out on the road. We found a secondhand store and bought some cookware, a toaster, an iron, ironing board, and bedding. Altogether we must have spent about twenty-five dollars. The owner of the store gave us a 50 percent discount because we were newlyweds. Then we went to Sears and Roebuck and got a good deal on some discontinued chinaware and bought some stainless steel flatware on sale. The only thing we paid full price for was a nice set of assorted glassware for five dollars.

Lena the bargain hunter was in all of her glory, making deals on what were already good deals. Over in the linen department, the clerk gave us a set of bath towels when we told her we were just married. I think that Lena was more exhausted from the excitement of shopping than she was from actually running around trying to get everything that we needed.

The little trailer was in almost perfect condition inside. The tip-out room worked just fine. The exterior was in terrible condition, and someone who didn't know what they were doing had repainted it a funny green color. It looked like a big green bug. It took me all day to paint the outside a nice shade of blue. All in all, it was worth the effort.

The next morning, Lena went out to look at the paint job. When she came back in, she actually smiled and said, "Danny, you did a really great job on the trailer. It looks super!" It made me feel proud to hear her say that, to hear her say more than just a few words at a time. I gave her a smile and a wink and went back to reading *Billboard* magazine.

Back in the day, *Billboard* kept track of mobile entertainment: horse shows, car events, circuses, carnivals, etc. There was a large advertisement for concession stands for sale, new and used. I spotted a popcorn stand for sale for a hundred dollars. That was a lot of money back then, but it was bound to be popular with carnivalgoers and make us a lot of money with whatever carnival circuit we joined. I called the number in the ad and wired the money after I had asked Lena if she thought she would be up to running it. She said sure, so we said our adoos to Diana and H.P. and headed to Atlanta to pick up the popcorn stand.

I couldn't believe that the popcorn stand was in such awful shape! The chrome was nearly all peeled off of the popper itself and the rest of the armature. I told the salesman that I wanted my money back—the stand was just in such poor shape. There were even scorch marks where the wires went into the unit.

The salesman called the big boss over, and he was real surprised that I didn't see a great deal tilting on its wheels just in front of me. This guy would have been great as one of them snake oil salesmen in the Wild West. "Why, young man," he said, "where do you think that you're gonna find a popper with such a big pot for anywheres near a hundred dollars? Look, I'm sorry the chrome is peeling so bad."

I peeled off a little piece of the chrome while he continued talking. He was sweating real bad, wiping his face with his shirt sleeve as he tried to save the sale. He went into the backroom and came out with some popcorn kernels and cooking oil. He cooked up a batch of popcorn, handed Lena and me little bags of the freshly made corn, and asked how it tasted. "That's what folks is goin' to pay money for, good-tastin' popcorn, not a popcorn stand that looks real purty."

The popcorn did taste pretty good—delicious even—with no hint of a burnt taste. But I still didn't want to buy such a crappy-looking popcorn stand. It would take a lot of work to make it look good enough to attract customers at one of the nicer carnivals. We haggled a bit back and forth, and finally the guy plopped seventy-five dollars in my hand. "Pal, I really didn't know the stand was in such bad shape. I'm just the middle man here, trying to make a living. Where are you parked, pal? Hey, Frank," the Big Boss yelled, "come out here!"

Frank came running out from behind a jumble of concession

equipment and piles of coiled electrical cables. He stopped in front of the popcorn stand and grabbed onto it as he nervously glanced at his boss and Lena and me.

"Frank, get the push cart to carry this here popcorn stand and go with these good folks and load it onto their 'vee-hee-kul.' Be careful now and don't scratch it up or nothing." He continued, "Pal, all you gotta do is git yourself some cans of that heat-resistant spray paint and go over the popper a few times. She'll look almost new. And the paint smell goes away after a few batches."

Lena looked at the salesman like he was speaking in tongues or something, gave me the same look, and started walking toward the truck. After Frank and me struggled to get the popcorn stand onto the truck bed, Lena and I both thanked him, and he headed back to the storefront. We sat in the truck for a few minutes, looked at each other and started laughing like kids playing.

"Wow, Danny, we made out like bandits! That crazy gadjo! And poor Frank!" Wow. Lena was actually laughing out loud, and poking me in the side. I couldn't remember the last time I'd heard her laugh like that.

As we were getting ready to head out, we heard someone holler out, "Hey, Mister! Wait!" It was Frank, breathless. He kinda staggered over to Lena's rolled down window and did a little bow like she was royalty or someone real special. "Here, Missus, these is fer you, fer being so nice and everthing." Frank handed Lena three cans of white heat-resistant spray paint. "Y'all take care now!"

"Danny, you should do like Frank, and bow to me more often."

"Don't think I ever have."

"Well then, it's about time you started." She was laughing again, and for the first time in months, I actually started to think that we had a chance, Lena and me.

We were talking again, and I was so happy not to be walking around on eggshells, always wondering if and how I should bring something up or try to talk to Lena when we were alone. Well, we were both getting hungry, so I stopped to this butane place and picked up some bottled gas for cooking. We pulled off the expressway into a rest area. Lena cooked us lunch while I copied down telephone numbers for concession agents and some places to spot the popcorn stand. After a wonderful, simple, delicious home-cooked meal, we set off to find a telephone booth.

I spent over two hours calling around, but just couldn't find a spot for our popcorn stand. Most carnivals have at least two popcorn stands in case one goes down, so's to protect themselves, because popcorn stands are popular with carnival visitors and provide a steady profit. But after a lot of calling around trying to spot our popcorn stand, I did find several shows that were looking for concession agents. Agents work the existing concessions, build a concession stand or joint with materials provided by and paid for by the carnival management. In return for the setup, the agents pay a percentage of their profits to the carnival. I asked Lena if we should hook up with a northern or western route show.

"Well, it don't matter to me, Danny. We need something to get started until you can make your own concession stand, something a lot bigger than the little corn popper on a stand that we got now."

I chose the Sherman Bros. Carnival, Northern Circuit. When we got to the current location, the guy I had gotten in touch with had left the show at the last spot they had played, so I wound up talking to John Sherman himself. He said that he felt real bad because we had come so far. He pointed to a trailer on the back lot. "See my brother, Bob. He might just have something for you kids. We're just getting started setting up the show, and probably a few more bodies wouldn't hurt."

I introduced Lena and myself and told Bob Sherman that me and Lena had been on the road before with different Sherman Bros. traveling shows. I mentioned that until I was eight years old, my folks and I traveled around the country with my mom's parents' dinner theater. Mr. Sherman asked where my grandparents were from originally, and I told him about them coming over to America from Italy, joining one of the Sherman Bros. traveling shows all those years ago, before they got their own gig.

I told Mr. Sherman that the same was true for my dad's family, that when they came to America from Bosnia, quite a few joined a Sherman Bros. Carnival to get to know their new country. I was kinda nervous and motor-mouthing, and I even mentioned that my uncle Vadim had disappeared on Ellis Island, leaving behind two trained bears and four singing monkeys.

Mr. Sherman seemed to take a liking to Lena and me right away, telling us that his family were immigrants too, and how they had worked hard and saved up and started their own traveling show. He finally stopped talking, took a few steps back, and with squinty eyes and a crooked little smile on his face, looked me up and down real carefully. "Danny, you look strong enough for just about anything we got goin' on here. But what the heck kind of Bosnian name is Miller?"

"Well, my dad's Old Country family name is Miloradovitch. They were Romanian Gypsies that had pulled up stakes and escaped to Bosnia in the 1850s, along with a lot of other Gypsies. And when my family came over to America from Bosnia, the Irish guys in the immigration shed on Ellis Island couldn't get a handle on Miloradovitch, so they just up and changed it to Miller."

"You two kids seem like you would fit in real nice with our crew. You both sound like hard workers, and you got the kind of personality and attitude we're looking for. Now, I'm goin' to share something with you that's a deal breaker for some folks. We run a clean show here, what some folks in the business call a Sunday school show: no crooked games, no dirty gal shows. We're a family-run business that offers fun and entertainment to decent folks. How's that sound to you? Do you think that you'd like to be a part of the Sherman Bros. family again?"

Lena looked over at me with a big smile and gave my right arm a little squeeze. "Yessir," I said, "that sounds great!"

"I'll make you two an offer: How about we set you up with a joint for your popcorn popper, and we'll start you off with thirty percent of the daily take? Sound fair?" Well, Lena and I were both so happy to hear that! We were finally going to have a routine to get into and money to build our life together.

"I'm thinking that's your rig parked over there, with the popcorn machine in the back. Pull on over to the green tent, and I'll meet you over there and introduce you to Sully. He'll hook you up with the juice. Tomorrow you can get started building a proper stand for that popcorn popper of yours. Kinda dress it up a bit. Make our guests want to check it out! You can pick up lumber, paint, hardware—whatever else you'll need—over at Keeley's Hardware, and put everything on our account."

I pulled over to where Mr. Sherman said to park, and he introduced Lena and me to Sully. We chatted back and forth while I jacked up the trailer to get it ready for Sully to hook us up. He gave us the juice connection, then disappeared under the trailer for a few minutes, banging around before crawling back out. "Hey, I can't find no drain pipe to hook up to. What gives?" I explained that we had just bought the trailer, had been on the road, and hadn't had time to stop somewheres to buy a drain pipe. Sully stood up, wiped himself off, and offered to go get an extra one he had on hand. He was back in a few minutes and had us hooked up in no time.

"One more thing, Sully: Where can we buy some kerosene?"

"No problem, Danny. I can fix youse up with that too. But I'm gonna need your can." So we wound up going to the store anyway to buy some food and a vented safety can for the kerosene. Lena was soon busy cooking dinner on this first night of our life together with the Sherman Bros. Carnival!

I ran over to Keeley's Hardware the next morning and got the materials I needed to make a popcorn stand. First, I painted the popcorn stand white, and for the top of the machine, I made a little gazebo with a red-and-white-striped canvas rooftop. I set it up and hooked us up with the juice. Ready to go! Then, all at once, I panicked: There was no oil, no butter, no bags to put the popcorn in, and no popcorn to pop and put in the bags! It was near opening time, so I went to the supermarket and got popping corn and oil. Where could I find white popcorn bags? Well, nowhere! So I went to the supermarket manager and asked if I could buy some small brown bags, explaining what I wanted them for. He only had ten-pound bags that we'd have to cut down. I asked Lena to take care of that and started the popcorn pot going.

We gave samples to all of the carnies and their kids and family members that came up to the stand, which turned out to be a good way to introduce ourselves and meet a lot of the folks that we would be working with. I had bought six boxes of salt, hoping that would be enough. Well, it was going pretty fast. Lena used one whole box on the samples, and I was thinking that the five remaining boxes of salt and the six pounds of butter should last through the night. It was gonna be close, because the butter pot held four pounds of butter, and if we were really busy, we'd probably have to reload it a couple of times. I told Lena to try to stretch what we had, to just use the small ladle that came in the cutlery set that we had bought.

All of the carnies were pulling for us, especially when they found out that we were newlyweds. All of the positive energy from their good wishes made us happy and helped to reduce the stress. We were both so excited, because this was our very first time working together in our own business. We just had time to change our clothes, and then the midway lights came on. I hugged Lena and wished her good luck. For the first time in a long time, I felt her hug me back.

Lena worked the popcorn concession with some of the other young gals, and that night I ran a four-sided concession joint that carnies call a pan joint. It was really more of a gambling joint.

Each of the four sides had a twelve-inch board with colored circles painted on it, with odds like 4 to 1, 6 to 1, etc., and a four-foot-by-four-foot board with a bunch of colored muffin pans. A player would put a nickel, dime, or quarter in one of the colored circles, then throw a ball at the muffin pans the same color as the circle he had placed the bet on. If the ball landed on and stayed in the muffin pan, the player would win.

There were six winners that first night, which is kinda rare, because the ball had to go into the muffin pan at just the right angle to stay there. The winners had all just bet with coins. A couple of guys had bet a dollar; another guy felt real lucky and put down a five-spot. All the guys who put down paper lost.

Lena was way on the other end of the midway. I was working the joint with a nice middle-aged couple whose teenaged son was helping them out that evening. I asked the kid if he would run over to Lena and ask her if she wanted something to eat or a cold drink. The boy came back and said that Lena already had a sandwich and a drink that she bought off a hot dog cart that was making the rounds. Right when he was telling me this, the cart came up to the joint. The owner told his son to give me a break. Generally the son would come by and give a break to whoever was working his dad's gambling joints. I gave the boy my money bag. Before the joint opened that night, they gave me a money bag with eighty dollars in it to start: coins, plus maybe two ten-dollar bills, four fives, twenty or so singles, and twenty dollars in change. Most of the customers had their own change to put down on the betting boards, and very few ever asked for change.

I ran over to the popcorn joint to give Lena a break so that she could use the restroom, which was about a hundred feet or so behind the joints. Lena gave me her money apron. I noticed that the butter in the pot was getting low, so I added the other two pounds of butter. I was glad that it had lasted so long! I felt a bunch of bills in the apron, and I knew that Lena was going great bangs. She didn't seem tired at all, so I used the restroom and then hurried back to the gambling joint. Wow, it was really packed, so I hurried in and thanked the owner's son and took over again.

This was one night that I was happy to see come to an end! I finally closed up the joint and went into the midway office for the count. Boy, was I lucky! I had pulled in two hundred dollars and some change. My share was seventy dollars that first night. I headed back to Lena, and she still had a crowd. As soon as the last drink was dumped, Lena came to me and said, "Come and take the money. We're closing up!" Then she handed me the money bag, and we almost ran back to our place. I dumped the apron on the couch and started counting. Well, Lena had been real lucky that first night. She had sold three hundred bags, at twenty-five cents a bag!

I looked up at Lena, and announced proudly, "We made fifty dollars' profit! Now, next time around, if we buy the supplies at a wholesale place, we'll make even more profit. But, the money we made was great for starters. You're fantastic with the customers, quick and always smiling!" I asked Lena if she wanted anything before the cookhouse closed up. She said no, that she was full of popcorn. She told me to go get something for myself, but I was just too excited to eat anything, so that was that.

That was the most conversation we had had in a long time. The three nights since we got the trailer, I had slept on the couch. Lena made up the bed and fluffed up the pillows and said, "I know that couch is hard; I can tell by sitting on it. You can sleep in the bed. It's big enough for two people. Just stay on your side of the bed."

This was a new-style California bed, and the sheets just tucked under the mattress, because the bed was built with storage space underneath. Whoever had it before us had taken great care of it. I was so surprised and happy when Lena said to go ahead and sleep in the bed with her, because that couch was real hard.

When we were looking at trailers, the dealer told us not to go by the faded outside of the one we wound up buying. He had bought it from an elderly couple who bought it to go on vacations. But the second year after they bought it, the man was in a car wreck, and he was no longer able to drive. So the trailer sat out in the weather for over a year, which is why the exterior was so faded. I thought that this was just a sales pitch, but when we checked out the inside, we could see that the stove burners looked new. When Lena opened the oven door, she said that the oven looked as if it had never been used. There was a warranty taped to the outside of the oven door that was hard to get off because the tape had been stuck to the oven door for a couple of years. The refrigerator was a regular house refrigerator. The trailer was just like what a carny would have ordered, except for the hard couch. Most carnies ordered sofa beds. We had really lucked out finding a trailer so cheap that looked so new inside.

During our time at that first spot, we made a profit of twelve hundred dollars. I had enough money to rig up my own pan joint on a trailer chassis, even though I knew that because of local regulations, I couldn't use it everywhere we would be playing on the current circuit. In the South, gambling joints aren't allowed, or you have to pay a *premium* to local law enforcement authorities to be allowed to operate without being hassled. So I had to come up with some other joints that could be used in shows on different circuits, maybe a joint that could be rigged up for various uses. This was going to require some planning, and I certainly had my work cut out for me, but I had been rigging joints since my early teens. While I was working away on my projects, Lena would bring me snacks. Little by little we started to conversate more.

But then one night when we were in bed, I guess I was having a nightmare and started rolling back and forth in bed, jerking my arms around, winding up almost on top of Lena, rolling back, and finally resting my left hand and arm on Lena's chest. She hit me in the face with an elbow, then pushed me so hard that I almost fell out of bed.

"You pig! Haven't you done enough already? Are you trying to kill my baby? What the hell is wrong with you? Get your sorry ass back on the couch, and don't ever try to touch me, not ever again, you bastard!"

I tried to explain that I had had a nightmare and I guess I was shifting around a lot, not realizing what I was doing. I hadn't meant to roll over on top of her and hadn't been putting the moves on her; my arm just wound up on her chest.

Well, things were pretty grim again between Lena and me for the next few weeks. She barely spoke to me, and often when I tried to talk to her, she would just walk away or look away and try to ignore me. The few times I tried to reason with her, we wound up arguing. It hurt me to see her so upset, so I just dropped the whole idea of talking about that night. The only saving grace was that we were busy packing up the carnival and getting ready to head up to the Alleghenies, then to the New York City area, so Lena and I were both too tired to argue about what had happened.

First mail call on the road, we got some letters from our folks, and I heard back from the radio show *Strike It Rich* that was broadcast live from New York City. I had sent for tickets and was hoping to be interviewed to be a contestant. In my letter, I had given them a real tale of woe, telling them that I was on the road with a pregnant wife, no money, and a real desire to win enough money to settle down somewhere and open a display-design business featuring my fantasy flowers.

I guess needing enough money to open my own business wasn't real heavy-duty stuff, like needing brain surgery or a new iron lung, or adopting a French war orphan. But the people at *Strike It Rich* said in their letter that they were interested in interviewing me, and pronto. I had just a few days to get to New York City for my chance at fame and fortune, or at least win enough dough to pay for my bus fare home. I'd been working hard getting the carnival ready for the road, and we were going to be on our way in another week or so.

This seemed like as good a time as any to feed Mr. Sherman and Lena some cock-and-bull story about going to visit a sick childhood friend and hop on a Greyhound headed to New York City. I was hoping to win a lot of dough, and—for one whole day—to forget about the miserable situation with Lena. God, was I ever unhappy. I had married Lena to do the right thing, and seemed doomed to an unhappy life with someone who would remind me regularly that I was the scum of the earth for taking advantage of her in Drake the Snake Man's little trailer.

What could I do? Toe the line, get used to the guilt trip I would be on for the rest of my married life, or leave Lena in the lurch, pissing off both families and winding up in jail, charged with aggravated assault and rape? At this low point, sometimes I even thought that a life behind bars couldn't be much worse than what I had ahead of me with Lena.

I hitched a ride with a carny to the Greyhound station and hopped on a bus to New York City. The *Strike It Rich* radio show was a big deal for ten years or so starting in the late 1940s. Warren Hull, a former movie star, was the host, which back then we called an emcee. That meant master of ceremonies. Probably almost as many folks tuned in to *Strike It Rich* as listened to the evening news, because they could see themselves in the contestants' shoes. Or maybe they were just fascinated by the pathetic stories some of the contestants told.

People in need of money—for medical treatment or to pay rent or bills or buy a car or a washer and dryer, refrigerator or whatnot—went on the show and told their sad story, then tried to win money by answering four easy questions. Each player was given thirty dollars and could bet any of their bankroll on answering each question after being given the category. If the contestant didn't win any money, the emcee opened the *Heart Line,* which was a phone line for viewers who wished to donate to the contestant.

The producers, Mr. Mark Goodson and Mr. Bill Todman, liked how I did in the interviews and run throughs before the real broadcast, and both said that I had a good personality and was easy to look at. Mr. Todman said that the very first television broadcast of *Strike It Rich* would be the next day, May 7, 1951. He asked me if I would like to stay over and be a contestant on the television show instead of being on the radio show. I remember that I was too embarrassed to tell the truth—that I didn't have enough money to stay over and also get back to the carnival—so I just said that my family needed me to return home as soon as possible.

I won sixty-five dollars when Warren Hull asked what part of a dog could somebody touch that would be cold if the dog was healthy. I answered "nose." The next question was "what is French money called?" I said, "franks." Right again! My daughter Drina's smart son, Andy, told me years later that the French word is spelled *f-r-a-n-c-s,* not *f-r-a-n-k-s.* But they're pronounced the same in English, so nobody knew I spelled it wrong in my head.

For the next question, they showed me pictures of different men all dressed up and asked me which one was a famous dancer, and what was his name. Well, I answered "Fred Astaire," so I was right again! Then they asked me what song is about what makes a cloudy day sunny. I blurted out "Imagination," so again I won! I decided to put most of my money on the next question, how to spell *solace*. I screwed up big time and spelled it *s-o-l-l-o-u-s*. That sounded as good as anything!

I headed back to the carnival with the sixty-five dollars that I had already won. Going to New York City had been like a brief but very welcome vacation for me from the sad state Lena and I were in.

After I got back from New York City, I apologized to Lena every day for more than a week for what had happened, and I tried to explain that I had been having a bad nightmare and hadn't been trying to touch her. "Truth be known," I finally said, "I wouldn't have tried anything with you because I just don't have no more sexual feelings for you, or for anyone, my girl."

"What a horrible thing to say, Danny," Lena said. "What have I done that would make you say such an awful thing?"

"It's nothing you've done or haven't done," I explained. "I just don't have the sexual desire or feelings no more that keep a normal guy going in the bedroom. I'm sorry, I just feel so much guilt over what I did to you that night in Drake the Snake Man's trailer. When I look at you—or any woman, really—in my head, all I see is that angry look on your face that night as you tried to push me away. I just have no romantical feelings at all. Not even thoughts."

"Oh, Danny," Lena said, "I'm so sorry. I don't know what to say, except that I believe you now, and I hope that when the baby's born, all that will change. You'll be so busy being a dad, you won't have time to worry about what happened in the past. You'll be a new man—good as new, anyway—when you see and hold our baby. Your old romantic feelings will kick in for sure." Lena came over and put her arms around me, pulling me into her bump. But you know, I felt nothing, absolutely nothing.

Lena's animosity had dissipated, having been replaced now with the often-awkward gestures and tone-deaf words spoken by people struggling to deal with uncomfortable circumstances. She hovered over me, cooked my favorite meals, adding every once in a while that I might do worse than to see a doctor about how to deal with my problem.

But it was a start, I guess, and we gradually settled into a pleasant daily routine, including some nice conversations about what each of us hoped the future would bring. Lena was now in her sixth month; one glance at her belly left no doubt about that! She was having more difficulty walking and doing her chores, so I bought Lena a good little car to help her get around. It was a small sedan, but it had plenty of power and a customized hitch for pulling the joint around.

I guess at one point I opened the door to bad luck by thinking out loud that things were going better than ever for us, moneywise anyway. One chilly Tuesday afternoon, I was working on the pan joint, putting up some new signage. Then all hell broke loose. All of a sudden, I heard a woman scream. A boa constrictor had escaped from its cage and slithered by Lena. As she panicked and turned around to run away from the big snake, she tripped over a spare tire and wheel that someone had discarded. She was rushed to the hospital, where she miscarried.

The snake's owner was a decent, hard-working guy named Ollie Stewart. He was devastated by what had happened and insisted on paying the hospital bill. Two weeks later, Ollie was gassing up his trailer at a service station when a drunk big-rig driver rammed the trailer, demolishing it and wrecking everything inside—basically everything he owned. Ollie won a big settlement from the trucking company's insurance company. Before he received the settlement money, Ollie had bought a new trailer for eight thousand dollars. When he finally got the insurance check, he paid off the trailer.

Ollie came to our trailer one afternoon after Lena had come home and handed her five thousand dollars in one-hundred-dollar bills. I wasn't home yet, and Lena tried to give the money back to Ollie, telling him that he had already done enough, that he had done the decent thing by paying her hospital bill. When I went to find him to return the money myself, he and his wife had already pulled out—lock, stock, and barrel.

Bob Sherman told me that Ollie's wife had said that she and Ollie just couldn't face me and Lena because of what had happened, so they left the carnival and headed off, hopefully for a life with happier circumstances.

Well, when I got home, still holding the bag with all of that money, Lena took a look at it, and said, "I guess you couldn't give it back to Ollie?"

"No, I had every intention of handing it back to Ollie and thanking him, but they had already left the carnival grounds."

"Well," Lena sighed, "it looks like we're rich! We can do so many good things with this money, can't we?" This time she hugged me really tightly. "I got your favorite kind of Italian sausage, along with bell peppers and onion! Tonight, I'm going to fix us a special dinner. We deserve it!"

At least we were at the point where we were speaking and communicating again. But communicating with our families was something else. Lena pretty regularly called her mom and brother. I still was so guilt-ridden about eloping that I had only called my family three times since we got married. Every single time that I'd call, my parents and brothers and sisters offered to send us money to help out, which I always refused by telling them that we didn't need no extra money, that we were doing just fine.

I still had no normal male feelings or desire toward Lena because of this guilt I had about forcing myself on her. The miscarriage had been a godsend to me, because I don't know how I could have loved a child conceived that way. How could I have such a thought—not loving our child? I don't know, but that's just how I felt. Having these thoughts about the miscarriage made me feel even more guilty. I had guilt about what I had done, and on top of that, I had guilt about feeling relieved that Lena miscarried. Lena confessed to me many years later that she had felt the same way about the miscarriage and how guilty she had felt about being relieved that it had happened.

Lena was still so young! But she was beginning to mature sexually and physically while I was still showing no interest in sex. A couple of months after the miscarriage, Lena came into our tiny kitchen and scooted a chair close to where I was sitting.

"Danny, I know now that what happened the night you had that nightmare was just an accident. But why haven't we even talked about being together as husband and wife since we got married? I feel bad because sometimes it seems like we take turns walking on eggshells when it comes to talking things through with one another. You know that you can come back to bed anytime that you want to."

Wow, what Lena just said really threw me for a loop! "Well, I didn't know that, not at all. Lena, I think I've already explained to you why I haven't tried anything with you. I have so much guilt about what I've put you through, I just feel cold as a cucumber. And the one time you thought I was coming on to you, you socked me and tried to push me out of bed! I just have no desire to be romantical."

Lena had tears streaming down her face and leaned over and put a hand on my shoulder. "Danny, please go see a doctor and get some help. There must be something you can do to be normal again!"

Lena's body was maturing, her sexual feelings developing, and here she was married to a supposedly healthy and strong Ludad guy who had no sexual desire at all for her.

I guess Lena figured that a doctor could just give me a pill or something to make me normal again, because almost every time I went into town to pick up a newspaper, she'd ride along and pick up a couple of what we used to call romance magazines, for women looking to spice up their love lives. She seemed to spend a lot of her free time reading these junky-looking things, and I'd see her thumbing through them in bed at night as she waited for me to come to bed. Pretty soon, she had a few stacks of romance magazines crammed into the bedroom closet. Every once in a while, I'd look through a few of them while Lena was sleeping or out on errands. I'll tell you, some of those covers and stories were real scorchy!

Lena had at least a half-dozen copies each of *True Romance, True Love, Modern Romance* and *Copper Romance*. What the hell: *Copper Romance*? Maybe Lena thought that the Black ladies would have some different ideas about how to go about seducing a Gypsy guy who had no interest in sex. Some of the stories had a happy ending: "This could happen to you, too. Keep looking for that special guy born to be your soulmate, to love you, and you alone." Others were more like: "Men are pigs! Be careful, girl! Don't let this happen to you!" One story even ended with a sympathetic lady friend with close-cropped hair and mannish ways comforting the unhappy young woman sobbing against her shoulder.

I don't know when or how Lena had started feeling something romantical for me. But I'm pretty sure that the romance magazines got her thinking more about sex and romance and made her long for what was missing in our marriage. Gypsy wives in those days had been raised not to talk about sex and emotions with their husbands. It was only after a few years together that Lena finally told me how much she really cared about me.

One night when we were both having trouble getting to sleep, I got out of bed and was sitting in a chair next to the bed, fiddling with some crepe roses I had made for a carny's upcoming wedding celebration. Lena sat up in bed, propped herself up against the headboard and was thumbing fitfully through one of her romance magazines. "Oh, Danny," she said, looking over at me with a look full of a lifetime's disappointment, "I think it's time we talked about what happened that night in Drake the Snake Man's trailer." Lena was finally opening up to me and sharing her feelings—past and present—about that night when we both had way too much to drink, and I forced myself on her.

"I just couldn't believe that you would do anything like that! You're a big, strong, muscular guy, just so much bigger than me. I couldn't fight you off, and besides, I was really sick from tasting all of those fancy alcoholic drinks. I thought that I was having a nightmare or something when you climbed on top of me and pulled my panties down, and your hands was all over me, and then you was touching my bad place. It was happening so fast, but I saw in the moonlight that it really was you. I started squirming and pushing your head away. Then I felt such pain in my bad place, I almost passed out. I know it wasn't a long time, but that night it seemed like you would never stop. When you rolled over off of me, all I could think of was pulling up my panties, getting the hell out of there, and getting home as quickly as possible.

"I was so sick, I felt like I was throwing up my whole insides. When I got home and made it to the bathroom, I noticed that there was blood all over my clothes and panties. I was confused, but then I remembered when Cousin Flora had told me about how messy losing your virginity can be. I put my dirty clothes into a bag, went out the back door, and threw the bag into the garbage. Sometime later, when my mom asked me what had happened to the pretty party dress, I said that I had given it to my cousin Tillie.

" 'Wow, my girl,' she said, 'after I spend all that money on that dress, you just up and give it away!' I was so afraid that she was going to try to get the dress back from Cousin Tillie, but she didn't, and that's all that she ever said about it.

"All the grand feelings that I had about you just went down the drain. I was so mad at you and at myself that I felt like I was foaming at the mouth. How could I not have known how evil you was? After I missed my next period, I thought something was wrong. I didn't know what, and I sure wasn't going to ask anyone. I went to the liberry in town and asked for some books on pregnancy. I looked through what they had but I couldn't find anything about missed periods. The beautiful older lady who lived across the street from us was out front when I got home. She waved and smiled. She had always been so nice to me, and I finally got up enough nerve to tell her that I thought I was pregnant, and she explained it all.

"Then I told your cousin Diana. She was really shaken up. She asked who the father was. She couldn't believe her ears. I didn't tell her that you forced yourself on me, and no one knows that to this day, not even Diana. When I started feeling worse, like being sick and vomiting, that's when Diana took me to the doctor. I used a phony name and address. The doctor asked me if I wanted him to be my doctor and deliver the baby, and I said yes. He said that he wanted to see me again in three weeks, and that when I came back for my appointment, I could work out some sort of payment arrangement with the office manager. The doctor told me that his fee for delivering a baby was two hundred and fifty dollars, and that I could make small payments and take up to seven months to pay.

"We didn't even have to pay him anything at the time of that first visit. That's when I decided that you and I should get married so that the baby on the way would have a mother and a father, no matter what kind of rotten father you would be. Diana thought that you and I was lovers or something, and I never told her different."

I was dumbfounded and didn't really know what to say. I went over to the bed and sat next to Lena, who was teary-eyed and shaking. I reached over, gently took her left hand, and held it for the longest time against the side of my face, as we both began to gently cry. We were caught up in the moment, and it was only later that I was surprised that she hadn't tried to pull her hand away.

It took me about a year and a half to work through my guilt and lack of sexual desire. I went to psychologists, medical doctors, got testosterone therapy, attended AA meetings: nything that I could think of or that I was referred to that might help me be a normal husband. I spent a lot of time and money trying to understand my guilty feelings and lack of normal sexual feelings toward my wife. But it was Lena who, by showing me kindness and forgiveness, rekindled my sexual desire and romantic feelings for her.

We traveled with the Sherman Bros. Carnival on the Northern Circuit all that season. After two more seasons traveling different carnival circuits, we decided to settle into something more stable, something that would let us put down roots in one place.

And that one place turned out to be California: orange groves, freeways, beaches, deserts, mountains, shopping centers, suburban sprawl, movie studios, movie stars, and maybe the first chapter of a new and better life for Lena and me.

8

Westward Ho!

It took us a good five days to drive to Los Angeles. We talked quite a bit about what each of us thought might the best way to get off to a good start in Los Angeles. We both settled on the idea of maybe finding work in a small display business, making the most of the event-decorating and setup skills we had learned while on the road with the Sherman Bros. Carnival.

We were one night out from L.A. when Lena asked if we could take a break from all of the driving and maybe spend our last night on the road in a motel. Not a bad idea, but there were a lot of no vacancy signs at the nicer places that weren't right on the noisy expressway.

We finally found a motel that had a room with a nice big bed for Lena to spread out in and a folding bed for me. There was even a 24-hour restaurant right next door. We got settled in the room, went over to the restaurant, and ordered a couple of steak dinners.

Lena seemed to be in the mood to talk. We had a nice conversation, not as give and take as in the old days, but it was a good start. We grabbed a Los Angeles newspaper and headed back to the motel. While Lena looked at the paper, I tried to get some sleep, but was having a hard time getting comfortable on the short foldout bed.

"Danny," Lena said suddenly, all excited. "The owners of a small display business put an ad in business opportunities, looking for someone to buy into their business. I'm not sure exactly what that means, but they're getting ready to retire and will take any reasonable offer. What do you think?"

"Sounds good to me! Just depends on what they mean by reasonable! Let's call first thing in the morning and find out more."

Wow! Things were falling into place already. We must have read that ad a dozen times before we settled down a bit. The next morning, while Lena showered and got ready, I called about the display business. I talked to one of the owners, Bill Willoughby. I had to ask him several times how to spell his last name, and he finally laughed and said to just call him Bill. He and his partner, Al, were looking for someone to buy into their business, Display Magic, hopefully agree to keep on the designers they had on the payroll, and take over after learning the ropes. We set up a time to go by and meet.

Lena and I headed to the Crenshaw District and met Bill, his partner, Al Kline, and their employees. We were real impressed with the work they did, mostly window and indoor display for local businesses. They had a large inventory of customizable floral arrangements and accent pieces in their showroom. Folks could check out the beautiful arrangements in the large display windows, go in and find something they liked, and the staff would customize the flower arrangement for any occasion. They did weddings as well, and Lena and I smiled at each other when we heard that, because we had done so many weddings in the Sherman Bros. traveling shows before and after we were married.

We still had the money from Ollie and our savings. Lena asked straight out what the deal was with buying into the business.

"Well, folks," Bill said, "we're just asking for a refundable deposit at the outset, because we want to find buyers who will be a good fit and develop a good working relationship with our designers. Of course, legally you could replace our designers with new folks, but spend some time with them and get to know them and their work. I'm pretty damn sure that you'll come to appreciate just how great our designers are! They've been loyal employees for many years, have become good friends, and we'd like to think that the new owners will respect the relationship we've built over the last two decades. Al and I will be around to answer any questions, explain the workflow, and introduce you to our favorite customers. If everything works out, then my brother the attorney will draw up the final sales agreement."

"Wow, Bill!" I almost shouted, I was so happy. These guys sounded like nice people, taking care of their employees like that, making sure that they would still have their jobs! "Tell you what," I said, "let me and Lena grab some lunch, talk over the deal, and come back to you with any questions. What do you think?"

"Sounds like a plan to me!" Bill said. "You might try Oz, just a few doors down from us," Bill and Al both agreed to meet with us again in the early afternoon, and finalize the deal if we were still interested.

So we were off to Oz! We entered the restaurant and stood just inside the doorway for a few minutes, trying to get our bearings, I guess. To Lena and me, it seemed like an unusual place. There were a lot of artsy types, mostly younger men dressed real casual, with a sprinkling of young women and older folks. We finally saw an empty table near the front window, and hurried over to grab it. Lena and I looked around, taking in the colorful characters talking in small groups at the bar and huddled together in booths along the walls.

A smiling young man wearing a tight shirt and even tighter blue jeans stepped out from behind the bar and brought us a couple of menus. He returned with a large pitcher of ice water and asked if we'd like to order anything from the bar.

We took our time going through the menu, and finally, we each ordered the New York Actor's Special, kind of a hip Los Angeles version of a New York deli pastrami on rye sandwich. We talked about Display Magic, what each of us thought about the employees, their obvious talent, what each seemed best at. Well, it didn't take long for us to decide to take Bill and Al up on their offer!

We hurried back to Display Magic and told Bill and Al that we were interested in taking their offer. Bill drove us to the bank that they did business with, and we bought a money order to cover the deposit. When we got back to Display Magic, we shook hands all around and signed some paperwork.

Six weeks later, a visit with Bill's attorney brother and filling out more paperwork there confirmed the good news: Lena and I were honest-to-goodness small-business owners, probably the happiest and most gung-ho new business owners in the entire city of Los Angeles!

How we enjoyed being our own bosses, talking with the customers and working with the designers! Both Lena and I pitched in and worked in the design studio alongside the regular designers so that we could make the deadlines. Lena was so thrilled to be able to help, and I was amazed at how talented and creative she was. She really enjoyed designing, coming up with her own designs and ideas.

We could concentrate on the creative side of the business because we kept on the accountant who had handled Bill and Al's finances, paid the employees, the rent, and any business expenses. He sent us a monthly accounting of everything.

We were so happy and were even getting new clients. We held First Monday open houses every month and invited folks from other neighborhood businesses to stop in on a Monday evening for finger food and soft drinks, to meet their neighbors, watch our flower-making demonstrations, and get some design ideas.

During our first few months as the new owners of Display Magic, Lena began opening up again and sharing more about her feelings, setting the stage for a new phase in our relationship. We began a romantic relationship based on the honest feelings, doubts, and hopes that we had shared with each other. We were like awkward teenagers at first, then as we became more comfortable with each other, romance bloomed and we were soon trying to have a baby.

Then something happened that changed everything, and our dream of being successful business owners had to be put on hold. After we had been in business for about eight months, faulty wiring in the air conditioner caused a fire that wiped us out. We had no way of starting over because the so-called accountant hadn't paid the insurance premiums for quite a while.

We found out later from the police that for some time the crooked accountant had been ripping off Bill and Al, other clients, then me and Lena. He'd paid the rent, and he'd paid the employees, but had been pocketing a lot of the other money that should have gone to pay taxes, insurance, and other business expenses. What a dope: He must have known that he would get caught sooner or later.

We had three hundred dollars in our personal savings account and a 1948 Cadillac convertible that we had purchased with cash just before the fire. We had three weeks until our rent was due. I decided to sell the car. There were lots of lookers, but it seemed like no one wanted to pay cash. Everyone wanted to make payments, like we were used-car dealers! Just when Lena and me were starting to get real nervous, Al Kline's son Mike made a generous cash offer, which we gladly accepted!

Then one day, Al came by and told me that his brother-in-law, Raul Varady, who had a display business in Chicago, was looking for a lead designer. "I told him how talented you are and how quickly you learn. It's a shame that the fire happened, but that's all in the past. The job pays three hundred dollars a week, and you'd be salaried, maybe work just a little overtime. It seems like you really love your work, and that's pretty rare these days. Well, Danny, sleep on it, and let me know." Al grabbed my shoulder, gave me a smile, and was out the door.

9

Varady Design

Should Lena and I stay in L.A. or go to Chicago? Either way, we were taking a big loss. Even after just a short time in L.A., we had gotten used to life without snow and wind chills and only catching glimpses of little patches of sky between tall Downtown Chicago buildings.

Time was running out, so I called Al Kline and asked him if his brother-in-law and and I could talk on the phone before Lena and I headed to Chicago. Raul was a fast talker, and he asked all kinds of questions about the work I had done, what had drawn me to the design field, was I a good listener with coworkers and clients, etc. Raul asked what I wanted to be doing in a year, in five years, and did I believe in following the client's vision rather than pushing my own ideas, etc. Whew! It seemed to me that Raul wasn't looking for someone who would just stick around long enough to make some connections, poach some clients, and then move on. He wanted someone permanent.

I guess he liked what he heard, because Raul asked if we could get together in Chicago mid-morning the next Monday and talk further. Raul said that he was really looking forward to meeting me to discuss the job and to see how he and I got on. "It's pretty much up to you, Danny. Hopefully after meeting me and checking out the creative lay of the land here, you'll decide that you still want the job!"

With just part of the money that Al's son Mike gave us for the Caddy, Lena and I were able to buy a great little one-owner 1946 Chevy pickup that was in really good shape. What a great buy: a thousand bucks for a pickup with only eighteen thousand miles on it—next to new!

Lena and I left Los Angeles in the wee hours Friday morning and arrived in Chicago early Sunday evening. We got a room and had a light meal before turning in early, giving me plenty of time to rest up for my interview at Varady Design the next morning.

We both got up way early that Monday morning and had a nice big breakfast before I headed out to meet the owner of Varady Design. Raul Varady turned out to be a plump little guy in his late thirties with a bushy Italian-barber mustache and a steady eye-to-eye gaze. He got up from behind his desk to pump my hand and said, "Have a seat, Danny. Glad to meet you! I've heard so many good things about you. I'm Raul Varady, the crazy guy who quit a fabulous job to go out on my own. I didn't have a clue what the hell I was getting into!

"Do me a favor: Danny. Feel free to let me know if I'm talking too fast, and I'll be glad to slow down." Raul finally took a breath, leaned back in his chair, relaxed, lit a cigarette, and looked me up and down, smiling.

"As far as I'm concerned, Danny, based on first impressions, our phone conversation, and all the great things my brother-in-law had to say about you, this job is yours if I haven't already scared you away! Maybe you can help us out, save the ship, and put some creative method into my madness."

Raul was a mile-a-minute talker, the kind of creative guy who's always trying to keep up with all the ideas swirling around in his head, and gets frustrated with himself if he thinks he's not getting through to someone.

Finally, I had a chance to say something! "Gosh, Raul, of course I'd like to work with you! It would be my pleasure. If you can give me a few extra days before I start, my wife and I can use that time to find a nice place to rent—a house or apartment—and not rush into anything. Lena's looking through the rental ads right now."

"You can start when you're settled in, Danny. Today I'll introduce you to your designers and show you the lay of the land, so to speak. About a nice place to live: If a one bedroom's ok with you, one of our employees just bought a bigger house, and their old place is for rent. If you want, I can call and find out more about it for you." I said fine, and it turned out that the little house sounded perfect. It was located in a nice middle-class neighborhood, and it even had a garage! When I got back to the hotel, Lena was already beaming because she had a list of six places for us to check out. She was even more excited to learn that we might already have a place.

When we drove over to see the house, we fell in love with it right away, even before seeing the inside! We parked across the street from the moving van that was still being loaded up. The guy who was moving out came over to greet us and took us on a tour of the little house, which was really more of a classy cottage, with white shutters, a steep roof, and a fireplace with a carved mantel. We loved it and called the landlord, who came over right away. We paid him the first month's rent in cash, and as soon as he had left, a couple of neighbors wandered over and started helping us move in furniture and boxes from the back of our truck. Seems to me that things were so much easier back all those years ago. The neighbors were all so open and friendly and welcoming, and soon we settled into our new place and new life.

I loved my new job at Varady! Lena worked with me part-time until she came down with what we thought might be a case of the flu. She was getting sick to her stomach a lot, and just didn't feel that great. Turns out that Lena was pregnant! At last, a new baby was on the way! So our little house would soon be home to three of us! We were so happy in our new home and would soon be even happier and a lot busier! Lena kept working with me on projects at Varady until her sixth month, then she stayed home and did some knitting and sewing and made lists of what she thought we might need to be ready to welcome our new baby.

We were so excited and happy when my folks called and said that they would be coming soon to visit and be there for us when the baby came. Mabel and John said that they were going to come and stay awhile at Christmas. Lena and I were planning to use my vacation time in the spring to go visit her dad and her brother Howard in Virginia. Since we'd arrived back in Chicago, we'd been in close touch with both of our families. Now that we were expecting our new baby, we talked with them on the phone every few days. The whole family was so excited and happy for us. Howard was so thrilled that he was going to be an uncle! We'd just come so far since those awkward first years after we had eloped—so much heartbreak and sadness, bad feelings, blame, and guilt. We'd gone through so many obstacles to get this far, and we were both hoping to go even further.

In August 1953, our son Andy was born. He was a healthy, happy, noisy, and always-hungry baby who came into the world weighing a pretty respectable nine pounds. We named him Andy in honor of Great-Uncle Andy Miloradovitch, who Americanized his old Bosnian first name when he arrived in Chicago in 1910. He kept the old last name, though, because he said he liked the way it rolled off the tongue.

Uncle Andy and Aunt Drina were the first in our family not to travel in steerage or third class when they came to America. They had saved enough money to be able to travel more comfortable, and didn't have to go through Ellis Island like the rest of the family did when they came over. Uncle Andy never talked about what kind of work he had done back in the Old Country. If someone asked, he would scrunch his brows, purse his lips, and say, "hard work, very hard work, and I was always busy." I liked to imagine that maybe he had been a pirate and had brought with him to America chests of shiny gold coins and other ill-gotten loot. Well, Uncle Andy and Aunt Drina had a lot of money, and it had to have come from somewhere!

They bought a guest house in South Shore, a real classy neighborhood in Chicago, known for its beautiful and unique architecture. I loved staying with them whenever our traveling show was in town. Uncle Andy seemed to really like kids, unlike a lot of other folks who were always ignoring us, asking us to stay out of their way, or shushing us, and telling us to sit and be quiet. He and my auntie had a lot of interesting, artsy-type friends who seemed to kinda act like big kids themselves, telling funny stories, laughing, dancing in the social hall to the jazz and "Negro music" playing on their spiffy gramophone.

Instead of leaving me and the other kids on our own, Uncle Andy would whistle for us to follow him into his study. There, us kids would sit Indian-style in a half-circle around Uncle's big carved mahogany desk and listen to his stories about his life back in the Old Country. As Uncle Andy launched into one story after another, he would hop around like a big kid, and gesture and hoot and laugh, or get real serious—depending on what kind of story he was telling.

At some point, Uncle Andy usually put one of us kids in charge, left the study for a few minutes, and came back with a large wooden box. With an exaggerated flourish, he would get a real serious look on his face and dump the contents—dozens of little pieces of wood—into piles all over the top of his big desk. Uncle Andy sorted through the piles, picking out pieces of wood, examining them up real close, keeping some, and tossing back the rest. He finally sat down in his big old wooden chair with upholstered arms, opened a drawer and pulled out a pocket knife and some carving tools. He continued with his storytelling as he whittled and carved—little wood slivers flying every which way.

When Aunt Drina finally came in to announce dinner, Uncle Andy let each of us kids choose one of the carved figures to keep as we filed past his desk on our way out. There were always plenty of the wooden figures to choose from, because Uncle Andy used to carve and whittle in his spare time. The little wooden figures were always unusual, one of a kind, and cleverly carved. He whittled and carved just about everything, from snakes, bears, and dogs to Gypsy wagons, even caricatures of the Orthodox priests who used to beat his parents when they were slaves in the monasteries back in Romania.

No two people could have been so happy and so in love as Lena and me were when our Andy was born! He spoiled us by being such a playful, curious, and easy-going little guy from the get-go, and he kept us too busy to dwell on our business and financial problems. Andy grunted and called out a lot while being fed, bathed, or changed, and he kept up the baby banter when he was alone again. He wasn't a fussy little guy, and didn't seem to want a lot of attention, finally looking away if someone held him too long or fussed over him. Andy became more and more independent after he could crawl and explore on his own. I guess he was trying to make sense of his surroundings in his own noisy way, expressing pleasure or frustration or surprise with a non-stop stream of grunts and groans, little giggles, wheezes, and chirps.

Andy, Lena, and me soon got settled and into a fine routine. My folks hadn't been able to come after all before Andy was born, so we invited them to spend Christmas with us. Lena's mom and John, and the twins were still planning to spend Christmas at our new place. One bedroom, a new baby, six house guests. No problem there!

We had already been planning on heading to Virginia in the spring to spend some time with Lena's family there. In the meantime, it was so wonderful and great to see my own folks. They were able to stay about ten days, because they were changing traveling shows. They got tired of playing the same old spots year in and year out.

Mom and Dad said over and over how much they loved our new house. They went on and on about how it was the perfect house in a perfect neighborhood. They thought that we were buying it and were real disappointed when we told them we were renting. Well, we had the hardest time saying goodbye when my folks left to catch up with their new traveling show. Saying goodbye was all hugs, tears, and more hugs. Mom and Dad made us promise to bring Andy soon for a visit.

We enjoyed their visit so much; same way we were so glad to host Lena's mom and John and the twins! They stayed on after my folks left. They were there a whole wonderful month, and even then, we really hated to see them leave. Family was a real joy when we were newlyweds! I don't think that happiness is there in Gypsy families so much anymore, what with all the divorces, drugs, drinking, and squabbling.

Lena and I always looked forward to getting out of the city and visiting family when vacation time rolled around. Mabel and John had hooked up with a new carnival and were going to be in Virginia Beach, Virginia, for quite a spell that summer. So Lena and me headed out there with Andy and stayed ten wonderful days. It was great to be with family, but it also made us appreciate our family life back in Chicago even more! John wanted us to come back on the road with them and open a concession stand. I was doing really well at Varady, and our little family was so happy in Chicago! Lena and I both laughed out loud when John tried to persuade us to go back on the road.

I was happy working in display and having a stable family life. In a business filled with creative folks with easily-bruised egos, I was considered not only able and willing to work outside the box, but easy-going and dependable. How much work we had to do at any given time varied from season to season, because the core display business is all about seasonal and holiday work. There were everyday display jobs, like window displays, designing and building sets, supplying real and faux plants and flowers to businesses, but holiday and seasonal work was where we made most of our profits. Getting ready for Christmas took up a lot of the work year. Spring displays were about twenty percent of what we had to do for Christmas. Summer, Easter, and fall together were also about twenty percent of what we did at Christmas.

Designers tend to come and go in large cities and move around a lot, being tempted by the promise of a higher salary, more responsibility, more assistants, etc. In the early years of my display-design career, my thing was to do freelance work and make extra money on the side when I wanted to do something different from my projects at Varady. I enjoyed being my own boss and took on jobs that were too small for Varady.

To earn even more money on my own, sometimes when family was visiting, we would make birch or willow lawn and porch furniture that was popular with folks living in the Chicago suburbs.

My salary at Varady eventually went to five hundred and fifty dollars a week and stayed at that because the company had over-expanded and was in a real financial bind. I stayed on because I was happy there, got along great with my coworkers, and I learned a lot. That's something that I rarely said later in my career, when I felt less need to listen to others, and my ego started to outstrip my accomplishments. Raul and his partner finally had to close when the money problems became too much to handle. Raul gave me a heads up on the closing about a month before our last day.

A few weeks after Raul had given me the bad news, Lena gave me some real good news: She was expecting again! The timing wasn't great, but we were just so happy to have another little Miller on the way.

Sooner than we expected, in September 1956, Lena gave birth to a beautiful, chubby baby girl. We named her Varda, and she was a real joy. She was so quiet, a lot quieter than Andy had been, and not nearly as active. Andy had turned three a month before Varda was born, and he doted on her. He spent a lot of time playing quietly near her bassinet, standing by it and singing to his little sister whenever he heard her crying.

I freelanced twenty-four seven for a while and enjoyed being my own boss. But with a growing family, I knew I needed to find a steady gig, a nine-to-five job that would give me a set schedule and more time to spend with Lena and the kids.

10

When Cousin Lonnie Came to Town

Just after New Year's back in 1957, my cousin Lonnie was in Chicago for a burial. For generations, many Romanian, Hungarian, and other Gypsies have been buried in the Chicago area, because this is where our families settled when they came to the United States from the Old Country. I had just come into my favorite bar, the High Note, where I was a regular. Since Varady Design had shut down, I was working any display-design or furniture-making gig I could get until I found a permanent nine-to-five job. When I was out and about on a job or had some free time, I would come to the bar to use their pay phone to follow up on job leads.

After my eyes adjusted to the dark and smoky bar interior, I saw my cousin Lonnie, who had moved away from Chicago many years before. Lonnie had been a role model for me when I was just a kid. Boy, I was really shocked when I saw him sitting at the bar, next to and almost part of this white-trash chippie who had breasts busting out all over. Lonnie's tongue was all over them. He didn't see me standing there, and I was speechless. The reason

I was so shocked was that I hadn't seen him in years, and here he was in Chicago all of a sudden, almost having public sex with a chippie.

In early 1942, Lonnie had been all excited to hear on the radio that one of his big heroes, Suicide Hays—the thrill-seeker, car-racer guy—was in town with a carnival over at Raceway Park. There were races pretty much every day while the carnival was in town. Lonnie dragged me and my brothers a half-dozen times over to Raceway Park to watch Suicide Hays race. Halfway through the last race we went to, one of Suicide's racing car's wheels came off. The car crashed into another race car, rolled over and over, caught fire, and almost made Suicide history. In his own way, Lonnie had always been a bit of a thrill-seeker himself. And he still looked the same. Lonnie absolutely had not changed, no way.

While he was lapping up whatever this chippie was dabbing all over her breasts, my thoughts wandered back to our lives during WWII. Lonnie's brother Georgie and I worked as pinsetters—bowling pinboys—in a bowling alley in Oak Ridge, Tennessee, a phony town which was built for the Manhattan Project, the Allies' WWII program to develop the atomic bomb. The government hired all kinds of men and women to live and work at Oak Ridge: laborers, skilled tradespeople, scientists, support staff, White folks, Black folks, Native Americans—and Gypsies.

Whether they had been construction workers, horse traders, mechanics, carnies, musicians, or craftsmen, Gypsies worked in Oak Ridge during the war at whatever jobs they were assigned by the government contractors to help set up Oak Ridge as a model American town. The town was built in a few months for the federal government by the Counties of Roane and Anderson. Modular and prefab buildings were used in the construction. Most of the workers' wood houses were built from kits, and even the sidewalks were prefab and made of wood.

We lived in a nice trailer park in Oak Ridge that my dad and my older brothers had helped set up. Housing, workspaces, recreational facilities, cafeterias, drinking fountains, etc., were segregated by race, of course, like everywhere else in Tennessee. Most of the White folks lived in prefab homes, and the Black workers and their families lived in dormitories and hutments—plywood huts with no running water. They didn't even have screens on the windows.

I'm pretty sure that almost none of the laborers and other blue-collar workers hired to live and work in the fake town of Oak Ridge knew that they were involved in a war effort to create a new type of bomb. There had been more than a few Gypsy families recruited by the government to live and work in Oak Ridge. I guess they were considered good workers for something like the Manhattan Project because they tended to stick to themselves and were known in the gadjo world as very secretive. Gypsies were probably the least likely to share details of their everyday lives in Oak Ridge with anyone in Oak Ridge or on the outside. When we were recruited to live and work in Oak Ridge, each of us had to sign an agreement not to talk about our time in Oak Ridge or even mention what kind of work we did there.

My dad and uncles and cousins worked in construction and did a lot of road work in Oak Ridge, laying asphalt and pouring concrete. Two of my cousins, Mulo and Dervo, each had a dump truck, and my Uncle Charlie had a big Chevy work truck and an old flatbed.

Charlie had six kids: Mulo, Dervo, Lonnie, Georgie, Flodia, and Leanna—the oldest. Lonnie had worked in road construction before, and he was assigned to one of the road-work details. His two sisters worked in a bakery. Both sisters were going out on the sneak with the same guy, a local gadjo who was known as Tennessee Billy. But it was Flodia that wound up falling head over heels in love with Billy and eloping with him.

It was still common back then for Gypsies who were Catholic or Orthodox to make a novena to ask a saint to intercede with God when someone was real sick or had recently died. Gypsies would sometimes make a saint's holiday every week, especially in the Orthodox Church, where they would tell you what saint's holiday it was on any given day. Raising a table for someone who was real ill was done before noon. If the holiday had to do with praying for a deceased family member's soul, the table was raised sometime in the afternoon.

If the person was very ill, folks would raise a table and promise God that if the sick person recovered, they would make this holiday for the rest of their lives. In the case of someone who had died, a novena was said to ask God to please have mercy on the deceased's soul and let him or her through the pearly gates.

Every saint's holiday featured a certain meat or fish main course, so there might be a lamb holiday, a fish holiday, or a pork holiday. Lamb and pork would be roasted; fish would be fried or put into a stew with all types of vegetables, fruits, nuts, etc., just like at Christmas and Thanksgiving. No one ever traveled on this type of holiday, even family members who didn't celebrate it. Folks just respected it and stayed home from work.

One particular sad day was a holiday my folks made for a family member who had recently passed away. My cousin Flodia had just eloped with Tennessee Billy, and she was planning to show up and see her folks alone, without her new husband. Uncle Charlie was still pretty riled up that his daughter Flodia had run off to get married to a gadjo. Gypsies at the time rarely married out of their race, and many, especially women, were shunned by their families when they did.

My mom was busy inside the little tent, about twelve feet by twelve feet, that we kept especially for holidays, because our trailer was too small to hold everybody who was supposed to come and make the holiday with us. Back then, most trailers were not much longer than twenty-four feet, if even that long. My mom was setting the holiday table when her cousin, my uncle Charlie, was saying his adoos. She called after him, "Flodia said she's coming. Aren't you gonna wait until she shows up before you cut out? You should at least pay your respects to the holiday." My mom was irritated because he wouldn't stay for the table.

From day one, Uncle Charlie hadn't been happy with his job at Oak Ridge. All the damn rules about this and that just didn't make much sense to him. He didn't get on well with the know-it-all gadjo foremen, and he resented them trying to tell him how to do the construction and road-building work that he'd been doing pretty much since he was a teenager. Uncle Charlie was also downright angry that there was so much socializing and mixing between the Gypsy and gadjo young men and women.

Early one morning while laying down a prefab wooden sidewalk, Uncle Charlie created such a ruckus that a slew of armed guards escorted him back to the trailer court and told him to pack up and be out of Oak Ridge by noon. The guards weren't going anywhere until Uncle Charlie was ready to leave Oak Ridge. My uncle packed his family and everything they'd need for the road into their trailer and big Chevy truck. Finally, wedged between government jeeps front and back, Uncle Charlie drove out the main gate of Oak Ridge, cursing the "evil gadje" the whole way.

Uncle Charlie pulled his trailer out of the camp about twenty minutes before a Greyhound bus dropped Cousin Flodia off at the edge of the road in front of the camp. Back in the day, Greyhound was the mode of public transportation for Gypsies, especially in little towns in the South.

Flodia arrived by Greyhound in the early afternoon and walked quickly toward her folks' trailer. By the time she got as far as our holiday tent, she saw the empty trailer space across the way and realized that her people were gone. I remember that my sister Kezia came out of the tent and got hold of Flodia and told her that her folks had left about a half hour before she arrived. Poor Flodia couldn't stop bawling.

Flodia had on a white dress with purple violets and shades of violet all over. She looked so gorgeous with tears in her eyes. Flodia really didn't eat much of anything at the holiday dinner; she held a piece of celery in her mouth while the tears ran down her face. That's something that I'll never forget. I don't remember many people who were ever that sad, even at funerals. Since her own family had left, my brother Luca took Flodia back to his place to stay with him and his family.

A couple of hours down the road, Uncle Charlie had a flat tire. He gave Lonnie a couple of bucks to go buy a tire iron and some beer. Hours went by, and Lonnie never came back. His brother Georgie ratted out Lonnie and told Charlie that Lonnie had taken a Greyhound back to Oak Ridge to marry a girl named Adeline that he had been sweet on. I used to see Lonnie and his gal have lunch together and dance together. I didn't know a whole lot about dating and love, but I knew enough not to squeal on Lonnie and his girl.

I saw Lonnie again in 1950, then on the evening when I entered the High Note Bar and Grill to get change to use their pay phone. This was in 1957, and back then all bars and restaurants had public phones. I had known Lonnie the whole time I was growing up, so I remembered very well what he looked like. He dressed really well—like the cool guys you see in magazines—and all the girls liked him.

As I was leaning over the bar to ask the barman for change, I looked Lonnie straight in his face and blurted out his name. He stopped licking those big breasts, started to raise up, and asked, "Danny, is that really you?" After zipping up his fly and making himself presentable, he stood up to shake my hand. Lonnie left the gal with the big breasts flat at the bar, and we went to a booth and started to talk about old times. We sat there and chatted for an hour, and I got so involved in catching up that I actually forgot why I came into the bar in the first place: It was to make a phone call to a new display guy who wanted me to help him with a large design project. When I remembered and dialed the guy's number, his phone just rang and rang; when I ran into the guy some months later, he wouldn't speak to me because he had waited and waited for me to call about the job.

Anyway, I took Lonnie home with me, and Lena cooked a wonderful dinner. She knew Lonnie's sisters and brothers, but had never met him. He wanted some booze, so I went out to a liquor store to get some.

While I was gone, Lonnie made a play for my wife. As soon as I came in with the booze, Lena came over to me and said angrily—pointing at Lonnie with a big skillet clutched in her right hand—"I want this jerk out!" I stood there with a puzzled look on my face as I was trying to figure out what the hell was going on.

Suddenly, Lena turned to Lonnie with a really angry look on her face. "Why are you still here, you son of a bitch? Get the fuck out of here," she screamed as she threw his jacket down in front of him.

Lonnie swooped up the jacket, managed to put it on by himself, teetered around a bit, then lurched out the back door, staggering along the side of the cottage to the path down to the road.

I had never heard Lena say a four-letter word before! I couldn't believe my ears. I knew that Lonnie was a hot bastard, but I didn't think he'd try something like that with my wife. Well, time does change a lot of people, or maybe it just reveals what people are really like deep down.

About a half hour went by. Lena was banging around out in the kitchen, muttering to herself and ignoring me, which in hindsight was probably a good thing. I decided I might as well close up and head off to bed. As I was closing the blinds, I looked out the window and saw Lonnie standing on the street corner, smoking a cigarette, trying to hitchhike. He stood there leaning from side to side. I hadn't thought about whether he had any money on him when we threw him out, so for old time's sake, I walked down to the corner to talk to him. "Don't you have no money?" I asked. "If you want, I can get you a cab."

"No," he said, "but never you mind, Danny. I'll hitch back to where I'm stayin' and I'll be fine."

I did feel sorry for Lonnie, I really did. The question that still pops into my head all these years later is *why* did I feel sorry for that bum? Why hadn't I just closed the living room blinds and gone to bed?

"Come on," I said, and motioned for Lonnie to follow me. I helped him into the work truck and asked him where he was staying. It turned out that he was overnighting with another cousin of mine, Lurie George, who lived out in Cicero. All I could think about as we were heading over to Cousin Lurie's was how pissed Lena was going to be with me. Lurie came running out of his house as Lonnie and I got out of the truck. He and his wife had been worried about Lonnie because he hadn't come home that night.

As soon as he got out of the truck, Lonnie said to Lurie, "Some broad rolled me in a bar where I ran into Danny. He saved my ass and took me back to his place." Cousin Lurie invited me in for a bite to eat, but I said that I had to get going.

I was so disgusted with Lonnie making moves on Lena that I felt like I was gonna throw up. I tried to calm down enough to drive home. As soon as I got back to the cottage, I could tell that Lena was real angry, not only with Lonnie, but with me, and more than she had been for years.

"You had some nerve taking that scumbag home!"

"Well, he don't live here in Chicago; he's just here on a burial. "I figured he didn't have no money for a cab, so I drove him to where he's staying, over at Cousin Lurie's."

"I'm so mad at you, you bastard! Maybe you should just go and stay with that lowlife! All the nerve you had to take him! Shame on your rear! What kind of man are you? A man makes advances on your wife, puts his hands all over her, and you take him home? You're made out of the same stuff as your drunken cousin. You're a real piece of shit!"

"Well, I can't explain it," I offered. "I did it for old times' sake. I've known him all my life, since I was five or six years old. I couldn't help it. I couldn't see him stuck out there. He had no money. He was real shaken up. I couldn't leave him to hitchhike like that," I said, starting across the kitchen toward Lena.

Her glare stopped me in my tracks, and I even took a few steps back, winding up with my butt against the door of the oven that in all the upset Lena had forgotten to turn off.

"Boy, you're such a great man! You have such honor! Old times' sake or not, you brought that son of a bitch into our house. We fed him, and he starts to devour me. I took that skillet and banged him on the head!"

Lordy! Lena was so wound up and was being so theatrical, puffing up her face and flailing her hands in my direction. Then, seeing how she was hopping up and down like a banty hen—and trying to imagine her going after Lonnie with a skillet—I couldn't help it any more and started to laugh. The angrier Lena got, the harder I laughed.

"You took a skillet and actually hit Lonnie on the head with it? Are you sure, because I didn't see no blood," I said, still trying to picture in my mind what that must have looked like!

Lena started to hit me, and I grabbed her hands and held her close and tried to kiss her. She pulled free, and I knew better than to try to grab her again.

Lena didn't speak to me for two full weeks. It took her a good three weeks to actually forgive me. But we made up. This was our second real falling-out, almost as bad as that time we were first married when I was having a real sweaty nightmare: I rolled over on Lena in bed before we were having marital relations, and she thought I was trying to force sex on her.

I was pretty disgusted with Lonnie when I seen him licking on that gal's breasts right out in public at a bar. I tried not to show my disgust when I recognized him. I thought he showed me at least some respect when he left the chippie flat at the bar. I was surprised that he didn't offer some explanation for his gross behavior, like maybe saying that he had had too much to drink. I guess he figured that he didn't have to explain, because I was another guy. But because of his behavior in the bar that evening and his coming on to my wife, I lost the respect and admiration that I had felt for him since I was just a kid.

I saw Cousin Lonnie once again, in 1989 in Atlanta, and he came up to me and reached out for my hand as if nothing bad had ever happened. I didn't shake his hand.

"Where's your wife?" he asked. The nerve of him to ask! I told him matter-of-factly that Lena had died almost six years before, and Lonnie said that he had lost his wife too. I felt like saying "good!" but I didn't. After all those years, I was still real upset with him. "Lonnie, I never did forgive you for that night. You're a real son of a bitch to have made moves on Lena."

"Oh, man, I was so fuckin' drunk," he said, in such a way that made it sound like he was so drunk that he found Lena attractive, not that he had come on to her because he was drunk.

"That was no excuse, you bastard," I spit out, and I walked away. I really didn't like to walk away, but I did. I just was hurt because I had known him for so many years when he disrespected me and Lena and got fresh with her. I should have decked him back then and finished the job Lena had started when she whacked him on the head with that big skillet.

I often wondered why I didn't take a poke at him on that street when he was hitchhiking. I had all the right in the world to do it, but that was me, passive to a fault, always thinking that problems would solve themselves. It wasn't in my nature. What was wrong with me? All my life, even when I was a kid, I never got my dander up. Even getting in small scrapes as a kid, I never struck back—never. No matter to what lengths bullies would go to make me mad enough to fight back, I never would, never did. I'd just walk away.

I never got in a real fight when I was young; maybe a little scuffle, but no fight. Ok, ok—only once, with Lonnie's brother Georgie. I was about 11. We were at a swimming hole in Alexandria, Virginia. There were three water moccasins in the water, and these guys swooshed them out of the water, and we were supposed to go in swimming, like skinny dipping. I said no way.

"But the moccasins is out," Georgie said.

"Oh yeah? Well, maybe their mother, father, sisters, or brothers are still in the water."

"Are you a sissy?" he asked, scrunching up his face.

I said, "Yes, a great big one, 'cause I ain't goin' in that snake hole." I wasn't going to get in a water hole where somebody had just chased some snakes out. Who in their right mind was gonna go in that water?

Georgie pushed me into the water, jumped in right after me, and started swinging like crazy. I got a few licks in, and he never struck back. That was the one and only time I got physical with someone until I was a lot older, and even then it was pretty rare that I would actually take a swing at somebody. What was possibly wrong with me back then that I just never got stirred up enough over so many years to get physical when something wasn't right? I just never got mad enough to follow through and throw punches.

Years later, I got decked when I stepped between my daughter Varda and her crazy dopehead husband, Marik, who was beating on her and tearing out her hair while she was holding their new baby. Marik pushed me back, kicked me in the balls, and slugged me hard enough to knock me down. I just got up, grabbed Lena, and drove us home.

Until my two younger boys were older, I had hit someone in anger only that one time when I was a kid. Just once growing up. I was never provoked into a fight, never got angry enough to fight. I was just raised that way, I guess. Even with all the provocation, I just would not get in any altercation whatsoever. Trying to figure out why has always left me feeling confused.

I did spank my number two son, Lash, when he was 15 because he stole some tools out of a neighbor's work shed and pawned them to buy dope. I took off my belt and gave him a good whack on the butt with it, which up to this day I believe was when he began to hate me. Lash has held a grudge and despised me all these years.

Another time, about seven months after his mom had passed away, I got physical when my son Earl wouldn't come out of the trailer to help me make some chairs. I took a broom after him and just barely caught his backside with the bristles. Lightly, that's how I remember it. He just laughed, hit me hard in the shoulders with both hands, pushed me down on the ground, and gave me a couple of good kicks. If any father ever had a good reason to beat the crap out of his son, I guess I did. But instead, I just jumped in my work truck and left for a few days to spend some time up in Washington state with my daughter Drina.

I was already a lot older by the time I finally flipped out and totally lost it. I punched Drina's no-good doper bed-hopping husband, Curtis Wheeler, and broke his jaw. He had given Drina the clap. Curtis told me that my girl had been fooling around and got the clap from someone else. I knew my daughter, and I knew what Curtis had told me was a damn lie. I felt so much anger toward him that something snapped inside me. I guess I reacted the way I did because I felt that Curtis had attacked my daughter's reputation, and she wasn't there to defend herself.

I'm not in no way making myself better than other men. Until I was a lot older, it was just never my nature at all to fly off the handle. Not even my folks had any nature like that. I can't remember any fights involving my dad or brothers or my immediate relatives. I just saw so many vicious fights among drunks on the carnival circuit, and when I would see how ugly people's behavior could be, it made me even more fearful of losing control and getting lost in anger. It's scary to think how your life can turn on a single decision. One act done in anger could end a life and change the course of so many others. I really tried to avoid taking on bullies, and I despised the meanness of people who picked a fight.

How can the most gentle person give in to such radical behavior; what drives him to go off the deep end? Just watching how someone's face and body change as they give in to anger shows how the anger takes over the whole person. You can see how their forehead starts to wrinkle, their eyes start to squint, they clench their fist, and they start to mumble. Their speech gets out of hand. They feel like they're a powerhouse. Something explodes in their brain. Boom, it happens. They come out fighting. Feeling remorse afterwards, they say that they don't know what came over them: "I don't know what happened; I'm not like that at all!"

Even though the craziness and the foolish impulse was in their own brain and drove them to pick up a weapon of some sort—a stick, a rock, a knife, or the fantastic, almighty handgun—how many thousands of people kill someone in a rage and afterwards never feel remorse? How many others finally feel remorse and ask themselves, "Why?" thousands and thousands of times over.

Just think about the many unknown perpetrators and their victims who are out there. Some people's crimes might be discovered quite by accident, by dogs or kids playing. There was a woman whose five husbands—twenty years' worth of hubbies—were found buried here and there in her yard. She told the police that she didn't know anything at all about that, didn't have the faintest idea how all those bodies wound up buried all over her property. "Things happen," she told the cops. "Men come and go. I've never been one to ask questions. Ain't like I had anything to do with them bodies gettin' planted in my yard!" The neighbors were jealous of her, so she said, never did take to her, got into knockdown, drag-out fights with each of her husbands. Maybe *they* were the ones who killed her husbands, one after the other, and buried the bodies in the poor widow lady's yard just to get her in a lot of trouble.

Now, did this woman go berserk at some point and kill each husband herself, or did she methodically plan each hubby's murder to keep collecting his Social Security benefits? But, even if she thought and planned real carefully, she was crazy in her brain to even think about doing what she did!

Even though my cousin Lonnie made a pass at my wife, I figured that he must have been crazy in his head to come on to Lena like that. It didn't give rise to an impulse in my brain to retaliate in any way. I didn't have it in me to get violent over it and attack him. I still felt sorry for him out of the love and respect that I had had for him. It was instilled in me that this was a cousin I held dear to me. Years later, when he approached me, my blood started to boil when I remembered the nerve he had to disrespect my wife. But right after it happened, instead of anger and a thought of revenge, I laughed and laughed when my wife told me that she had conked Lonnie with a skillet.

Up until that time I decked my rotten son-in-law Curtis, it was never gonna be me to lose it over someone else's craziness and go bonkers in my own brain. I had never snapped before, never, even at that crucial moment after Cousin Lonnie had come on to Lena, when I really should have beaten him up and thrown him out, or at least certainly not have given him a ride! Oh, how my blood boils when it crosses my mind, and it really does still cross my mind.

There was a wonderful singer, Lonnie Johnson, way back when. I stopped listening to his beautiful music because when I heard his name on the radio, I would think of Cousin Lonnie, and thoughts of that evening would take over. Lena never made any connection between the two Lonnies. I think that name rested on my brain because I really believed that I didn't do right by my wife. I could have been a righteous and angry husband and beaten Lonnie up for assaulting Lena. I didn't even ask Lonnie what the hell had been going through his mind that made him think that coming on to my wife was a good idea.

Maybe reliving over and over and rethinking that night and feeling my blood boil is my penitence to this day. How it sits there on my brain all these long years. It's there, believe me, because as I've said, part of me—maybe even the better part—still believes that I didn't do what a stand-up guy would have done that terrible night so long ago.

11

Silvestri Art Manufacturing Co.

There was a fancy bar called Delby's in Chicago that I stopped at one afternoon on my way to deliver paper roses that a former coworker had asked me to make. The bar owner was really impressed with the roses and asked if I could make a half-dozen or so giant roses to put up on the large mirror behind their front bar. He was planning a surprise birthday party for one of the barmaids, whose name just happened to be Rose. I left, spent about an hour making the roses, then scooted back to the bar. I crawled up a short ladder to reach the sides of the mirror and tried my best to use cellophane tape to make the flowers stick to the mirror, but they kept tilting to one side or the other. I just couldn't get them to stay put in the positions where I wanted them.

A good-looking guy stepped away from the crowded bar and came around to the foot of the ladder. He smiled up at me and told me that he worked in the display business. "Let me help you, pal! Looks like you're having a hard time getting those stems to stay put. I'll show you a little trick!" I stepped down from the ladder, introduced myself, and the good Samaritan shook my hand and said that his name was John Spain. He grabbed one of the giant roses and the roll of cellophane tape and quickly climbed up the ladder. John reached down for more roses as he worked his way around the mirrored wall. Wow! This guy was good!

All John did to make this work was bend the end of the heavy wire rose stems and make a little crook—like at the end of an umbrella handle—which gave the cellophane tape something to hold onto. With the little crook taped flat against the mirror, the roses remained upright. John crawled down off of the ladder and asked who had made the beautiful paper roses. I told him that I had, and that I had done quite a few display projects working for others and on my own. "Man," he said, real excited, "we could use you where I work!"

He took me to the bar's telephone booth, got George Silvestri, the owner of Silvestri Art Manufacturing Company, on the line and told him about me and my giant handcrafted roses. John finally looked over at me, smiled, and waved the telephone receiver in my direction. I grabbed it and introduced myself to Mr. Silvestri.

"So, Danny, you make these giant flowers by hand, without using any machinery?" Mr. Silvestri got right to the point.

"Yes, sir. I started making crepe-paper flowers as a little kid. My grandparents had a traveling theater show, and I was put to work making crepe-paper roses. As a young man, I built sets and concession stands and did display work for several different traveling shows. I just finished a display stint as lead designer with Varady Design. I don't think you'll find a better fit for your retail unit, Mr. Silvestri!"

He seemed pretty impressed and asked me to stop by to see him soon. I called the Silvestri personnel department and made an appointment to meet Mr. Silvestri and show him samples of my work.

Two days later, clutching my design portfolio, samples of my fantasy flowers, some small-gauge wire, and rolls of crepe paper in various colors and shades, I headed over to Silvestri Art Manufacturing Co. and met with Mr. Silvestri. He took one look at the samples I had brought and called in his business partner, Bill Martin, and Bill's staff. I stood there and made sample roses and other flowers by hand as they watched how smoothly my fingers moved and how quickly I finished each flower.

Bill took his designers back to the work area, and Mr. Silvestri asked what kind of salary I wanted to start working for him. I said three hundred fifty dollars a week, and he said how about three hundred for starters until he could see how to use me. I was so excited that I said it was a deal before I'd taken another breath.

I couldn't believe my good luck! Lena was going to be so happy! I was so overwhelmed, I couldn't even think straight. This was like singing a song in a high school production and the next week winding up on *The Ed Sullivan Show*. The only time I had been as excited as I was about landing a job at Silvestri was when Lena and I were first married, and I went to New York City to be a contestant on *Strike It Rich*.

I was the new designer kid on the block at Silvestri Art Manufacturing Co., known in the display-design trade as Silvestri Design or simply Silvestri. It was the most creative, innovative, successful, and prestigious display company of them all. The company's designers had won all sorts of awards for their innovative display products and imaginative displays for retailers and the entertainment industry as well as for public seasonal displays.

Silvestri was the company that in the late 1950s designed and imported from Italy strings of tiny white waterproof and weatherproof lights for retail and domestic use in the U.S. They were called Italian lights even when later on they were manufactured in Hong Kong. In late 1959, George Silvestri partnered with Joe Kreis, the display director at the Saks store on Michigan Avenue, to try out a new idea they had come up with for Christmas decorations. They strung Italian lights—smaller Christmas lights than Chicagoans had ever seen before—to outline every branch of the half-dozen or so elm trees in front of Saks. When the switch was flipped, the effect was pretty amazing: Pedestrians stopped to look, and cars slowed down. Mr. Silvestri and Joe Kreis had together created a Chicago Christmas tradition. Within a year, other Michigan Avenue merchants were also using Italian lights to decorate the trees in front of their stores.

By the early 1960s, Silvestri Italian lights were a big seller all over America and transformed how cities big and small decorated for the Christmas holiday season. The lights could easily be set to either blink or burn steady. They were soon available in many colors and also were lightweight and easy to put in a wide variety of locations. Many trees on Main Street, USA, were soon covered with Italian lights and looked like something out of the *Nutcracker* story. Silvestri was hired to decorate much of downtown Chicago. We did all of the trees along State Street and Michigan Avenue, and these displays were in the news all over the world. Until I saw them all lit up, I hadn't realized how gigantic some of those trees were!

I started working at Silvestri before the Italian lights were introduced, but back then the company was already famous for its department store displays and mechanical animation figures. Probably the most famous animation figure was a Santa Claus that smiled, winked, waved, and lifted a bag of toys into and out of a sled pulled by reindeer that also moved their heads and opened and shut their eyes. Over the decades, Silvestri introduced all sorts of mechanical figures that had even more intricate animation routines.

These animation figures in display windows drew quite a crowd. A lot of folks admired the window displays for a while, then went inside to see more and wound up buying something that caught their eye. Silvestri was known in the display-design field as having the finest and most imaginative animation figures in the United States.

Mr. Silvestri loved to introduce his more elaborate holiday window displays to merchants and to the public by personally throwing the switch and shouting, "Showtime!" The beautifully lit and decorated display windows wowed the crowds of people who had been waiting outside the store in the dark. They oohed and aahed when the display lights came on and the animated figures started going through their routines. It all looked like something out of a fairy tale!

I was pretty damn excited as I arrived early at Silvestri Design for my first day of work. I was beaming like a newlywed as I headed to the human resources department to complete some paperwork and be issued an employee badge. Mr. Silvestri himself met me there and offered to give me the grand tour of the company.

I was amazed at the size of the factory! The Silvestri building had seven floors. The first floor had the shipping department, the company offices, and a very elaborate and impressive showroom featuring items they manufactured on site as well as original displays created by the staff.

On the second floor was the plaster casting and sculpture department, where they made life-sized figures like Michelangelo's *David* and such.

The third floor housed the wire and welding department, where they made all of the display armatures, frames, and fixtures.

The electric department was up on the fourth floor. That's where, in the late 1950s, the first Italian lights were made and assembled into strands of varying lengths. That's also where I ran into John Spain again—the guy who had helped me with the giant roses at Delby's bar and got me the interview with George Silvestri. John had headed a team that designed and put together the famous Silvestri lamps of various sizes and designs. John became a really good friend, but he left to work at another company after I had been at Silvestri for only about a year or so.

The electric department had an elaborate showroom in the Chicago Merchandise Mart, featuring plastic and silk flowers imported from Paris, plus what I call fantasy trees and flowers, and all kinds of electrified display items and lamps. Later, they had Silvestri's entire array of Italian lights on display and also some good-quality imported items that were manufactured in Taiwan or Italy to Silvestri's strict quality control standards.

On the fifth floor was the display department, where the workers made a wide variety of display components used to create all kinds of displays, from window and indoor merchandise displays to all sizes of theatrical and movie display items. They also did specialty medical mannequins in the display department; there were designer-artists who painted eyes, muscles, and whatnot on mannequins to be used in training medical students. Some of the heads and torsos had parts that nested inside the mannequin, like the heart and other internal organs; these were all hand-painted. I was so impressed to meet all of these talented people.

Graphic design, advertising, art and illustration, photography, and photo processing were located up on the sixth floor.

On the seventh floor was a down-sized but full-featured printing plant with various types of modern and antique printing presses.

Oh, how excited I was, thinking about what my life would be like working for such a high-class company! At the beginning of my first day, I was shown my work table in the design atelier on the fifth floor. I was already set up right next to Edie Tanaka, a beautiful young Asian lady who was busy painting eyes on some large doll heads that I found out from her were actually milliner's heads that would be used in stores to display hats and scarves and maybe jewelry. Edie was also one of the artists who worked on the medical models.

My work table consisted of two wooden horses and a four-by-eight-foot sheet of thick plywood covered with brown paper. My boss told me to go ahead and go out and purchase or order whatever I needed to get started making paper flowers.

First on the list were several widths and thicknesses of crepe paper to make samples. Then I walked over to the Wholesale Florists Exchange to get the florist wire that I needed. I didn't realize at first that they actually had tons of the stuff! I only bought one twelve-pound box, plus floral tape. They had in stock so many types of wire that I had never seen before, and so many different gauges. They had thirty-six-inch-long heavy specialty wire, cotton-covered wire and paper-covered wire. To make flower and foliage stems for my freelance projects, I had used any kind of wire that I could get my hands on, and I covered the wire with thin crepe or art paper.

Mr. Silvestri had told me previously to just go ahead and

make an assortment of roses and other smaller flowers, and the designers would incorporate them into whatever designs they were working on. The designers at that point in time were putting together kinda generic displays that could be modified to use on various holidays and occasions. There were a lot of small display items that could be combined in different ways: ball-like trees, hanging trees, complete topiaries, and every type of garland imaginable.

Mr. Silvestri suggested that I go by the Chicago Merchandise Mart and check out our company's showrooms there and find out just what display-design people were buying. I saw trees there covered with all kinds of flowers, from tiny orchid blooms to large roses and magnolia flowers. In addition to every kind of flower imaginable, the Merchandise Mart also carried a wide range of decorator trees, including willow trees, manzanita trees, magnolia trees, and birch trees. I decided to take some manzanita branches back to Silvestri and make an assortment of decorator trees featuring vibrant colors, fantasy flowers, and brightly colored birds.

While I was waiting for them to be brought out from the back, I had what I thought was a brilliant idea: to make a three-dimensional, living copy of the large fantasy-garden mural on the wall of the Silvestri showroom's entrance, not knowing that the mural was about to be changed out by the designer in charge of decorating the showroom space.

Later, back at Silvestri, I asked the lead designer, Jack Jones, if he thought it would be all right if I did the three-dimensional version of the mural. "Well, I don't think that Mr. Silvestri wants you to design anything for the showroom itself. And about the mural, it's going to be switched out soon for one with a totally different look. We don't have any permanent display features in the showroom, just display items for sale. But, Danny, we're getting ready to put on our fall show, so if you can manage to design and make a willow tree as beautiful as your willow tree sketches, that would be wonderful! Mr. Silvestri said for me to let you do whatever you want to. Go for it!"

I chose some long green sprigs of plastic foliage and fourteen-foot-long annealed twelve-gauge wire to use as stems for the foliage. Using the stemming machine that had a treadle like an old-fashioned sewing machine, I started attaching the sprigs along the length of the wire, using green thread. I bundled together some of the wire stems with and without foliage, finally creating the willow tree trunk by making a large bundle out of some of the smaller bundles by running them through the stemming machine. The base of the tree trunk was only about two and a half inches in diameter. I stuck the bottom in a redwood planter tub filled with plaster of Paris. I set the tree at an angle, then formed the foliage into a pattern that made the tree look like it was branching out like a real willow tree. The branches were of different lengths at different heights, and the tree looked totally natural and real. This tree, the first of many, made a spectacular impression on coworkers and customers alike. There were several variations too. One was sprayed orange and highlighted with gold.

The lead photographer, Mark Kuebler, came down from the photo studio and said that he was photographing some display pieces for fall, and he wanted to take the willow tree up for some photos before we experimented with different looks. So we loaded it into the freight elevator and headed up to the photo studio. "By the way, Danny," Mark said on our way up, "Mr. Silvestri is showing some auto industry bigwigs around, and he said that he'll meet us up in the studio."

Mark pulled down a seamless backdrop which was a beautiful shade of sky blue, and then he placed the tree on a green grass matte. I started working with the willow branches, forming the tree into its final shape. Mr. Silvestri came into the studio, accompanied by a group of real nattily-dressed men, who he introduced to us as Ford Motor Company representatives. Mr. Silvestri was already busy designing and planning the 1958 Ford Circus traveling show. As they approached, I started to move out of their way, but Mr. Silvestri told me to stay put.

One of the visitors said that he thought that the willow trees would look wonderful in the showrooms of Ford dealerships across the USA. That was when Mr. Silvestri introduced me as one of his lead designers, someone who he could count on to always be trying out new ideas. He explained that I had just finished working on the willow trees, several of which in different colors and shapes would be featured in our new fall line. Mr. Silvestri told the visitors that the design supervisor liked this sample in green so much that he wanted to have it photographed just the way it was for the next spring catalog.

One of the Ford gents asked the price of the individual trees and the bulk price. After Mr. Silvestri said that we'd have to get back to them about the prices, another of the visitors said that he was sure that Silvestri would give them a good price, and maybe they should do a small order of two hundred trees just to see how they went over in the local dealerships. But, he added, not in the redwood planter, but in a more formal-looking planter urn.

After the visitors had left later that afternoon, Mr. Silvestri told me to come to his office later with Jack Jones. He told us then that Ford wanted two hundred trees and asked us to price out the project, taking into account my time to actually complete the design, plus preliminary expenses, new equipment costs, shipping, etc.

All I knew at that moment was that this project could be a real feather in my designer's hat if I managed to pull it off. My main problem at that point in my career was trying to do as much as I could by myself; I had a real difficult time delegating any of the tasks that a large project required. I figured that I was part of a team, but sometimes I wanted to do more than carry my own weight. That's why I often put in a lot of overtime hours. I had to move fast getting this project underway, because that week was the spring lay off, when we would take some time off and rest up for all of the work that we would have to deal with in the next season.

The foliage had to be created from scratch, and we would need extra machines to deal with all of the foliage assembly.

There were six workers who didn't take the week off. One was a new guy, a helper who in this case would spend his time feeding the wire rods for the foliage into the stemming machine. We designers didn't actually do all of the production for shipping purposes. Someone would physically place a large pipe in the center of each urn so that the tree trunk could be placed in the exact center to secure the tree that would be shipped separately, with instructions on how to assemble the tree, and how to arrange the foliage and branches to achieve the classic willow tree shape and appearance. Different clients told me over many years that assembling our designs on site was a welcome break from their regular everyday duties.

Ford got back to us within a matter of days following the initial shipment, congratulating us on a job well done. I was happy and pleased with everything that I had accomplished in the short time I had been at Silvestri.

I went right on designing for the fall collection: foliage sprays with dried and preserved real autumn leaves, and floral arrangements of all shapes and sizes. I put together some fantasy designs as well as some that were more traditional and formal. What I never did was make a floral arrangement without first checking out the designs in the previous years' fall lines. I read all of the various notes about what had been successful and what hadn't been so popular. I always found some plain-jane designs that could really be turned around using a little imagination and maybe different textures or materials, maybe some dried flowers and leaves in addition.

The next big order for the willow trees was placed by Sears, Roebuck and Co., and that order was for another two hundred trees. The sales people had different territories all over the US and Canada, and since the large willow trees wouldn't fit in a briefcase, the folks in sales had a large portfolio with large and small photos of everything in our lines. The major retailers like Sears usually purchased Christmas items about two years in advance. Most national chains had the same traditional Christmas season appearance. A decorated sales floor in

Wisconsin was pretty much identical to a sales floor in upstate New York. The two big exceptions were Florida and California. Retailers there usually bought from nearby display companies, and their holiday displays reflected local customs and tastes.

By June, we had to come up with ideas and samples for that year's Christmas line. June was when the major department stores and chain stores as well as the locally-owned stores and specialty stores bought their display items for the Christmas season. Silvestri was known for the most unique and lavish display items. Even used Silvestri display products were highly desirable because they were of great quality and workmanship. And Silvestri display products didn't come cheap. Prices were at least 25 percent higher than for our competitors' products. A fully decorated six-foot Christmas tree from Silvestri was 50 percent to 75 percent more expensive than a tree put out by the competition. The big selling point for our pre-decorated trees was that the ornaments were hand-made, hand-blown, and imported from artisan shops throughout Europe. We had exclusive rights to these ornaments, so our clients would never see the same ornament or a knock off or copy anywhere else.

The company eventually branched out into niche markets, such as high-quality statuary and urns and flower pots for cemeteries. One of Mr. Silvestri's cousins had a business in California that manufactured concrete statues and fountains, as well as planter boxes and other garden décor. Many years before, the company had made carnival plaster dolls and animals to be given away as prizes at the midway concession stands of traveling shows. Even back in the beginning, Silvestri made items that stood out from the usual, such as the famous Sailor Girl doll with her hands in her pockets that was in high demand all over the USA. Other popular items were the lying-down collie and standing bulldog figures that were probably Silvestri's first stand-out products.

Department stores came to Silvestri for new display and merchandising ideas. They purchased elaborate urns, vases, and statues made out of plaster of paris. Then, their display people would apply their own finishes, textures, and colors. Soon, local and chain stores were purchasing finished vases and urns filled with plastic, paper, and silk flowers, then fantasy-flower trees and floral pieces celebrating the arrival of spring.

Over the years, Christmas decorations were introduced, and Silvestri created some products that are still considered to be cutting edge, such as Italian lights. These popular lights can now be ordered with battery packs, so the lights can also be used on weatherproof outdoor wreaths, Christmas trees, and decorations.

Some of our best ideas came from buyers and sales reps who were well-traveled and dealt with a lot of different people and listened to their suggestions and ideas. One department store buyer said that we should make a doll about eighteen-inches-high that would have a little motor inside that could make parts of the doll move, like maybe an arm and hand to play a harp. Working on that idea was the start of a whole department at Silvestri—the animation department. Within a few years, Silvestri had a large inventory of animated elves, angels that flapped their wings, fairy godmothers with sparkling wands, dogs and cats that opened their mouths and sat up and sat down, and other figures that had moving body parts and eyes that opened and closed and rolled. Valentine's Day was a time when a lot of the newer animation was tried out, like a cupid that could shoot arrows into a large red heart.

Some of our bigger clients had stores scattered all over the United States and Canada, so Silvestri opened facilities in New York, Los Angeles, Miami, in the Midwest, and in several cities up in Canada. We had a growing sales force that worked out of these different locations. When they were in town, they would come and share ideas with the designers. One rep told me that the stores out West especially wanted some new Christmas decorations that would be more modern and stand out. At one point, I put together a wreath from dried real flowers, silk and paper flowers, sprinkled glitter on it, and put a Christmas ribbon on it made by a gal who was the best and most imaginative bow designer anywhere. Mr. Silvestri saw it and went bonkers over it. He said to make a matching garland and some trees of different sizes with the same flowers and glitter.

Over time, I became known for my roses made from paper and silk, and also for my silk camellias. Sometimes, I would spend a week to ten days making just one kind of flower for a large order.

I was rewarded with regular raises, and for special jobs, I would receive a bonus of from two hundred fifty dollars to twenty-five hundred dollars. The first time I brought home a twenty-five hundred dollar bonus check, Lena had to sit down real quick before she fell over.

When I did have some time off after completing a big order, I would use some of the bonus money to take Lena out on the town. She spent so much time at home being a mom and housewife, taking care of everything when I was away on business. I hadn't bought a new suit for myself in years, so I finally broke down, went downtown to Bonds and bought a suit made from blue shadow stripe wool. The slimming jacket had a classy one-button lapel roll, which I'd admired so much on other guys. I also purchased a dark-blue tie and an off-blue Arrow-brand shirt that I had seen in a display window on my way into the store. The salesman and I were both amazed that the suit didn't need any alterations except for hemming the trouser legs. On my way home, I stopped at Thom McAn and bought a beautiful pair of black featherweights with a square toe.

I was already feeling great when I got home, but Lena had some wonderful news that sent me over the moon: She had found out that day at the doctor's that we were expecting a baby! So now our night on the town was going to be a real celebration!

Lena and I invited our next-door neighbors Betty and Bob Arndal to join us on our night out on the town, and the four of us headed downtown to see a movie and have a late-night dinner. We decided to get in line at an art house theater to see *The Boy With the Green Hair,* a 1948 movie, because the line of people waiting to see it was shorter than the lines outside the other theaters. We were so happy to be out for a movie and dinner that we didn't stop to think that maybe the reason the line at the art house theater was so short was that it was kind of a screwy movie! It had bombed at the box office when it was first released.

I got in line to purchase tickets while Lena, Betty, and Bob waited at the lobby doorway. A guy behind me tapped me on the shoulder, and as I turned around he said, "Pal, you're a real looker in that suit!" I said thanks, and turned back around, and he tapped my shoulder once more and handed me his business card. He told me to give him a call some night when I was free and we'd get together over a drink. "Pal, I'd really love to run my fingers through your wavy hair." I was so clueless about his intentions that I just thought that my hair must really look good. It wasn't the first time that someone had commented on my thick wavy hair, and not the last time. But what that guy said and how he said it really stuck with me.

I bought the tickets and went back to where Lena and our neighbors were waiting. Bob asked if the guy behind me in line had tried to pick me up! I gave him a strange look, not knowing what he meant. I told Bob that the guy had said that he really liked my suit, and I let it go at that. It was only some time later that I figured out what Bob meant.

The next bonus check from Silvestri that I received was for one thousand dollars, so Lena and I decided it was time to go house hunting in the Chicago suburbs. We found a house under construction in Cicero that the builder-seller had stopped working on because of financial difficulties. We took over the house and spent a month and a half putting up the plaster wallboard and ceiling. We found a company that specialized in building garages of all types and sizes. Within two weeks, the head honcho and his crew had finished the garage, which was a large two-car garage with built-in wooden workbenches that would be perfect for working on display projects right at home. As soon as the garage was finished, we put a lot of our belongings in it and gave our landlord a thirty-day notice that we were leaving.

Our life in Chicago was fantastic! Lena and I had a beautiful new home, two great kids, and a baby on the way! We had nice friendly neighbors that we did a lot of things with, and coworkers who had become good friends. My job was going great guns. I had created a lot of buzz in the design industry with my fanciful fantasy flowers and trees. Some months my performance bonuses were more than my regular salary.

Lena and I believed that we were well on our way to achieving our goal of putting down roots and living a settled life. A lot of folks believe that they belong where their family is. But our families were scattered all over the place, or on the road, on the move. Lena and I really wanted to find a place where our own little family could grow, prosper, and belong. That just wasn't going to happen easily for us like it did for folks who stayed on where they were raised, or had a place they were from that they could always return to. Lena and I were both born while our families were on the road, and the road was the only home we had known for many years.

12

You Could Be Movie Star!

Chicago, 1958

An Italian Admirer

It was a beautiful, wondrous spring day in Chicago. I was on my way to work in my brand new Chevy Impala convertible, convinced that I was about the coolest cat in all of Chi-Town. Silvestri Art Manufacturing Company, where I worked, was just around the corner, at 1147 West Ohio Street. I turned left onto Racine Street and parked right at the corner to get some breakfast at a luncheonette that was popular with Silvestri employees. As a matter of fact, I almost never parked in the luncheonette's parking lot. It was just too damn hard to get in and out.

In the 1920s, and for many years, this particular neighborhood around Grand and Racine was the home turf of several Chicago crime families like the Nittis. Frank Nitti was one of Al Capone's top guys, in charge of strong arm and enforcement operations. If someone refused to pay protection money or tried to take on the Chicago Outfit, Nitti's men would take care of him. The Nitti family owned a lot of businesses, and the Nitti name was everywhere: Nitti's Pharmacy, Nitti's Bakery, Nitti's Fine Furnishings, Nitti's whatnot. Back in the day, this luncheonette had been frequented by some of the Nitti soldier guys. Once in a while, I'd walk past tables where some of them—old guys now—still got together, hoarsely speaking Italian and checking out the ladies at the tables around them.

I walked through the crowded parking lot toward the front door. I was smiling because I smelled spring in the air, and I just felt so damn good about my life. Lena had just given birth to our second son, Lash, who was already sporting a full head of hair. I had a great job as a senior designer for one of the country's top display-design-and-manufacturing firms. We worked on everything from upscale window displays to broadcast, movie, and theatrical sets. I worked with a bunch of great, talented people, doing something that I absolutely loved. And I was a good designer, not afraid to think outside the box.

I went into the luncheonette and plopped down in one of their comfortable, oversized booths, the kind that little kids love to bounce around in. There was quite a breakfast menu: three or four pages of big and bigger breakfasts to choose from. I finally decided on the farm breakfast. I motioned to a passing server and ordered breakfast. I wasn't that familiar with the servers, because I usually just ran in to buy cigarettes.

My server had just hurried off when the owner, who I had never paid much attention to, sat down across from me in the booth and started speaking Italian. "Hold on," I said, "I don't understand what you're saying, so let's speak American, ok?"

The old guy looked surprised, like he couldn't get over the fact that I couldn't speak his lingo. "Well, my friend," he continued in English, "I say that my name is Guido, and I ask what is your name."

"Well, Guido, my name is Danny, and it's a pleasure to meet you," I said as he reached across the table and shook my hand. He was leaning over the table, staring at me, like he really couldn't believe that I wasn't Italian or couldn't speak Italian. I had thick wavy black hair, a big nose, a mustache, and dark skin; I guess I looked like I might be Italian. A lot of guys who looked like me in the Chicago area in the 1950s *were* Italian-Americans, and some could speak Italian. I didn't want to go into the Gypsy bit, so I just settled in, relaxed, and listened to the old guy's stories for quite a while, telling him as little about myself as he would let me get away with.

As much as I loved my job, I usually wasn't in a big hurry in the mornings. I was salaried, so I didn't punch a timecard, and as long as I made good progress on my projects, I could take some extra time for myself. I never really was called out for being late, because I often worked late on my projects and was usually one of the last people to leave at night. I always went way beyond the call of duty.

It was not uncommon for the days I spent working on design projects in other cities—planning, supervising, and fine-tuning installations—to stretch into weeks. Silvestri was the place for all this to happen and for my design talents to be put to the test. I sorta went overboard at work, taking on any new project that they threw at me, taking on more than I could handle and still have a good home life, at least what I thought at the time was a good home life.

My wonderful wife never complained, and she told me over and over how happy and proud she was to be married to me. Lena was overworked and stuck at home, while I was totally obsessed with my work. I really didn't know how to cope with it, how not to constantly think about work, so I just started working even more hours. I thought that when I reached a certain point and felt that I had finally achieved my goal, everything would fall into place. But that never happened.

Anyway, this particular morning, I took my time and enjoyed the old man's attention and conversation. I finally opened up a little more about myself and told Guido that I was a Gypsy. He let out a little whoop, smiled, and quickly asked what my family name was. As soon as I said "Miller," the old man slid out of the booth, hurried over to the cash register, and brought back a little piece of paper. It was the receipt for an awning repair that my dad had done for him. It turned out that my dad did repair work on Guido's awnings—at the luncheonette and at his home! I was flabbergasted! Even though he was semi-retired, my dad had all the work he wanted. He was known for being able to repair awnings on the spot.

"I meet your dad long time ago, and he tell me his name is now Tom Miller, and that he and his folks come to Chicago from place called Bosnia. I never heard of Bosnia so I ask him where the hell that is. That whole Bosnia thing—how you say it—threw me for loop, because we was speaking Italian all the time. I never ask your dad how he speak such good Italian."

"Well, pal," I said, "That's quite a story, a long story that I'll share with you another time."

The old man smiled, settled back into the large leather-upholstered booth, and launched into one story after another about his various dealings with the storefront Gypsies he had gotten to know over his many years in Chicago. Now, this was in 1958, and Guido's family had been in Chicago since before the First World War. He went on and on about the Gypsies he had met, done business with, been ripped off by, and gotten into knockdown street fights with. Guido knew many of the storefront Gypsies who were still around, probably most of them, he said, and expressed a lot of disgust for them, calling them the most ignoramus people on the planet.

At one point, he smiled at me, slapped his right hand down on the tabletop, and said, "You and your dad—Gypsies! You don't seem anything like storefront Gypsies here in Chicago, not even close. Last thing I think!"

The old man continued and told me about the Tene-Bimbo Gypsy gang that got its start over on Maxwell Street. This was one of the city's oldest streets, famous like Delancey Street or Havemeyer Street in New York City. Maxwell Street was famous for all of the storefronts selling factory seconds and thirds, where you could find new pots and pans with dinks and dents and chips in the porcelain finish, irregular socks and shoes—all kinds of junky stuff that couldn't be sold in a regular store, even on sale. Then, there was the goods that appeared on the street out of nowhere, probably stolen from cargo holds, freight cars, and trucks— good quality undamaged stuff from all over the world that vendors sorted through and bought at below-market prices to resell at a pretty big profit.

Guido went on to tell me about the many storefront and basement fortune-telling dives up and down Maxwell Street, shady businesses that Guido said must have paid off the cops. Those were the days of the Chicago Machine and rampant official corruption everywhere, which was no secret at the time. There were men of all ages wandering up and down the street, doing auto body work and fender repairs on the spot. The gals sitting on porches would flirt with passers-by, and the Gypsy tough guys would roll the johns and steal their wallets while they were busy feeling up the gals in all the right places. Guido knocked the Tene-Bimbos to no end.

"I lose my wife twenty years ago and I only have one woman after her, after fifteen years, for two years. Her dad was muckety-muck in Tene-Bimbos. All she want was my money and my business. She lucky I just kick her out on her keister! I tell you, my friend, I no put up with no woman since that."

"You were lucky, pal, to get rid of that gal before she got rid of you!"

"What you mean?"

"Well, there was a guy at work talking about some gals who were part of the Tene-Bimbos. They would find older guys with money and marry them, then kill them after persuading the old guys to sign over everything. The cops were called by a nephew of one of the victims, who reported his suspicions about his uncle's death. So the cops opened an investigation and a bunch of the gang members were arrested and charged with murder."

"The sons-a-bitches! Well, like I say, I'm fine without woman in bed, and I'm happy guy."

Right away, Guido got a look on his face that I'll never forget, as he said to me, "Get the picture, pal?"

I looked at him, all confused, because I had no idea what he meant about getting the picture!

"Oh, knock it off," the old guy said, making a face.

I was thinking of all this today—April 5, 2009—after my brother Gussie said exactly the same thing to me: "Knock it off, Danny!" I did knock it off today—I stopped nagging my brother—because one time a couple of years back, he was visiting from Indianapolis, and I yelled at him for borrowing my work truck and bringing it back with the front bumper all banged up. I got up in Gussie's pudgy face back then and really lit into him. He told me to knock it off, and when I didn't, he stepped back, punched me in the face, and knocked me to the kitchen floor. That time, my neighbors saw Gussie rush out of the kitchen door, thought he was a crook, and called the police.

This particular morning, I just sat there looking at Guido, wondering what I had said to piss him off.

The old man continued, "You know exactly what I mean!" I laughed, and he said, "You make fun of me?"

"No, not at all. I just don't understand what you're getting at!"

"Well," he continued, "if I tell you I think you're handsome guy, what you think about that?"

What should I think? I wondered. He looked kinda irritated.

"I'm sorry, pal; I lost you. I just don't know what you want me to say."

"Well, come later, my friend, after five, and sit and talk with me."

He took my right hand so tenderly and so softly in both of his hands. *So strange,* I thought.

"Promise me you'll come back. I must talk to you, Danny, I must."

I worked until about seven o'clock that night, saving some finishing touches for the next morning. As I walked to the car parked by the luncheonette, the old man was sweeping water out the side door. He didn't notice me right away, and then he walked over to me real quick.

"Danny, come and have coffee with me, please."

I said that I was already late getting home.

"Please," he said, "just one cup coffee. I have to 'splain what I tell you this morning."

I closed the car door and followed him. He told me to go around to the front because he was washing down the kitchen. I'd seen him do that many times before, but never paid him any mind. I went in through the front door. He came in from the back and poured me a cup of coffee and sat down with me.

"You really not understand what I talk about this morning, do you, my friend?"

I said no so softly that he leaned into me and asked, "Are you married?"

"Yes."

"Children?"

"Yes, three—two boys and a girl."

"Well, you look like hot papa! I got the hots for you, Danny!"

My mind was full of all the things that I had done that day at work, and I was already thinking about everything I had to do the next day. I just wasn't getting what he was trying to say.

"Danny, I like men. I like sex with men. But I have no sex with men in long time. I see you crossing street. You come in here many times for cigarettes, but we never talk."

He spoke English with an Italian accent so heavy that he sounded as if he'd just gotten off the boat from the Old Country. That's why he was so hard to understand.

"I see you don't understand my English so well."

Guido slid over closer to me and put his right hand between my legs, under my crotch. Wow. Wow. Wow! What a feeling! I actually froze. My cock was stiff as a board. I didn't know what to say. What could I possibly say to him as he sat there cradling my balls in the palm of his hand through my baggy pants?

I hunched over to stand up and said, with more confusion than anger, "I have to go *now*!"

He took his hand away as I stood up, and said, "I really

didn't mean to scare you, Danny. I like you very, very much. Come in some morning now and have breakfast on me, ok?"

If I never ate breakfast again, I wasn't going to go back in that place!

Line One, Hollywood Calling

About two months after my encounter with Guido, we were juggling so many projects at Silvestri that my coworkers decided to save time on our lunch break by just going to eat at the luncheonette, which was catty-corner to our workrooms. Whether we were eating in the luncheonette or I was just walking by on my way to work, I tried real hard not to glance over at Guido and risk catching his eye. He tried many times to get my attention, so I even took different streets to get to work. One day, while my crew and I were walking back to work after lunch, a guy in a suit came out of the luncheonette and ran after us, shouting my name. He had something in his hand and was hollering, "Danny, Danny, wait up!"

I stopped in my tracks, and he approached me. He was a dark-complected and handsome guy with a nicely trimmed mustache. "Hi, Danny! I'm Aldo. That's my dad over there," pointing over at Guido standing at the door of the luncheonette. "We've been trying to get in touch with you. It's been a good two months since my dad told me about what happened. Please, just give me five minutes of your time. My mother-in-law is a screenwriter, and she just finished writing the screenplay for a new *Wuthering Heights* movie. My father said that you would be the perfect Heathcliff. I can see now that my dad's right. You'd be great for the part. Please call me!"

Aldo grabbed my shoulder and handed me his business card. Because of our heavy workload at Silvestri, I honestly forgot about the card. About four days later, as I was parking my car, Guido came over to my car, made an Italian hand gesture, and said, "You no call my boy! He can make big movie star outta you!"

The old guy handed me another card. The first chance I got

back at work, I called the number on the card and got Aldo's wife on the phone.

"Oh Danny, Aldo's been adamant about getting to talk to you! Like my father-in-law, he feels that since you're a real Gypsy and so handsome, you'd be perfect for the part! I'm dying to meet you as well. How's chances that you could come over for supper tonight? I cook an outta-this-world-delicious pasta!"

"What time?" I asked, completely surprised by her invitation.

"How about seven tonight? That would give you and Aldo time to talk. My mother was so excited that maybe a new Heathcliff has been found. She really has no say in picking who plays what when they cast the movie, but she was so excited when Guido mentioned that he had met this Gypsy decorator guy named Danny who could become a movie star! He's such a movie buff! He really thinks that you're the one for the part of Heathcliff! *Wuthering Heights* is one of his all-time favorite movies, and I guess a lot of folks feel that way."

I stayed at work until six-thirty and then moseyed over to Aldo's place, about nine blocks from Silvestri. Guido met me at the door and did everything but kiss me! I didn't know that he lived there too, and I was a little embarrassed by all of his attention. He introduced me to his daughter-in-law, Selena, a very beautiful lady, and I also met her and Aldo's little baby girl. Aldo had called home to tell Selena that he had to work late and wouldn't be home for dinner. So Selena, Guido, and I went ahead and had a delicious pasta meal without him. Guido went over and plopped down in a big chair in the living room and just as quickly fell asleep. I chatted a bit with Selena, then I gave her my business card and went home to be with my family.

About noon the next day, Aldo called and apologized for not making it home for dinner the night before. He asked if I could meet him that evening at the bar across the way. We met about seven o'clock, and we talked about this and that and about his little baby girl that he and Selena had waited four long years for. He told me about his mother-in-law, Margaret, her screenwriting career, and some of the Broadway shows that she had also worked on. I'd never even heard of most of the shows that Aldo mentioned, but there was one show that I remembered, *Pajama Game*, because I had taken my wife to see it one time we were visiting family in New York City.

Well, anyway, to get to the nitty gritty, Aldo asked me if I could get him a set of black-and-white still shots of myself to pass on to his mother-in-law. I told him that wouldn't be a problem. I figured that since there were professional photographers working at Silvestri, I could just ask one of them to shoot some head shots of me. The first guy I approached, Michel Auberry, told me to come up to the photo studio after work and he'd be glad to take some head shots of me. The very next day, Michel showed me six different poses that he had taken of me and went ahead and made some beautiful glossy prints for me to take over to Aldo. I met Aldo that evening, and he gave me some release papers for me and Michel to sign so that the movie people could have the right to use the photos.

"By the way, Danny, have you ever done any plays?"

"I did plenty of sets in school but never acted in a play."

"Well, that's a surprise, because you don't seem at all nervous when I talk about the screen test."

The next day, Aldo called me at work around five o'clock, which was the normal quitting time, but I usually worked late preparing the next day's projects. He said that his mother-in-law, Margaret, wanted to set up a meeting with me, so we decided to get together that Saturday evening at her place in the Oak Park area of Chicago. As we came up to the door, Margaret, an elegant older woman, greeted me with open arms. Margaret lived in what had been her parents' home. Once she had hugged me, she said, "You look just great for the part! Let's go in, sit down, and see how you read the dialogue."

Aldo and I settled in, and Margaret made us some margaritas, which was a pretty exotic concoction for the Chicago suburbs. Margaret then rolled a portable recording machine into the room, put a 33 1/3 lp recording blank on the turntable, lowered the recording head onto the blank, and we started. I read into the microphone the typewritten words that she had given me to say. A few times, I would fumble over the words, or Margaret would tell me to talk louder or slower. She asked me to giggle, to laugh, to shout, to cough, to talk in a high voice, then to say something in a low voice. We recorded both sides of the blank.

When Margaret played it back, it felt really strange hearing my own voice. I sounded like my cousin Eppie! I'd never heard myself like that before. Margaret commented on the strength and quality of my voice and its softness. She finally put some goo on both of the recorded surfaces of the record and put it in a beige sleeve. She typed a label and stuck it on the sleeve.

"Danny," Margaret said, "I'm sending your glossies and the recording to my colleagues in Culver City, California. Keep your fingers crossed! I have your phone number and address, all of the info that they need to get in touch with you. I do wish you luck! You're a very handsome and charming fellow, Danny. I think that you'd make a fine Heathcliff! But as I've said, it's the folks in Culver City who would contact you about doing an actual screen test. I think that you'll be hearing from them, I just feel it, because you have so much going for you. It's been a real pleasure meeting you!"

We took our leave of Margaret, and Aldo led me down the stairs. There were a lot of beautiful artificial flowers mixed in with the live plants and flowers in the gardens. Aldo drove me back to my car parked at Silvestri and asked me to join him for a drink. We sat at the bar, turned toward each other and clicked our glasses.

"Danny, you're a handsome guy. You know, my dad's got a big crush on you."

I was so startled that I didn't even blink.

"Don't you know?" he continued.

I just looked dazed, I guess. "Not really," I said.

"What more can I tell you?"

"A whole bunch." That's when I ordered two more margaritas and we moved to a booth. We were the only two in the whole bar.

Aldo leaned over the table and started, "Well, about twenty years ago, my dad started to fancy men."

"What do you mean 'fancy men'? Explain that to me, Aldo. How could that be, because you've got two sisters and a brother, right? So how can he fancy men? And he's an old guy!"

"My dad's not as old as he looks. He's only sixty-seven, although I know that he looks a lot older. He's had a really hard life, both back home and here in America. When he worked in the olive groves in Italy, he worked so hard and so long in the hot sun that he wrinkled early. His gray hair is premature. But being old doesn't really have that much to do with a man wanting another man."

"But he's got children, so how did that happen if he likes other men."

"Well, Danny, I'm kinda tired, and I feel self-conscious talking about my dad this way! Can we maybe do this another time?"

"Sure, that's fine with me," I said, more confused than ever.

Well, it was about three months later, at the time of the June Christmas show, that I received a call from Aldo's mother-in-law, saying that the folks in Culver City wanted some more recordings of me talking, and this time, they wanted a really wide range of emotions. She invited me back over to her place and said that Aldo and Selena would also join us.

I rang the fancy chimes doorbell; Aldo opened the door, reached out and grabbed my hand and shook it hard.

He closed the door behind us, asked to take my coat, and grabbed my shoulder. "Hey, Danny, good luck! I'm so excited for you!"

"Me, too," Selena added, reaching over to give me a big hug.

Margaret brought in a big fancy tray of margaritas and hors d'œuvres. She handed me a cocktail, then leaned over to say, "They must really be interested in you, Danny, to want more voice recordings of you."

This time, I read more passages, made more types of sounds—enough to fill two recording blanks on both sides.

Selena stayed with Margaret while Aldo and I walked about six blocks to a bar, where we ordered more margaritas. By now, I was hooked on margaritas. We were both feeling the drinks.

Aldo began, "Boy, it's been quite a while since I've seen you, Danny, and you're even hotter-looking than I remember! Hollywood's gonna go crazy for you! I'd hate to give my dad any competition, but I'd really like a roll in the hay with you myself! You see, Danny, like my dad, I'm turned on by men also."

Wow, did my eyes open wide! "I didn't know," I blurted out. "Wow!" I sat back and started to sip my drink. I didn't know what to think.

"I'm making you feel uneasy, and I apologize for that, but you're easy to talk to. I got this gal I see about once a week, on Wednesdays—that's my night out with the boys, so to speak. Sometimes it's sex with a gal, sometimes sex with another guy, and sometimes it's three-way time. I like my three-ways!"

I don't know why, but now I was interested, and I wanted to find out more. When I opened my mouth, it sounded like someone else asking, "What exactly is a three-way, Aldo?"

"Well, that's when I have sex with two gals, or with a gal and another guy, or with two other guys."

Again, I heard this strange voice ask, "So what do youse do?"

"Me and two guys? Well, at first, I watch while they go at it, then I might start stroking their rears, and maybe reach over and grab one guy's cock while it goes in and out of the other guy's ass or mouth. Sometimes, I grab their balls. Then I might stand by their heads while one or both suck my dick. Then we switch, and it's me doing the sucking while one guy plays with my balls and cock or sucks me. Then we work on each other until we all have an orgasm."

Yikes! I couldn't believe my own ears, but I knew somehow that Aldo wasn't pulling my leg. "So how long have you been doing this?" This time, it sounded more like my normal voice.

"About four years, but I've been letting other guys play with my dick since I was fifteen."

"Wow!" That was becoming my word of the night.

"Just before I got married, I started playing with guys. I really got married to see if my wife could maybe straighten out my sexual appetite. But I still wanted to be with guys. I always had this desire to touch another guy. I started fantasizing other guys when I was twelve."

Again, "Wow!"

"I really didn't get another chance until I went to Michigan to visit my sister, and I had to share a bed with her husband's twin brother. He was staying there that weekend while my brother-in-law worked on his car. Anyway, that first night, it just happened: He took my hand and placed it on his crotch, and that's how it started. I've loved every experience ever since. My dad doesn't know about any of this, so I trust you not to blab to him!"

"Oh, I certainly won't!"

"I gather that you're not interested?"

"No," I answered, maybe a little too quickly.

"I could tell. I guess I knew that the first time we talked. But I figured that you looked so damn sensuous, it was worth a try. You really fooled me, or I guess that I was just hoping. Anyway, my dad genuinely likes you. He said that your dad repairs his awnings for him, and does the kind of quality work that's pretty rare these days.

"Danny, do me a favor and stop in and have coffee with my dad. Be nice to him. He's kind of a lonely old guy. He really wants you to make it big, to be a real movie star. And that's still very possible. So be nice to my dad; he won't bite! He told me that you're the first guy that he's admired in years, so just be a friend to him and stop in and sit and have coffee with him, ok? He said that your own dad is a handsome man and must have been a ladies' man in his day."

"How right he is," I kinda mumbled. When he was younger, my dad was a very sensuous, masculine guy. He was a charmer and popular with the ladies. After taking in what Aldo had told me, I did stop in now and then and have coffee with Guido.

My dad had heart surgery around this time and was out of

commission and stuck at home for over a month. Guido really missed my dad's company and managed to get out to Cicero to visit him a few times. When my dad was able to get around with one of his caregivers again, he would stop in sometimes and have coffee and a prune Danish with Guido. They would share stories about life in the Old Country.

Sometimes, Aldo would join them over coffee, and he told me that he was surprised how similar the stories were that the two old men shared, almost interchangeable. Different countries and different cultures—well, there was the Italian connection—but the stories they shared were about their families, the women they had been with, and the struggles to make it in a new country.

About the time my dad was first able to get out and walk around in his neighborhood, some real cold weather hit Chicago. The wind seemed to chill folks to the bone. Not the best weather for my dad to venture out in, but my mom knew that dad was getting stir crazy. Mom always bundled Dad up real good before they went out into the cold weather.

One day I dropped by to see my folks and tried to persuade my dad to not go out into the cold weather. As he stood there putting on his overcoat, then lighting a big cigar, I knew my words had gone in one of his hairy ears and out the other. I left and hurried to work, skipping my usual breakfast stop at Guido's place. I was getting into the elevator at work when someone called my name. When I turned around, there was Aldo. He grabbed me and started bouncing up and down, yelling, "They want you to do a screen test! A screen test! Call my mother-in-law! I had to rush over and give you the good news myself!"

Boy, was I happy, and Aldo was really carried away! He grabbed me again and kissed me right on the lips. I didn't mind because I had such a happy feeling. I called Margaret, and we wound up driving all the way to Milwaukee for the screen test. I read a bunch of lines and did a few different accents and talked at different volumes and changed the pitch of my voice. It took only about forty-five minutes from start to finish. It's a little more than an hour-and-a-half drive from Chicago. On the way home, I guess we were all lost in our thoughts and dreams, because not much was said. When I dropped Margaret off, she gave me a big hug and a kiss, started up the walk, then turned to me and said with a smile, "You owe me big time, Mister!" She disappeared up the walk and the staircase, and I went ahead and drove Aldo back to his place.

As soon as I parked in front of his house, he grabbed me and pushed me down in the seat and started kissing me. "There, I've been wanting to do that for a year now," he said between kisses. We finally sat up, and Aldo headed up the stairs to his place. I wasn't upset that Aldo had kissed me; I can't remember feeling or saying anything. Looking back, these brushes with gay men didn't seem to disturb me in the least. Did I return his kisses? Again, I can't remember. I guess at the time, I just tucked away my feelings.

Guido died just before summer. I went to the funeral home to see him. It seemed that his wrinkles had disappeared. Aldo asked me to say the eulogy at the old man's funeral, and I was proud to do so.

Falling Stardom

About six weeks after the funeral, Aldo called me one Sunday at home. "I just made Italian sausage sandwiches with the sausage that Selena's mom makes. I'm so in the dumps. You think that you could come over and keep me company? I really need to have somebody here with me."

Aldo sounded pretty solemn and depressed, so I decided to go over for a visit. As soon as I entered his place, he held me really tight, and I mean tight! He had tears rolling down his cheeks, and he was holding his face against mine. My face was getting drenched with his tears. Aldo held me so tight for so long that finally I had to push him away so that I could breathe. He began hugging me again. The baby was in the stroller crying, sort of a frightened half-scream. I was waiting for Aldo's wife to rush out, so I pushed him kinda hard and said, "Aldo, the baby!"

He released me and grabbed the baby up in his arms real quick-like, because the baby seemed like she was choking from crying so hard. Aldo tried to give her a drink but that only made matters worse. Then, all of a sudden, the phone rang, and the baby stopped crying and trembling almost instantly. I guess she thought that it was mommy. The phone just rang a few rings, then stopped. When the baby had calmed down even more, Aldo gave her a bottle of juice.

He started embracing me again and sorta swooshed me over to a big over-stuffed chair. He sat down, then pulled me down into his lap and held me like I was a toddler. Aldo held me close to his chest while my feet dangled over the chair. I was really uncomfortable, but he just kept holding my face to his chest. "I miss my dad so much," he sighed. "I'm just so glad that you're here for me, Danny. I feel like I've known you all my life. My father loved you so much. You were his favorite guy, and now you're my favorite guy. Oh, Danny, how much I love you! All my years, I've never loved a guy like I love you. Please lay down with me, Danny; I'm just so tired."

He took my head in his hands and kissed me and held me real tight. Then, we went into the bedroom and he took off my shoes. When the phone starting ringing again, Aldo got up and ran to answer it. I just laid there. After about ten minutes Aldo came back into the bedroom, lifted up the baby and put her in a big playpen. He came and laid beside me and cuddled against me. Then he started to unbuckle my belt. I pushed his hand away.

"Please, Danny, please. I just want to feel you."

I heard such sorrow in his voice that I just laid there and let him open up my pants and put his hands around my testicles. He pressed my testicles and stroked my pubic hair with a couple of fingers. I was getting hard, and Aldo started groaning almost like he was having an orgasm. "I just knew it, Danny: You're all man!" He slipped my shorts down a little ways and started to lick my thighs and groan and say stuff in Italian as he licked all around down there. I finally tried to push his head away and got mad when he wouldn't stop. "Aldo, this has nothing to do with your dad. You just used being sad as an excuse to lure me over here!"

I pulled up my underpants and trousers, and as I started to buckle my belt, Aldo pleaded, "Please, Danny, just let me kiss it once. Just once. Please. Then I won't bother you anymore." He even kissed the cross on a chain around his neck, like maybe he was making a promise to God. Aldo opened my fly, and pulled out my cock and gazed at it like it was a god or something. "You're uncut! I just knew that you were, Danny. God, that thing is so beautiful!" He gently kissed the head, and I pushed him away.

"I'm sorry, but that's enough, pal," I said in my movie-tough-guy voice. "I was just trying to be nice to you." I opened the bedroom door and I left like lightning. I said to myself, *Oh, God, please forgive him; he needs help! He's so very sick all the way around!*

That happened on Sunday. On Tuesday, I got a call from Selena that I don't think I could ever forget, will never forget, because I stood with my mouth wide open for at least two minutes after I hung up! Aki, my young Asian assistant, said, "Hey, Danny, you're all pale! Did you get good news about the screen test?"

"No, sorry, kiddo," I muttered, turned around, and walked over to the other side of the work area. I went to talk with Mike McAuffrey, just to hear myself talking, to see if I sounded okay. But I couldn't stop shaking. "Oh, Danny," he said, "you work too many hours. You didn't leave until after nine last night. You're overdoing it! You can't take it with you, and you'll wind up spending it on doctors! Look how you're shaking. You're gonna have a nervous breakdown and won't be able to work at all." I nodded at Mike, gave him a pat on the shoulder, and—at a loss for words—wandered back to my work area.

I started cutting out some patterns for giant fall leaves as I relived the call from Selena.

"Danny, this is Selena! Is my husband a fuckin' queer? Come on, Danny, tell me: Is Aldo a queer, a faggot, and are you one too?"

"Selena, what are you talking about?"

"I found a used condom on the bedroom floor. Aldo told me that he missed me so much that he jerked off. I feel like taking it to be analyzed to find out if it's your semen or his."

When I was thinking about all this later, I almost had to laugh. *What a stupid, crazy bitch: Like there was a twenty-four-hour semen analysis place in the neighborhood that would be able to tell her whose semen it was and look up his address and phone number in their* "Unabridged Semen Directory." *Hahahaha!*

Selena continued to press me: "Aldo said that you came over Sunday. He told me that you was here when I called. When I came home, the baby said, 'Daddy and Danny go sleep in the bedroom.' What the fuck was you doin' in the bedroom with my husband?"

"Nothing!"

"What do you mean 'nothing,' you fuckin' queer?"

I was like I had been hit and was unconscious and looking down at my body. I finally managed to say, "Hey, hey, hey! Cool down. Aldo was just showing me pictures of Guido and their family from years ago. He spread the photos and albums all over the bed." Aldo had actually done that the last time I had gone over to see how he was doing.

Well, hearing that sorta started to calm her down. But she continued, "Please, Danny, Aldo just won't explain the condom. He said that you had been here hours before. So, what gives? And the baby said that the two of you went to sleep in the bedroom, so my innocent angel must have seen you two get into the bed."

I started to sweat and my palms got all clammy because I wasn't used to making stuff up and lying like that.

"Please, Danny, I think that you take Aldo like a friend. Is there something really wrong with him? Please, if he needs help and he's really queer, let me know! I'm ready to jump out the window!"

"Come on, Selena. Why would you do that? You got that baby to live for. Your husband has never said one vulgar word to me. He just told me that you two waited so long for the baby and that you and the baby are his life. All he did was cry when I was there."

"Well," Selena added, "he does get those crying jags."

"I think you really don't have a problem with Aldo. His problem now is that he's still feeling the loss of his father. They used to kid and joke and talk about everything with each other. They were closer than any other father and son; they were like brothers, but brothers who are always there for each other and never fight. He really needs your love now. He was so sad when I was there; I hated to leave him. He was so pitiful.

"He begged me to stay until you got home, but my own family was waiting for me to come home, and all that crying was hard for me to take. It really upset me, because I liked Guido a lot. Everyone in the neighborhood loved him and the stories that he used to tell. Look how many people from the neighborhood were at the funeral! There were more Grand Avenue people there than family, and the flower car was so loaded that the rest of the flower arrangements had to go in those two Ranchero cars, remember?"

"Yes, Danny, I know that he misses his dad a lot; we all do, but you're right: They were so close, and he still gets so emotional about losing his dad."

"Please, Selena, believe me, if there's something queer about Aldo, I've never seen it. There is nothing feminine about him!" The more I lied, the more I sweated. I had to put her on hold several times; that's how long we were talking. That must have been the most nerve-wracking telephone call that I've ever had! Oh, how much I lied! Finally, we finished up our conversation and I hung up.

I think it was less than an hour later that Aldo called. I wasn't quite over that call with Selena.

I picked up the phone, and Aldo said, "Danny?"

I said, "Yes?"—a long, drawn-out yes.

"Danny, I don't know how to start."

I told him to slow down. "Aldo, your voice is really trembling."

"Danny, I just came from my mother-in-law's. My wife is threatening to leave me! The baby told Selena that me and you went to sleep together."

"Yeah, Aldo, I already know all this. Selena called me earlier and told me everything. She thinks that there's something terrible wrong with you, that you and me had sex together. I told her that the bedroom door was open so that you could watch the baby while you showed me your family pictures, like you done the time before. I didn't lie to her there, because you had shown me a lot of the pictures. So, what's the deal with the condom? Did you have someone else over for sex after I went home?"

"No, no. You had me so excited that I put on a condom and beat off. But I just told Selena that I jerked off because I missed her. Believe me, please, Danny!"

"I believe you. I just hope that your wife is convinced."

"Well, I don't know about now. Selena's mom went ballistic on me when I dropped the baby off to her. She put the baby in the stroller and took her forearm and knocked me down and started kicking me, calling me a 'fucking queer.' She just kept kicking me and yelling that she should have known that you and I was having sex, because everybody knows that those designer and decorator guys are all queer. She kept calling you 'that fucking queer great phony movie star guy.' When I was trying to get back up, Margaret was still taking swats at me, screaming that she hadn't wanted Selena to marry me because she suspected that I was a 'faggot.' She screamed, 'Faggot movie stars, all of them!' as she got in a few last kicks.

"Then, she said that your movie star career was down the toilet. She picked up the folders with your sound recordings and head shots and threw them in the fireplace and turned up the gas jets, the fucking cunt! I stood there and saw the folders fall apart in the flames.

"Danny, She just wouldn't let up, and started yelling about how the Culver City people wanted you to go New York City for a final screen test and to sign you up. 'Now your fucking fake movie star lover is really fucked,' she yelled after me as I left. I was too upset to think of anything to say, so I just got out of there.

"On the way here to call you, Danny, I was thinking about what a witch Margaret is, and how she used to yell and scream at her husband all the time, always trying to get him to work longer hours, do what the bosses wanted, move up the corporate ladder, and make more money. So my father-in-law smoked too much, drank too much, and worked too much, probably knowing that it would kill him. But at least then he wouldn't have to live any longer with that conniving shrew bitch of a wife. I know her: She just won't be happy until she breaks up my marriage. But, it's all my fault: I really fucked up!"

"No, Aldo, you should be fine. Your wife and baby need you. Go home. Decide what's important in your life. If you want to be a good family man, husband, and father, cut out the Wednesday-night messing around. Stay home with your wife and baby." Well said, I guess, but advice that I later pretty much ignored in my own personal life!

I wondered about that conversation with Selena. Had she really believed me, and thought about what I had said? *As if she would ever listen to me,* I thought to myself.

Well, as it turns out, Selena *did* listen to me. Aldo called me at home to tell me that when he got home after our conversation, Selena gave him a big hug and apologized. "Danny, I'll never forget the magic you must have worked on her! She just won't stop apologizing to me! So far, so good, and thank God for that!"

As far as I was concerned, the movie star dream was over, and I was too busy at work to really give that whole fiasco much thought.

13

When It Rains

I didn't realize that a lot of my success at Silvestri was due to my being part of a close-knit team of folks who helped and supported one another. We shared our ideas, our tips and tricks. And it was our combined experience, design abilities, and teamwork that made Silvestri Design the giant creative powerhouse that it had become. When I thought of everything I had accomplished as part of an award-winning design team, my overactive ego kicked in. I saw myself as the King Bee, perfectly capable of leaving behind the worker bees, hopping on my high horse and riding off on my own to accomplish great things. Hahaha!

This attitude led me at times to downplay just how much of my success was due to my creative and very talented coworkers. I often ignored suggestions and advice that could have really helped me be an even better designer.

I began breaking the hard and fast rule that I had followed since I first started doing display work on the side while working back at Varady: to never do any design work on the outside that would conflict with what I was doing for my employer. I actually recommended Silvestri to some potential clients who had wanted to hire me for jobs more suited for a larger display company to take on. But then, finally, faced with bills piling up and a growing feeling that I was stuck in a creative rut at Silvestri, I started doing freelance work that pretty much was the same as what I was doing nine to five. My King Bee complex had me thinking that Silvestri was just another client competing for my time and talent. If I took on enough work, eventually I would find one very special company that would pay the King Bee what he was worth.

I met the owner of Ber-Tals, who had just opened a four-story women's apparel store catty-corner to Marshall Field's: 10 West Randolph Street, at State Street. I did display at the specialty store for three years in a row: spring, summer, fall, and Christmas. The owner was especially pleased with my window displays. Media types and all sorts of folks used to stand out on the sidewalk and photograph my imaginative, edgy work. One of the favorite window displays featured hot pink poinsettias from twelve inches to thirty-six inches in diameter, with black velvet leaves and gold-colored glass balls for the centers of the flowers. This window was so spectacular that one of the local TV stations filmed it and showed it on the evening news broadcast.

One of the three display guys I was working for told me to make some floral samples for Bill Miller, who owned a small display company. I made him some magnolia sprays that sold as fast as I could make them. Bill tried to hire me full-time, at three hundred dollars a week plus one-third of the net profits. I was really strutting around like a big rooster, so full of myself.

I told Mr. Silvestri that I was thinking of quitting, and he told me that if ever I should listen to someone's advice, I should really listen to his. "Danny, you are extraordinarily talented, but listen to what I have to say, ok? Look, Bill Miller will get tons of orders, but he's always short on cash and won't be able to front you the money to buy all of the materials to complete the orders."

When I told Lena about the offer from Bill Miller, she gave me a troubled look and said, "Danny, we're doing so well, I think that you should listen to Mr. Silvestri."

Well, I didn't listen to Mr. Silvestri, and I didn't listen to Lena either. I went with Bill Miller's offer, and took with me Myra Ainonen, who made such beautiful bespoke gowns and other clothing for the animation figures. This was the week that Ber-Tals was featured on *The Ed Sullivan Show,* so Myra designed some exquisitely-dressed animation characters for Ber-Tals. I also took with me Gabe Contreras, another fabulous designer. Well, the money problems that Mr. Silvestri had predicted happened soon enough. We got a huge order, and when the supplies were being delivered, we employees had to pay so that we could complete the order. We couldn't keep paying up front, and on the strength of all the orders, we managed to get a couple of credit lines with our suppliers. But we were soon falling behind in the payments and were getting demand notices almost daily.

One day we came to work and there was a sheriff's department padlock on the door. Behind the locked doors there were also some giant crepe-paper flower arrangements that I had made for Mr. Silvestri. He had given me the money to buy whatever I needed to do the job for him. We never heard from Bill Miller, and he pretty much disappeared from the Chicago display scene. I had even lost some floral assembly machines that I had bought with my own money. I was way too embarrassed to go back to Silvestri, but Myra and Gabe returned to work there.

I contacted some of my freelance window trimmer buddies, made display items for them and managed to snag some display gigs on my own. One client was the Morris B. Sachs clothing store downtown on State Street. Sachs ordered man-made fur coats in birch-tree colors—gray and black. The whole idea was to have the window and floor mannequins wearing the gray and black coats in a setting I would put together, featuring fantasy birch trees and furniture made out of birch wood.

Off I went to Wisconsin to get a truckload of birch tree trunks and limbs. From the smaller trunks and limbs, I made rustic yard chairs, love seats, and tables to be used in the fall displays. Then, I made rustic gates and fences for the display windows and the display ledges inside the store.

As was the case even in good financial times, and in so many other stores and companies, the Sachs display director was always told to keep using old displays, like recycling previous years' Christmas trees by adding new ornaments and ribbons. But one year, old Mr. Sachs was feeling a need for something fresh, bold, and eye-catching to promote sagging fur sales: maybe a campaign that would catch people's attention and draw them into the store to check out the furs. This particular year the displays were so spectacular and popular with shoppers and passers-by—and the fur sales so successful—that Mr. Sachs himself congratulated the display director and his staff.

The next Christmas season, Mr. Sachs hired me to design some new Christmas trees that would really stand out and catch people's attention. I made dozens of fiery orange and yellow trees covered in blinking Italian lights for all of the street-side display windows. More than a few people driving by the windows called the fire department because they thought the store was on fire! The trees were in all of the windows and also up on the display ledges throughout the store. For a month or so, passing motorists would pull over and call the police or fire department, and folks riding by on buses would jump off and run to a phone booth to call in a fire at Sachs!

All this impressed Mr. Sachs. He called me the morning after we made the evening papers and news, telling me that the fiery Christmas look had really gotten a lot of attention and that the store had to hire more employees to handle all of the customers attracted by the displays and all of the publicity. Mr. Sachs' office got a lot of calls from other retailers asking who had made the displays or to say how original and attention-grabbing the displays were. It was only toward the end of the Christmas season that different departments reported to the main office how many customers had commented on the displays and also wondered who had designed them. Quite a few folks who either owned a retail store or were planning a special event had asked for my telephone number. The season was almost over before Mr. Sachs heard how many people had asked for my number, but even at that late date, I got a couple of new steady customers.

That year's Christmas season had more sales volume than any previous Christmas season. Mr. Sachs encouraged me to keep coming up with new ideas, a lot of which I worked on right at home. We had had our new house now for over a year, but I just was not making that much freelancing and we were getting behind on our house payments. I struggled to hold things together until the next holiday season. I thought just how great it would be if I had a display shop of my own! Lena was so much in love with the house and our wonderful neighbors, but I jumped the gun and decided to try to find a retail space of my own that also had living quarters big enough for our growing family.

I found an empty building on Addison Avenue that used to be a drugstore with living quarters in the rear, with a full basement plus another smaller storefront next door. Well, I just had to have it. Without really discussing it a lot with Lena, who was always busy with housework and keeping track of the kids, I filed for bankruptcy and gave up the house. Lena was plenty upset that we had lost the house that she loved so much, but she went along anyway with my plan. We moved everything into the new place at the height of the holiday season. It took a long time to get the showroom ready. Then, with a lot of help from Lena, I made all sorts of floral arrangements and also decorations and home décor items to sell retail.

Lena didn't like the idea of moving into a store, even though it had three bedrooms. There was a large, very old-fashioned kitchen and a dining room and living room combination that looked like something out of an old silent movie. But Lena was soon happily buzzing around, working with me and fixing up the new place and getting the kids settled in. She had the kids and me, so she was pretty happy. She actually made most of the flowers and was much faster with her fingers than I was.

We finally opened on December 9th. On December 19th, I was stopped at a red light near our place. A drunken woman with no insurance skidded on the rain-soaked street and demolished the back of our station wagon that I used for deliveries. The station wagon was totaled, plus I got a severe whiplash and was totally unable to do any work.

By December 22nd, we had sold all of our stock and were down to the bare walls. My medical bills were sky high. We didn't have insurance, but not because we believed in the old-time Gypsy superstition that having insurance might bring us bad luck. Insurance was expensive, and we could barely afford the basic necessities and business expenses. Lena and I were caught up in getting the new place ready and were working seven days a week to grow our business and provide a good life for our family.

Now, we were thinking about what we could sell after Christmas. Lena made some beautiful floral arrangements but also had to do the household chores without much help from me, plus take care of the kids.

Within just a few months after the accident, we were running out of money. My dear friend Myra Ainonen came to visit me and the family. She was still working at Silvestri.

"Oh, Danny," she sighed, "Mr. Silvestri and all of your friends and coworkers sure do miss you at work."

What could I say? I had tears in my eyes and a lump in my throat. My time at Silvestri had been the happiest and most exciting period of my career. "I know, kiddo, I miss you folks too."

"Anyway," Myra said, "I came by to invite you and Lena to my naturalization ceremony next week! I'm just so darn proud that I'm finally going to be an American citizen! You two have always been so kind to me, and I also want to invite you to the dinner I'm hosting after the swearing in. My family, friends, and coworkers will all be there. Danny, you and Lena just have to come!"

Of course Lena and I were going to be there to help Myra celebrate her first day as an American citizen! We wouldn't have missed that for anything! We could ask our neighbor Rose to come over and watch the kids so Lena and I could go out on the town like real adults! Lena was so excited! She spent the whole day before the ceremony buzzing around, asking me and her gal friends what dress she should wear and what shoes and accessories would go with it.

Lena took fifty dollars out of the old sugar bowl she had hidden in one of the kitchen cupboards—her emergency fund—and took Varda with her to buy a new coat to go with the dress she was going to wear for Myra's special occasion. As we got dressed for Myra's ceremony, I filled Lena in on just why this was such a special day for Myra, a day that she had looked forward to even before coming to the United States.

Myra had come to the USA from Finland in the early 1950s. She and her two sisters were like a Finnish version of the Andrews Sisters. The Ainonen Sisters made recordings and sang on the radio and performed all over pre-WWII Europe. But in the early 1940s, they made a big mistake and accepted an invitation from some muckety-muck in the Finnish government to sing for an important foreign visitor. That foreign visitor turned out to be none other than Adolph Hitler, making a hush-hush visit to Finland. Singing for him got the Ainonen Sisters blacklisted just about everywhere in the free world. The sisters' singing career was pretty much over. Nobody wanted to listen to "Hitler's songbirds," which is what a lot of people called them. They disbanded, and Myra finally made it to America in 1952.

The ceremony itself was very emotional for everyone there, so by the time we got to the restaurant to celebrate, we were all pretty hungry. After everyone in our party had ordered dinner and drinks, Myra stood up and thanked everyone for joining her and her family in celebrating this special day.

At one point, Myra opened up her purse and pulled out a plain white handkerchief all tied up into a little ball. She set it down in front of her, carefully undid the knots, and finally we saw what was inside: a little pile of what looked like dirt. Turns out it *was* dirt: the first American soil she had touched the moment she got off the ship from Europe, soil that she had scooped up from a planter box on the dock in New York City.

Myra wiped tears from her eyes, dipped into the little pile of American soil with a finger trembling with emotion, tasted it, and said, "I am an *American!*" We told the waiter about Myra's citizenship ceremony, and he went over to the center of the dining room and announced that "the pretty lady at table seven" was a brand-new American citizen. Everyone in the restaurant stood up and applauded Myra. All of the genuine emotion and pride that folks felt for Myra was very touching! Lena and I stood up with everybody else, and Myra just couldn't stop crying. What a wonderful evening that was! It made us all feel so proud to be Americans, something that by then we took for granted most of the time.

14

The Hazy Bright Lights of Hollywood

About a week after her citizenship celebration, Myra came by to visit again and had some wonderful news for us. She had received a call from a former coworker now living in San Diego, Larry Moreno, who told Myra about a lead designer position available in Los Angeles. It was with a small but very successful display-design business run by a good friend of Larry's and the friend's brother.

The brother, who did the actual design work, had just died. Larry's friend handled the business's finances and was looking for a talented, take-charge designer with an outgoing, people-pleasing personality. Larry thought that Myra might be interested, but Myra said that she was happy where she was and had so many friends and family that she wanted to stay close to.

But—and it was a big but—Myra told Larry about me, my flower-making and design skills, my leadership abilities, and my willingness to give my all to projects of all different types and sizes. I can just hear Myra ticking off my good points: dedicated family man, handsome, hard-working, good communicator, and a real people person. I'm pretty sure that she also mentioned my present circumstances: recovering from an auto accident that had made it impossible to continue to keep a start-up display business in Chicago up and running, forced to sell everything just to pay the bills, looking for a new start.

Wow! Myra had a way with words, and she must have used the right ones to sell Larry on me. He called to talk with me himself, to find out more about me and to give me more details about the job. We hit it off right away and had a nice long conversation.

Larry said that he knew a Mr. Carl Jelm in Hollywood, California, who was married to the sister of Edmund "Pat" Brown, the Governor of California. Mr. Jelm and his brother Hollis were business partners in a design studio and artificial flower business, Hollis of Hollywood. Hollis had just died, and Mr. Jelm was looking for an extraordinary floral designer to take over as partner and lead designer. He said that from what Myra had told him about me, I sounded like I just might be the guy. I told him it would be weeks before I'd be up and around, and I thanked him for contacting me. He said the pleasure was his, and that if it was ok with me, he would tell Mr. Jelm about me and give him my phone number.

"Now, Danny," Larry said, "don't expect him to call you straight away. Carl's got a lot to deal with right now. And he's still not sure if he even wants to continue to run the finance end of the company. He might just decide to sell the business and find someone to buy it lock, stock, and barrel. I'll be playing golf with him in Palm Springs this weekend; I'll tell him about you, and we'll take it from there. And, if you're not a golfer, you better become one, because a lot of our business out here is conducted on a golf course and over drinks in the clubhouse."

I never did get a phone call from Mr. Jelm, but about a week after I talked to Larry Moreno, Mr. Jelm himself showed up at the door of our now-closed display-design studio and introduced himself. He must have been pretty impressed by what Larry and others in the industry had told him about me! Mr. Jelm was looking around and saw a few scattered floral pieces and picked them up and said that I was exactly what he had prayed for, and that he could really use me in his new solo venture in Hollywood. I showed him photos of more of my designs, and he went bonkers. Mr. Jelm handed me his card and said to give him a call when I was ready to go out to Hollywood. He would even buy me an airplane ticket to go to California so that I could get out there faster and get the ball rolling.

As soon as I could move around better, I called Mr. Jelm, and told him that I was ready. He wired five hundred dollars for my family to live on while I was in L.A. The next day, American Airlines called to confirm the roundtrip ticket. I called Larry Moreno and thanked him for making the connection. I asked him more about Mr. Jelm. I found out that Mr. Jelm was the founder of a home for wayward boys in Chino, California. He supported the home financially and was a prominent contributor to various other charities and causes.

Mr. Jelm more or less settled into handling the design company's finances, but he had done quite a bit of design work himself before he brought his designer brother aboard. Besides doing display design, he had done a lot of movie studio work over many years. Mr. Jelm had helped design a lot of the jungle scenes for the Johnny Weissmuller *Tarzan* movies and still had an exclusive contract to furnish living and artificial floral displays and movie greenery—grass, foliage, trees, etc.—for Metro-Goldwyn-Mayer (MGM) productions.

Carl Jelm's brother Hollis's design company was known in the trade as Hollis of Hollywood; in the design business, that's what Hollis himself was called. Hollis specialized in artificial floral pieces. Both Mr. Jelm and Hollis had previously worked for 20th Century Fox. Boy, was I beside myself! How impressed can you get? Well, I was beyond impressed! So was Lena, when I told her all about what was going on and who I would be working for. Usually nothing or nobody really impressed Lena, but this time, she got real excited for me and for us.

I left the very next morning and landed in Los Angeles late that afternoon. Lenny Squires, one of Mr. Jelm's drivers, met me at the airport and took me to the Hollywood Plaza Hotel on North Vine Street, right in the center of old Hollywood, where Mr. Jelm had reserved a room for me. He had given me a choice of hotels in Hollywood, and I chose to stay at the Hollywood Plaza, even though it was no longer as spiffy and popular as it had been in 1939, when my folks and I had dinner there a couple of times with the friends we were staying with in Hollywood. For many years in the Golden Age of Hollywood, the Hollywood Plaza hosted broadcasts, shows, and major entertainment industry events. Because of the many broadcast studios and theaters in the area back then, the hotel was popular with visiting radio and stage actors.

The main reason I decided to stay at the Hollywood Plaza was that one of my dad's old nightclubbing pals, Maxie Rosenbloom, had lived there since the early 1940s with his entourage. They had a suite of rooms on one of the hotel's upper floors. Maxie was a former light-heavyweight boxing champion and at one time owned one of Hollywood's most popular nightclubs, Slapsy Maxie's, over on Wilshire Boulevard. After he retired from professional boxing in 1939, Maxie turned to acting, becoming a popular character actor in radio and movies.

Back in 1939, my folks and I took a train from Chicago to Los Angeles to attend our friend Esther Bornstein's wedding to Sammy Haddad, a Canadian transplant to L.A. who was a prosperous electrical contractor. Sammy was a real busy guy with a lot of connections. He belonged to a lot of organizations and maintained close ties to the Canadian and British expat communities in Southern California. Maxie Rosenbloom was another of the many wedding guests, and Sammy introduced him to my dad. Dad and Maxie hit it off right away, and they were soon fast friends.

We stayed on for a week or so after the wedding and spent a lot of time with Maxie. I really enjoyed hearing his stories about boxing and his life in Hollywood. He took us to the beaches, over to Catalina Island, and up the coast as far as Santa Barbara. We even got to go see Maxie perform a comedy skit when he was on a radio show hosted by the famous comedian Fred Allen. Maxie was always happy to get us tickets to any radio show that we wanted to go to.

As much as I enjoyed spending time with Maxie while we were staying in Hollywood, I was happy enough just exploring the area with my folks: going to tourist attractions, meeting interesting new people, enjoying foods that I had never eaten before, and going to the movies in the evenings.

This time around, going on twenty years later, I was really looking forward to staying at the Hollywood Plaza, spending some of my down time with Maxie and his friends and trading stories about everything that happened during my last visit to Los Angeles.

Mr. Jelm himself picked me up the next morning at 10 a.m. in a classic Ford Woody Wagon. We shook hands, got into the Woody, and before we got underway, he reached over and handed me a check for two hundred dollars to cover expenses for my week in L.A. I was so moved by this act of generosity that I got a large lump in my throat. I was speechless and so choked up that I could barely manage to squeak out a timid "thank you."

We headed over to Mr. Jelm's office building at 6122 Santa Monica Boulevard, just a few blocks from Hollywood and Vine, which back then was probably one of the most famous intersections in the whole world. We parked in the rear of the old brick building, next to a brand new white Cadillac convertible with red leather upholstery. I followed Mr. Jelm as we got out of the Woody and headed into the building through the rear entrance by the loading dock.

Mr. Jelm showed me all around his building: the design area, workshops, warehouse area, showroom, office, and an even larger office that he would be taking over. All of the big warehouse area in the rear would be mine to set up any way that I wanted to. Workspace and stockroom areas—I would be the guy deciding how to set up and organize everything. Oh, he had my head reeling! Just to get the ball rolling, Mr. Jelm told me to make some sketches of where I wanted the lighting and work tables in the design area. He said that he would bring in some carpenters and electricians to do whatever I wanted to be done, and he would work things out with them to do everything to my exact specifications.

"Then go ahead and sketch out how you want the entrance and showroom area to look, and we'll go on from there. Look, Danny, I saw what a great job you did with your studio in Chicago, and I have every confidence that with more money and more help, you'll turn this old place into the design center for Hollywood." Again, my emotions got the better of me, but this time at least I smiled and thanked him with a handshake.

In the middle of me telling Mr. Jelm what I needed to get started, a phone on a nearby counter started ringing. That room was so big and so empty that the ringing phone sounded like an alarm bell going off. Mr. Jelm grabbed the receiver, talked for a few minutes, then turned and told me to just walk around and get a feel for the place. "Danny, check out the fridge and grab a soft drink. I'll be on the phone for a while, so here's some paper and a clipboard. Go ahead and walk around and take notes."

Mr. Jelm was on the phone for over an hour. I walked through the entire building, hit all of the floors, made sketches, and wrote down suggestions for how to set up everything. When Mr. Jelm finally finished the phone call, he apologized for taking so long and told me that he wanted to see my sketches and hear my ideas as we did a walk-through of the entire building.

I know he was trying hard to make me feel at ease as we walked around on the old creaky floor in that big empty building, but I was still more nervous than hungry when he said, "How do you feel about having some lunch with me? It's already 12:30." I said fine. "You just follow me," he said as he stood up. I was right behind Mr. Jelm as he walked toward the exit. On our way out of the building, he showed me the water and gas cutoff valves, master light switches, etc. He locked the rear door, and we headed out to where he had parked the station wagon.

The white Cadillac with red leather upholstery was still there. Mr. Jelm walked over to the driver's side of the Cadillac, turned and tossed me a set of keys. "Danny, these are the keys to the station wagon. I want you to have full use of it while you're here in L.A. That way, you can just pick up any supplies that you need to get started. Feel free to drive around and get to know the area. Check out the sights. Some are probably pretty much just as you remember them. But I think that you'll see that Hollywood has changed a lot since you were here back in thirty-nine!

"I'll give you a list of my suppliers and the folks I have credit with. I also have credit at the Richfield Oil gas station at Hollywood and Van Ness. If you need gas or anything else, just ask for Scotty, the guy who runs the place. I know that you're a good family man, Danny, but ask Scotty about where to go to have some fun while you're here, some good spots to unwind and enjoy yourself before the work piles up. I want you to be happy working here!"

Mr. Jelm pulled out of the parking lot, and I followed him just a few blocks to Santa Monica Boulevard and Vine Street, and into the Brown Derby parking lot. We had a wonderful lunch, and we ate and relaxed while Mr. Jelm continued to compliment me. He explained how he had spoken to some of my colleagues. "Danny, they just couldn't stop saying such nice things about you, how talented you are and what a wonderful, warm, and loyal human being you are. And a fantastic family man to boot.

"When I first saw your flowers and designs, I knew right then that you're the guy I've been looking for. So many designers are so excitable, so emotional, so hard to deal with day in and day out with all of the creative fireworks. You know, I've been looking for just the right guy to put in charge since shortly after my brother Hollis passed away about a year ago. After we finish lunch, you can follow me over to where my brother's display business was. I know that his designers and staff had a hard time trying to keep the business going. Again, I think they just didn't have his people skills, and certainly not his design skills, so his clients have pretty much found other design firms to work with.

"After you finish setting up the design center, we'll do some radio and television spots, have some open houses and presentations at industry events. But I'll tell you what, Danny: Once people meet you, see your designs, see the incredible work that you do, and find out what a nice guy you are, they'll drop their current designers and come over to you. I'm sure of it! You know, Hollywood can be a pretty stressful place; there's a lot of drama. I'm not just talking about on screen, but behind the scenes. Folks will be glad to deal with a nice guy: a good stable family man, talented, imaginative, easy to work with, no tantrums, no drama. That's you!"

By now, my head was spinning from all of the compliments. If I had been a hard-drinking man, I would have downed a few more just to even my keel. "Anyway," Mr. Jelm said, "I won't be back until Thursday morning. I guess when I get back, I'll just meet you over at the design center."

Wow, after that lunch—which I guess was what they call a Hollywood business lunch or power lunch—we headed over to Mr. Jelm's brother's closed-up business. We went into the huge building where there were piles and piles of design stuff, all disorganized and jumbled together. It looked like there had been a lot of work going on, then everything came to a stop, and the workers just dropped everything right where they were working. There were loads of rubber palm tree bark, all sorts of dried and preserved foliage, banana palm leaves, branches, manzanita trees, and all kinds of paper and silk flowers.

A lot of the flowers were all crushed and messed up, like someone had dragged something over them or just accidently stepped on them while moving stuff around. Gosh, there was so much to take in: furniture, art work, cabinets, tables, other display fixtures, bowls, vases, urns in different colors, even kinda cheesy-looking artificial fruit. But what really blew my mind was ream after ream of crepe paper in so many different weights and textures, in literally a rainbow array of colors, some of which I had never seen in crepe paper before. There were roughly eighty or so rolls on heavy metal pipes, sticking out about four feet along one long wall. There was not only a huge range of colors, but different shades of each color. I started thinking about all the work that would be necessary to carry all this heavy stuff, load it onto trucks, then unload it at the new place.

Mr. Jelm must have seen the look on my face, because he quickly said, "Danny, just take what you feel you'll need right away over to the new place. I own this building now, so we'll use it as a storage area for supplies and finished seasonal items like Christmas trees and wreaths. Anyway, you decide! This is your ballgame now. I have absolute confidence in you and your expertise. I imagine that you're trying to make sense of everything that you have to do, so just go back to the hotel, get your muscles loosened up, and do whatever you can to relax. I could have one of my drivers take you around town and show you the sights this afternoon. How about Lenny? You two seemed to really hit it off."

"Wow, Mr. Jelm, that sounds great!"

"Look, Danny, I don't want to keep you too long from your family, so for the next six days, work with the moving crew, draw up some plans for the move, tell the guys exactly what you want done. In two weeks, they should have everything done, from the lighting, laying the floor tile, building the showcases, whatever you want done. Remember, it's your ballgame, so start playing ball! I'll send you another round-trip fare to come back for—let's say a couple of weeks. When you come back, I'll have my secretary help you find a place for you and your family to live." Mr. Jelm shook my hand and said that he would see me Thursday afternoon. We said our adoos, and I headed back to the Hollywood Plaza.

I had a call from Lenny, who came and showed me around Hollywood for a few hours. He drove me down Hollywood Boulevard, Sunset Boulevard, and finally into the madhouse traffic of Downtown. Lenny knew Los Angeles like the back of his hand. We were back at the hotel though by 5 p.m. When I picked up my room key, the desk clerk gave me a piece of paper with a telephone number scrawled on it. I called the number, and Mr. Jelm answered. "Danny, are you going to have enough cash to last until I see you Thursday?" I told him that I had plenty of money to see me through.

I really enjoyed my week planning the move to Mr. Jelm's office building and driving around with my new sidekick, Lenny. It was great seeing Maxie again too, and playing catch-up. I showed him some pictures of Lena and the kids, and Maxie sent me home with some pictures of his own: a couple of him and Sammy Haddad and my dad, even a cool photograph of him back in his boxing days, autographed and made out to Lena. She was so excited when I gave that to her. She treasured that photo and always packed it carefully on our many moves through the years.

I finally flew back home to Lena and the kids, who I had missed a terrible lot! They were all so glad to see me and gave me a wonderful homecoming, with a lot of good food, good friends, and good conversation. I told a lot of stories about my trip, describing the different people I had met and all the places I had seen. I passed around some postcards of the Brown Derby, the studios, the big buildings, the zoo, the palm trees, and the beach areas. Andy and Varda were so excited about moving to California!

The short time back with my family went by so fast, and before I could really think that much about it, I was back in L.A. for another two weeks. That was such a busy two weeks, because I worked through a lot of nights getting the new showroom, offices, and workrooms all set up. I did so much myself and got even more done with the crew: wallpaper in the showroom, carpeting in the offices, lighting throughout, custom work tables, every type of shelving. We were soon ready to start bringing over supplies from the old building. Mr. Jelm was more than pleased with my work orchestrating the move and preparing to open for business. We were now finally ready for the employees to start! I worked so hard non-stop because I was anxious to bring my family to California as soon as possible.

I found a fine family home for us in Baldwin Park—more affordable than Hollywood, but still a beautiful area—with good schools for the kids, and not a very long commute to and from work. Mr. Jelm very generously advanced me the down payment. I signed all the papers, and I went ahead and caught the next flight back to Chicago.

Lena had already gotten a head start with all of the packing for our move, recruiting family and neighbors to pack our furniture and household items into a big van. Lena and I said our adoos, and I guess what this move could mean for our future finally hit me. I brushed away tears as we pulled out of the parking lot behind our building and headed for what I hoped would be a new and good life for us in Baldwin Park, California, in our new-to-us beautifully landscaped three-bedroom home.

Once we had arrived, got all moved in and settled in, our new home seemed like a dream come true: The weather, the house, the neighborhood and the neighbors—everything seemed so perfect. Well, almost everything: We decided that the dozens of beautiful red and purple geraniums planted all along the front walkway had to go. They were full of spiders that seemed to like hopping onto people walking by. The kids especially were too scared to go in or out through the front door. Without the geraniums, the yard looked pretty drab. We had so much on our minds that we didn't even think of just spraying the geraniums to kill the spiders!

Oh, we were so anxious, but so hopeful too, for our new life as a family in California! There were some good schools for Andy and Varda. Lash was now ten months old and was already walking around and getting into trouble exploring his new home. It was a new start for our little family, and a new direction for my career.

From the get-go, it seemed like almost everywhere we were invited, we wound up brushing shoulders with celebrities. Lena and I had so many delightful encounters with Hollywood folks, who treated us like old friends. We had a lot of wonderful neighbors as well, many of them involved somehow in the entertainment industry.

Our nextdoor neighbors, Fred and Jeri Shields, had built sets and fake towns for almost every John Wayne Western ever made. Jeri's sister Jayne was married to Mr. George Liberace. She died in a private single-engine airplane crash during messy divorce proceedings. The crashed plane wasn't actually found—out in the desert between Las Vegas and Los Angeles—until six months later, in November 1960. Jeri got most of her sister's clothing, and she gave Lena a few items of clothing that my wife cherished for many years.

There had been a lot in the trade papers about a new feature-length Cinerama movie about to go into production. According to all of the media hype, Cinerama was the latest and greatest widescreen movie process. The name inspired Mr. Jelm to call our new business Flowerama, since designing and making flowers was the main part of our design business.

We had many prominent people and celebrities as clients and customers. I think that one of the most elegant and prestigious clients was Mrs. Samuel Goldwyn. I remember her first time in our showroom as if it was just earlier today. She carefully examined everything on display and finally purchased a close-out group of high-quality artificial plants that she was going to put in planters in the entrance foyer of the MGM offices. I was honored to do the installation myself. Mrs. Goldwyn was very pleased with my work and told me with a big smile that she wished that I worked for her fulltime. Mrs. Goldwyn recommended me to many of her friends and associates, who contacted me, asking for my help redoing their home or business decor or designing floral arrangements and decorations for a special event.

In those days, the Goldwyn companies rented out production sound sets and studios to various television and movie companies like ZIV—a company that specialized in productions for first-run television syndication—and others whose names slip my mind. These were companies that offered local markets alternatives to network programming, some of good quality, some not. We got a lot of work making sets, on-screen flowers, trees, foliage, furniture, and whatnot for the Goldwyn companies, as well as for productions from the independent media companies using the Goldwyn production facilities, and also for other major Hollywood studios.

Many of the productions were sort of anonymous cookie cutter productions churned out like products on an assembly line—not very original or innovative. Most of the time, I was dealing with a production company and didn't even know the name of the movie I was working on until I saw it later on and recognized my work.

Some of the companies we worked with did produce quality

and award-winning movies and television shows that at the time of production didn't really stand out from the productions that were churned out willy-nilly. A good example of that was *Elmer Gantry,* starring Burt Lancaster, filmed in late 1959. My design team and I made a lot of garlands with celluloid flowers for the scene where the revival tent catches fire and burns down. But in the first take of this scene, the celluloid flowers didn't burn quick enough, and we wound up using yards and yards of chiffon-type fabric soaked in kerosene that ignited a lot better. But anyway, I was proud to have been a part of the team working on this movie.

We made a lot of floral arrangements for the 1960 movie *I Passed for White,* and we did florals and other incidental design pieces the same year for the movie *Pepe,* starring the wonderful Mexican comedian and actor Cantinflas.

I also did regular work on *The Loretta Young Show,* including the episode where she's an invalid in New Orleans at Mardi Gras. At one point, she tries to defend herself against an intruder by throwing a kerosene lamp at him. It misses the bad guy and hits a large matchstick-look bird cage with a bunch of flammable foliage inside that I had made. The birdcage planter was about twenty-four inches tall by twenty inches wide or so, and I was told to make two of them, which would make it easier for the cameramen to shoot what would look like just one birdcage from different angles.

When I was already working on the second birdcage planter, I ran out of some of the foliage, so the set guy said to just put in what I had. The second planter had larger plants and different foliage—a totally different look. When I finally saw this episode of *The Loretta Young Show* on television, it was easy to see that what were supposed to look like different shots of the same birdcage were actually two different birdcages shot from different angles.

Anyway, Loretta Young liked my work so much that when she opened up a string of ladies' self-improvement studios, part of The Loretta Young Way, I was hired to do a lot of the interior design and decorating. One location was running ads offering free trips to Hawaii for the lucky winners of a contest. I outdid myself and redecorated the interior with giant palm trees. The palm fronds were made out of banana tree leaves, and the palm tree trunks were actually yucca tree trunks wrapped with rubber tree bark, which made the trees look like the real thing. I placed orchid and wood-rose arrangements throughout the interior.

Flowerama was becoming popular with quite a few of Hollis Jelm's former display-design clients. My team and I created a Hawaiian theme for Spice Islands company's booths and displays at various state fairs and conventions. Flowerama was awarded the blue ribbon for best exhibit design at a big Los Angeles convention, and Mr. Jelm had the blue ribbon framed and displayed on the wall in his office. If anyone was pleased with anyone, Mr. Jelm was surely pleased with me.

But not everything went smoothly. There was a big night club opening being planned in Hollywood, and the owners contacted Mr. Jelm and ordered two twenty-foot artificial palm trees to stand on either side of the entrance for opening night. They also hired us to design the interior of the club and give it a tropical look. The palm leaves that we had in stock were pretty old and very dried out, so I told Mr. Jelm that I didn't think that these leaves would survive any heavy winds and rain. This might have been the first time that I actually irritated him. He told me that the dried banana leaves had survived other installations where they had powerful fans blowing on them to make it look like they were in tropical breezes. His tone was like "and you're not going to tell me anything different. Just go ahead and do as I say."

Mr. Jelm had a vendor make the palm tree trunks out of aluminum, and my team went ahead and wrapped them with the rubber bark. I worked on the palm fronds and made them as secure on the trunks as I could without any wires, braces, etc. showing. Anyway, about three weeks after we installed them in front of the night club, Los Angeles experienced some of the heaviest winds it had seen in years. The winds basically shattered the banana leaf fronds and blew the debris all over the sidewalk and street.

I went ahead and asked Mr. Jelm if we could maybe use the heavy plastic fronds that I had suggested in the first place, the ones that I thought would last through whatever kind of weather we might be up against. These fronds were plastic but looked just like the real thing. I don't know what was going on with Mr. Jelm, but this time around he vetoed my suggestion again, and we wound up using some other fronds that he bought on the cheap. These didn't work out either. The wind bent the wire skeleton that the leaves were constructed around, and they were pointing in all different directions at weird angles. The leaves I had suggested had a steel wire that would give with the wind and not bend like the cheaper annealed wire did.

Mr. Jelm was annoyed with me again, as I was with him. I was the designer, and I kept up with the latest trends and with what worked and what didn't. I had a lot of pals in the display business, and we liked to share tips and ideas. From time to time, Mr. Jelm would putter around in the design workrooms and make floral pieces that weren't well-designed at all, that looked like something kids would bring home from a crafts class at school. He proudly put the pieces out front and center in the showroom, but they never sold. So he would get discouraged and give up for a while, then start in again. Well, he was the boss, so he pretty much could do whatever he wanted.

Back in October 1957, when I was still with Silvestri, the Russians launched Sputnik, the very first successful space satellite. People were so excited—and I guess scared, too—because all over the country, people would stand outside, maybe even up on a rooftop, and try to catch a glimpse of Sputnik as it passed overhead. This was way before personal computers and search engines, so when rumors started up, it took a while to find out if they were true or not. There were all kinds of dopey rumors going around about Sputnik: that it was a spy satellite taking pictures of everything and everyone as it passed overhead, that it was equipped with death rays, that it was going to crash to earth and kill a lot of people.

Inspired by the shape and antennas of Sputnik, I started working on a huge rose-colored sphere almost ten feet in diameter. We hung it from the ceiling in the middle of our display showroom. I started at the base with maidenhair fern, added six-inch crepe-paper roses, then graduated from six-inch roses to one-and-a-half-inch roses strung on five-foot-long wire that stuck out like the antennas on Sputnik. When I had added some foliage, we turned on the motor that the ball was suspended from, and we had our very own dressed-up, revolving Sputnik.

Our hip-loooking Sputnik almost made it onstage at the 1960 Academy Award ceremonies! That year, a huge tent was set up in front of the RKO Pantages Theatre in Hollywood. (The 32nd Academy Awards ceremony was held on April 4, 1960, to honor the films of 1959.) The theater is just behind the famous Hollywood Walk of Fame where so many movie and entertainment greats have stars set in the sidewalk to honor their achievements. Everyone attending the Academy Awards had to pass through the tent to go into the Pantages Theatre. Each year back then, a different studio hosted the tent and had to make the inside look like the Taj Mahal, or a river steamboat, or a French chateau, or whatever inspired the design people in charge of the décor.

This time around, it was 20th Century Fox that was hosting the circus tent activities. The circus tent housed all of the broadcasting equipment—monitors, auxiliary power units, lighting, etc.—as well as a large refreshment area and tables holding the special bags of luxury items that all attendees would be taking home with them. This was also the place where the winners would be interviewed by reporters from all over the world. The tent had actual walls and beautiful furnishings, and everything was designed and set up so well that that people walking around the different areas in the tent could have easily forgotten that they were in a big tent!

Film art director and production manager John DeCuir was in charge of designing and setting up everything. Mr. DeCuir had been nominated for an Academy Award in 1956 for Best Art Direction/Set Decoration for the 1955 Fred Astaire movie *Daddy Long Legs.* He was up for another Academy Award at the 1960 ceremonies.

On one of his many visits to the Flowerama display showroom, Mr. DeCuir saw our ten-foot revolving rose ball, to which the final touch had just been added—fluorescent day-glo paint that was only visible when exposed to black light. Mr.

DeCuir was so impressed by the whole concept that he ordered a copy of the revolving ball for the area in the tent where the best costume design awards were to be handed out.

Mr. DeCuir had designed a spiral staircase that the fashion models wearing the different outfits nominated for an Oscar would walk down, turn around, then step to one side, so that all of the nominated designers' designs could finally be seen. He planned to hang our revolving ball in front of and above the staircase. Mr. DeCuir hired me and my design team from Flowerama to work with him on the installation and setup of the ball and other interior and exterior design elements for the award ceremony.

Since Mr. DeCuir was up for an Academy Award—Best Art Direction (Color)—for the film *The Big Fisherman,* he left early to go home and get dressed, leaving me in charge to see to all of the last-minute details. "Don't worry, Danny, don't worry at all. You'll do just fine. You're probably one of the most talented designers I've ever met, and you're a natural leader." I was beaming, and what he had just said—and how he said it—reminded me of what Mr. George Silvestri had told a vendor from the prestigious Max Eckardt glass ornament company: that I was "the finest faux foliage man in America."

Some of the Academy Awards attendees started arriving later that afternoon. Electricians were working on the wiring harness for the giant revolving ball, and my crew and I were making last minute adjustments to the décor. I was bending over a cluster of manzanita branches and straightening out some of the silk flowers when I heard a very familiar deep and resonating voice say, "Absolutely lovely, gentlemen, absolutely lovely. Well done!"

I looked up and saw Miss Bette (BETee) Davis sweeping by, a big smile on her face. I turned to acknowledge her and thank her for her kind remarks just in time to see her beautiful full evening gown skirt get snagged on a couple of manzanita branches. Miss Davis stopped and was very kind and gracious as we scurried around her, bumping into one another, finally calming down enough to slowly and carefully pull her beautiful gown off of the branches. What a classy lady! I don't think I could have been any prouder or happier if I'd been awarded my own personal Oscar!

When we were just getting ready to hang the revolving ball, some nebun phoned in a bomb threat to protest actress Ingrid Bergman's attendance at the Academy Awards. We had to stop our work while the police and the Academy's own security guys were searching the tent for a bomb. Ingrid Bergman wasn't everybody's favorite actress. Back in 1949, she had created a big scandal when she left her Swedish husband and their daughter to live with Italian film director Roberto Rossellini. While the Awards ceremony attendees were arriving and winding their way through the tent into the theater, a lot of people sitting in the freebie bleacher seats at the entrance to the Awards booed when Miss Bergman arrived. Even back then, there was no shortage of holier-than-thou nutcases trying to make life miserable for the rest of us.

The police and security guys moved a lot of stuff around while they were searching the theater auditorium and circus tent for the bomb. With the whole rigmarole of the cops and security guys looking for a bomb inside the theater, the electricians didn't have a chance to finish hooking up the giant revolving ball to the wiring harness and electric motor that was supposed to make it revolve. So throughout the ceremony, the ball was just sitting over to one side, like a big beach ball.

I had called my friends, relatives, and former coworkers back East, telling them to watch the Academy Awards ceremony and check out the revolving ball. But all I saw from offstage during the ceremony were a couple of bare wires hanging from the ceiling wiring harness and revolving. I was so disappointed, but it could have been worse. Because the camera crew pulled in closer to the models, the ceiling area was never in view, but everyone could see the rest of the set that I had designed. It was a beautiful oriental motif. There was a huge Oscar statue off to the side, and there were some very elegant black manzanita branches decorated with silk millinery roses.

It was my great pleasure many years after the 1960 Academy Awards gig to be introduced to Miss Bergman. I was visiting friends in L.A. for a week and decided to spend some time with a former coworker from Austen Display, the artist John Tucker Mertz. John had been retired for years from the design field and had a beautiful house in a prestigious gated community in Dana Point, California. I was having trouble finding the street where the entrance to the gated community was, so I drove back into town and stopped at a phone booth to call and ask for better directions. John patiently explained how to find where he lived and added, "Now hurry over, Danny. I want you to meet a very special houseguest of my next-door neighbor. She's a beautiful and charming lady you share an Academy Award memory with!"

Huh, I said to myself. *Who could that be?* With the new directions, it didn't take me long at all to find John's place. He was sitting out on his rear patio talking to a stunning woman with beautiful hair and a no-makeup fair complexion. The lady looked up and smiled as I approached. My God, it was Miss Ingrid Bergman, who John introduced as a longtime friend of his next-door neighbor! There was a little trowel and gardening gloves on the table in front of her. "So, Mr. Miller, Mr. Mertz informs me that I should apologize to you for interrupting your beautiful design activities at the Academy Awards!"

"Oh, please! Ingrid, dear, what are you talking about?" John gasped, pale as a ghost.

"Well, Mr. Miller, I do apologize for whomever phoned in that bomb threat. I think that perhaps they were not very happy with one of my films." I can still see that twinkle in her eye and hear her school-girl laugh. What a charming and gracious lady!

Lena wasn't real happy, though, that I didn't ask for Miss Bergman's autograph.

Over the many years that I was active in the design field, I met a lot of other celebrities. Like other folks, some were friendly and pretty down-to-earth; others were full of themselves and were their own biggest fan. Carol Burnett, Vicki Lawrence, and anyone else I met from *The Carol Burnett Show* were all just real nice folks.

Liberace was a true gentleman, and he often treated the dancers in his shows to dinners in good restaurants and nights on the town. He had a fleet of limos and fancy tour buses to take the chorus gals and crew on special outings. Bob Newhart seemed real shy but had a very dry sense of humor, asked a lot of good questions, and was a nice guy to do business with.

Dinah Shore was one of nicest and most down-to-earth celebrities I've ever met. I was making some final changes to floral arrangements for an outdoor charity fundraiser that Miss Shore was hosting at her beautiful home. We were chatting back and forth, and all of a sudden, I inhaled a flying insect and started coughing and choking. Miss Shore brought me a glass of water, and made me sit until I calmed down.

The compliments I received from Dinah Shore and many other famous clients went to my head—no surprise there! I became a real swaggering know-it-all. I really puffed up with pride as I thought about all of the jobs I had through the years: upscale window display, fine interior design for individuals and high-end department stores and retailers selling luxury goods, major design work for the Ford Motor Company—and, to top it off—working on the interior and exterior decor for several Academy Awards ceremonies. I sure had a good opinion of myself. It didn't happen big time right away, but eventually my inflated ego would get me into a lot of trouble.

While me and my team were busy doing our thing at the 1960 Academy Awards ceremony, Mr. Jelm himself undertook the design and installation of the various floral displays and design elements for the two The Loretta Young Way studio locations that I hadn't worked on. One day at work, I got a phone call from a guy at The Loretta Young Way who I had met and worked with at the beginning of that project. He was calling to tell us to "come and pick up the crap" that Mr. Jelm had set up. Gosh, that was the first time I had ever heard someone call our work crap! Something was obviously majorly wrong. I headed out with some assistants to see what we could do.

When we got to the first location, I almost plotzed! I

had never seen such unprofessional and messy design and workmanship! If there had been a hole big enough, I would have crawled into it. I was really shocked and embarrassed. I just had to call the guy from The Loretta Young Way and apologize. But before I had a chance to do that, I was told that there was a telephone call for me. It was The Loretta Young Way guy who had called to complain about Mr. Jelm's work—the guy I was just about to call.

He started out by apologizing for being so abrupt with me before. "Danny, I have a feeling that you didn't work on the displays for the last two locations, because your work at the other studios was so fantastic. Lucky for both you and me that Miss Young only visited the other locations, and she was really impressed with the fine job you had done."

I had to smile at that, and I guessed that the crappy displays were the work of Mr. Jelm and Eddie Monday, one of our least-talented and most unprofessional design assistants. I remembered a similar situation that arose when we had first opened Flowerama. I had gone to a popular beauty salon in Beverly Hills whose manager had called to ask if we would be interested in redoing and upgrading the entrance to their place. They wanted me to redesign the displays in the planter boxes on either side of the entrance and create two elegant floral pieces for the salon's front windows. I made the two window pieces, done in shades of pink and purple. I had to go consult with another client, so I told Eddie to go ahead and finish up the two planter boxes. The foliage was ready to go; it just needed some straightening out. A middle school student could have easily finished the job.

When I returned to check on Eddie's progress, I was surprised to see that he had redone everything. Instead of following my directions and my color scheme, he had done all of the planter colors in yellow, orange, and blue, and he said that he thought that these colors were "brighter and prettier" than the colors that the salon owner and I had chosen. Eddie just never learned to follow directions and the client's wishes. "The customer is always right" is the perfect motto for the display industry, because it's our goal to create for our clients a design that they like, that complements and enhances how they see their business. The salon manager was pretty unhappy with Eddie's work and the fact that he didn't want to listen to what she wanted. So I stayed until late that night trying to follow the design that we had come up with together. The owner was ecstatic.

Weeks later, a very elegant lady who owned a fancy specialty shop for women called The Red Tree came into the atelier. She had an idea for a display that would serve as a visual depiction of the name of her shop. She wanted me to spray-paint a manzanita branch fire-engine red and put it into a fancy-looking pot; the color, shape, and size were up to me. She planned to place it in front of a bright white wall at the rear of her shop so that it could be seen from the entrance. We had a great inventory of manzanita branches in different colors and sizes. She chose a large branch that had been sandblasted and had a smooth finish that would look stunning spray-painted a bright-red color. Since I was so busy with other projects at the time, I told Eddie to go ahead and work on this for me.

When I came into Flowerama the next morning, I immediately got busy spray painting a Christmas dwarf back in one of the workrooms. I had just started when I heard the announcement that I was wanted up front in the showroom. The very elegant Red Tree lady was standing next to a multi-colored manzanita branch, tilted at a weird angle in a planter box painted with splashes of about half a dozen colors. Yikes! So I guessed that the lady had changed her mind after all about what she wanted. It was totally different from the design that we had decided on.

When I approached the lady, she said, "Danny, you know that this isn't at all what we agreed on." When I returned to the work area and fetched Eddie, he went up to the lady and asked if she liked his work. She replied by waving him off and saying that all she had wanted was for the manzanita to be painted red and put into a pot. Eddie got right up in her face and blurted out, "You're crazy, lady! This is beautiful!"

"It might be to you, but it's not what I wanted!"

Then I turned to Eddie and said, "To you, it's beautiful, but what counts is what the client wants. She just wanted us to paint the tree red, put it in a pot, and anchor it with plaster of paris."

Eddie just rolled his eyes, threw his hands up in the air, turned around without saying anything, and flounced off in the direction of Mr. Jelm's office. I apologized to the nice lady, thanked her for the opportunity to make things right, told her that I would get right on her project and deliver and install it myself as soon as I was finished. She beamed, grabbed my hands, and said that I was the greatest.

You know, in the greater scheme of things, a red manzanita branch in a fancy container made in Taiwan probably doesn't count for much. But at that moment, that's what was all-important to the Red Tree lady. And pleasing her was just as important to me.

I started from scratch and delivered the tree the next day. The lady was happy to see her own idea brought to life. My goal here was not to sell the client on a design that I had come up with in my own imagination, but rather to create something just as the client had imagined it.

When I went back to the office, I found out that Eddie had quit, all upset because I had hurt his feelings and hadn't stuck up for him in front of the Red Tree lady. I admit that I could have handled the whole situation a lot better. After all, I had reprimanded him right in front of the customer, which, as the boss, you just don't do, no matter what business you're in! So much pent-up frustration with Eddie just came out. He was always goofing up, and I spent a lot of my time cleaning up Eddie's display messes. Mr. Jelm felt sorry for him and kept him on for far too long, but he certainly wasn't pleased with Eddie leaving the way he did.

Eddie's know-it-all attitude and lack of respect for me and the client's wishes showed me that Eddie had a totally distorted idea of what a designer does and how a designer plies his trade.

Mr. Jelm wasn't very happy with me at this point, so when Eddie returned and begged to have his job back, Mr. Jelm relented and rehired him. I sure was sorry that he did, because Eddie never changed. Rehiring Eddie showed me what little regard Mr. Jelm had for me and what I expected from my coworkers. My philosophy was this: share my design and marketing skills with the new hires and coach them as they worked with me on a project. Most of the new people welcomed my advice and tips and appreciated my sharing with them the tricks of the trade that I had picked up over my years as a designer. Most of them were grateful; others, like Eddie, grudgingly took my advice and weren't shy about complaining that I was stifling their creativity.

Here's where my big ego stepped in when common sense would have told me to just cool it and get on with my life. I approached Mr. Jelm and asked him why in the world he had rehired Eddie. Hadn't he noticed that Eddie didn't seem too keen on listening to advice and following directions? Hadn't he seen that Eddie's pieces weren't up to our standards? I could hear my big ego talking out of turn, *Humph! No one else sees what you see in Eddie. I mean, no one likes working with that jerk!* Talk about poisoning the well water! Mr. Jelm shrugged his shoulders and looked embarrassed. I immediately felt like I had forgotten my place, that it wasn't right for me to talk this way to a man who had been so kind to me and my family, who had helped us move to Los Angeles, who had advanced us the money to buy our home there, who had always had my back until Eddie Monday came to work for us.

Mr. Jelm said, "Well, we can't all be Mr. Danny Miller, I guess." I took that as a dig against me. I think the problem was Mr. Jelm's own stubbornness to admit that he had been wrong, together with me riding my high horse a lot. Anyway, after this mean-spirited conversation, I never again felt the rapport that we once had, and we weren't as friendly to each other as we used to be.

I really screwed up big time handling the whole Eddie situation. In just a matter of a few weeks, Mr. Jelm wound up getting rid of Eddie for good. Mr. Jelm had noticed that a lot of times when Eddie was leaving for the day, he'd have his car trunk open and would spend some time back there before finally closing the trunk and driving off. The other designers and I had noticed that from time to time materials would go missing. We couldn't figure out what was going on and thought that maybe some stuff had been left behind on a job or was left in the van when they were bringing supplies back from a job site. Well, Mr. Jelm was leaving early one day and caught Eddie stuffing a bunch of fabric rolls and silk flowers into a friend's car trunk. He thought at first that Eddie was taking some stuff to me on one of the jobs I was working on. But when Mr. Jelm looked into the trunk, he saw that these were supplies that had nothing to do with the job I was doing.

Eddie was gone and almost forgotten, because we had so many design associates coming and going, people who would stay long enough to learn the ropes and then head off to find something better, or so they thought.

We had a wonderful new client, Sally Kaspersky, who wanted me to make some floral pieces for her new home. Originally from Brooklyn, New York, Sally and her husband, David, had arrived in Hollywood just after the war. David was a musical director at one of the big studios. Sally's in-laws weren't that crazy about her and were always putting her down, never giving her credit or praising her in any way.

But Sally had an excellent design sense and was doing things to the décor of her new home that were quite ahead of the time. In her bedroom, the wall covering was a textured cloth material, and the design matched her bedspread exactly. Her bedroom was also the first that I had ever seen that had an entire wall of mirrors, which reflected the beautiful view from her windows and also made the room seem twice as large as it actually was.

It was quite a privilege and challenge to design floral treatments for various rooms in Sally's beautiful home. I felt like she was working with me like a colleague rather than as a client. After the first floral arrangements, some of Sally's in-laws complimented her on her good decorating sense.

To celebrate Sally finally getting some compliments from her in-laws, she said that she wanted to treat me to dinner, mentioning some ultra-high-class dinner places that offered top entertainment. I told her that she didn't have to do that, but how about us having a nice lunch at Janetti's, the Italian restaurant next door to Flowerama? Sally agreed that the food at Janetti's was great, and that she had never been disappointed on the many occasions that she dined there on her visits to Flowerama.

"All right, Mr. Designer to the Stars, I accept your kind suggestion," Sally said, standing up and making a little curtsy. I took her arm and escorted her next door to the restaurant, beaming and walking like I was the King Bee with his Queen.

We settled into a comfortable and delicious lunchtime, and partway through the meal, Sally commented that while she had bought some arrangements made by the other designers at Flowerama, she thought that I was the most talented. She just came out and asked me if I would be interested in us going into business, with her as an equal partner.

What she was proposing really fed my ego and raised up my high horse even higher. Of course, I was flattered and all, but I told her that I was basically happy at Flowerama, and it would take a lot of money to open our own place. "Oh, Danny," she said, reaching across the table to grab my hand, "you wouldn't have anyone holding you back, and you'd make so much more money. I've got the bucks and a good design sense, and you have the actual know-how. Just think about my offer, deal?"

"Deal." Truth was, I was tempted to accept right then and there. Mr. Jelm had become more reclusive, distant, and impatient since the Eddie incident. "Danny, think about my offer, talk it over with Lena, and whenever you've made up your mind, just let me know. Now, let's order dessert!" Sally still had that exuberant Brooklyn accent even after living so many years in Los Angeles. She always managed to sound so excited!

A week passed, and I got a call from David Kaspersky, telling me how great I was, and that Sally was buzzing around, all excited, hoping that I'd take her up on her offer. David assured me that when I was ready, money wouldn't be a problem, and that he would support us in any way that he could. His studio connections might also open doors for us.

To be honest, the reason I was hesitating was that the Kasperskys' compliments and those of so many others put the idea in my brain that maybe I should hold out and wait to be hired as a set designer at one of the big studios. Then, I'd really be acknowledged as the great designer that I had become. Wow, talk about me being my own best fan!

With all of these big thoughts swirling around in my little brain, it was hard to decide exactly what I should do, what the right thing to do really was. I didn't want to hurt or disrespect Mr. Jelm. He had done so many nice things for me and my family, too many great things to be able to list them all. On the other hand, this offer from the Kasperskys was probably too good to pass up.

The money was there and the business would almost be a self-starter, considering all of the wealthy and influential people that Sally and her husband knew. Their friends were like a Who's Who of prominent Hollywood society, business, and entertainment big-wigs. Right off the bat, we'd have a bunch of potential clients, influential people with a lot of connections. Thinking about all this, I was totally wrapped up in my own little universe.

Going into business with Sally was beginning to sound like a pretty good idea! While working at Flowerama, I had already done a lot of design work for clients who happened to live in the Kaspersky's swanky neighborhood: folks in the movie and entertainment industry, the legal field, the arts, and sports. I reconnected with some of Hollis Jelm's former clients, and added quite a few new clients through networking and socializing as well. At one point, I did a bunch of baseball bat and glove arrangements for a big party at the baseball player Sandy Koufax's beautiful home just down the street from the Kasperskys. He was a nice, outgoing, guy-next-door type who didn't act famous at all.

I designed the entrance and garden areas of the Sunset Lanai apartments, mixing high-quality artificial flowers and plants with the real thing, and I did some really elegant but modern-looking arrangements for their foyer. I did more traditional displays for some of the big law firms along Sunset, some of whose partners were neighbors of the Kasperskys. So a lot of people in that area already knew that I did great design work.

I personally did a lot of the sets and floral arrangements featured on *The Perry Como Show, The Ed Sullivan Show,* and so many others.

I was spending more and more time after hours with Sally and David and friends of theirs, either at the Kaspersky's beautiful home or with some of their friends who hosted what were basically hook-up or swinger parties. There was a lot of heavy drinking, nude swims, pairing off, even dope smoking. I got caught up in the kind of activities that Sally and her husband would never have participated in or tolerated at their own gatherings!

I was so stupid and self-centered, so eager to be the center of attention, that I usually didn't even ask Lena if she would like to go with me to gatherings at the Kasperskys. How she enjoyed herself when we went out on the town with Sally and David! Most of the time though, when I was invited to a dinner or party after work, I actually told Lena, who was stuck at home with our kids, that I was working late on an important project a long drive away.

Sometimes, when I had to work late at a client's business close to home, Lena would have a neighbor come over and watch the kids, and she'd bring me extra supplies, even at two or three in the morning. We often wound up trimming department store windows after the stores closed, and we worked through the night and early morning hours before the stores opened up again. Lena would sometimes give me a worried look and say that I looked tired, that I was working too hard.

How wrong she was! I was busy partying and doing my own thing. Not only was I lying to Lena sometimes when I told her that I had to work late, but I would meet all sorts of women at the parties and other events that some of Sally Kaspersky's friends invited me to. I started having one-or-more-night stands with some of the women I met there. I was so angry and disappointed with myself, because more than anything, I was so proud to be thought of as a good family man. More times than I can count, I intended to go home to my loving family. But I didn't slow down on the partying and drinking and screwing around. I was a good-looking and well-dressed guy. Sometimes, all I had to do while talking with a potential date was to lightly graze my crotch area with my right hand, and the hard-on I had been hiding suddenly wasn't hiding any more.

I just went along with the flow of the crowd that I was with. I was easily led, because in the back of my mind, I always had the thought that maybe, just maybe, along with getting laid, I would get a job offer that I couldn't refuse. So several nights a week, after a G-rated gathering at the Kasperskys' beautiful home, my so-called friends and I would go to someone's place and pair off. So many times I wasn't even turned on all that much by whatever women expressed an interest in having sex with me. Pleasing my partner rarely crossed my mind; I just wanted to get my rocks off and go home.

I would stay at these loud parties until the wee hours, drinking margaritas, screwdrivers, and vodka martinis. Sometimes, I was too drunk and lazy to get naked. I would just unzip my trousers, sit back in a comfortable upholstered chair, and let a lady or two satisfy me orally. Many nights, the women I had had sex with just conked out, and I hurriedly got dressed and cut out. I would come up with an excuse—like early appointments or work to do—to go home to my family. Some of the gals would actually beg me to stay longer, but finally I would put my foot down and leave. There were some nights that I was too drunk to drive. I would stagger to my car and sleep it off, all crumpled up behind the steering wheel or in the back seat.

I was so disappointed in the person I was becoming. I'd look at myself in the mirror and see this worn-out-looking boozer with bloodshot eyes, matted and uncombed hair and several days' worth of stubble. I started getting sloppy at work. But you know what? If Mr. Jelm had looked at me crooked, said anything, or asked me what gives, I probably would have just jumped on my high horse and ridden off into the proverbial sunset. As screwed up as I was, I still felt higher and mightier than anybody else. I was the go-to guy for making faux flowers and doing good design work, but not so good that I couldn't have been replaced.

Too many times after partying all night, I staggered home smelling like booze and cigarettes and still managed to convince Lena that I had pulled an all-nighter to complete a display job. When I finally sobered up and looked around and saw Lena cheerfully making me breakfast, I felt like the biggest fool in the world. None of my sexual adventures left me with any feelings that could compare to what I had with Lena. I thought of the love and support my wife gave me and all the wonderful ways she could please me.

One of those ways was definitely not oral sex. I guess part of the rush, thrill—whatever—of screwing around was to experience the different types of sex acts that I would never in a million years ask my wife to do. I became almost addicted to having women perform oral sex on me at these swinging parties.

Lena and I had over many, many years what I look back on as beautiful, natural sex. I always felt that everything we did in bed could be considered to be real lovemaking. I'm sure that while she loved me very much—and as good as our lovemaking was—she still had a lot of negative feelings about sex itself. That's just the way our generation was raised, by parents who had brought a whole bunch of sex-is-a-necessary-evil hang-ups with them to America from the Old Country.

Gypsy girls are raised with a real double standard: We want our girls to marry young and start a family, so we encourage them to always dress and behave like they're older than they are. That's a good way to attract a guy who has marriage on his mind. Young girls from some clans are encouraged to wear way too much makeup and jewelry to make themselves look even older and more attractive to potential husbands. Some get engaged before they are really old enough to get married, and they miss out on the pleasures of just being a kid. On the other hand, sex, even in marriage, is often considered a bad, Garden-of-Eden thing that you have to do in order to have children. And having kids is all-important in Gypsy culture.

Most of my affairs were short-lived by mutual agreement, but I did meet several ladies that I went out with for quite some time. One was a beautiful, thirty-something blonde, single and available, who had on several occasions worked as an on-set stand-in for Miss Lana Turner.

One other special lady in my life was Miss Elena Verdugo, who played Dr. Marcus Welby's nurse on the *Marcus Welby, M.D.* television show. She was a lady friend, not a sexual or romantic interest, but a delightful companion who often very gently and diplomatically ironed out some of the rough spots in my what they call social graces.

And then I fell in love—total, all-consuming love—with a beautiful, exciting, and creative lady artist. At a gallery opening over in Beverly Hills, I met Adina Meldola, a wonderful thirty-something single Italian-Jewish lady from an old and once-wealthy family, who was a well-known and successful working artist. She had recently moved to Los Angeles and was an artist-in-residence at a local university. Boy, did I fall for this lady!

This was the perfect affair, maybe not a match made in heaven—I was married, after all—but everything went so well for quite a while. Adina had no desire to get married. She must have been one of the first independent, think-outside-the-box women that I had met, a true free spirit. She seemed more like a student than a teacher, because so many of her friends and associates were young and active in the arts: as painters, sculptors, writers, screenwriters, musicians, etc. We were from different backgrounds but had a lot of the same interests: going to flea markets and exploring neighborhoods, taking in classic movies at revival house movie theaters, making the rounds of art galleries and dance clubs. And did we ever dance great together!

Adina and I had such a passionate relationship, I can hardly remember what else was going on in my life. I was always in a good mood at work and basically just did my thing and avoided any more confrontations with Mr. Jelm. I got home late, even on weekends, and poor Lena was often left alone with the kids. Of course, I wasn't interested in—and no help at all—dealing with anything or anyone that didn't have to do with work or getting laid. Until I met Adina. Yes, we had a great sexual attraction, but for me anyway, it became so much more. I had found a free-spirited and open-minded woman I could have passionate and satisfying sex with, a woman who was also educated and multi-talented. Of course, I fell head over heels in love.

Things were going so great with Adina; each of us was the one that the other had been looking for, without knowing it, I guess. But as good as things were going, everything came to a screeching halt when Adina announced over a late-night dinner that she was pregnant!

I was dumbfounded, speechless. "But what are we going to do?" I asked gently, kinda sheepishly. "Well, *we're* not going to do anything, Danny. I intend to have this baby and raise him or her myself. I've told you that I don't want to get married. But I do want to come home to children every night. I do love children. I'll always be grateful to you, Danny, for giving me my first child. But I don't think it's a good idea for us to see each other again. Maybe in the future, when this baby is old enough for you to see what a beautiful, talented, perfect child you helped create."

I didn't know what to say. I was off the hook so to speak, but how could Adina even think about raising a kid without a man in her life? But then again, what kind of father would I be? I was already a pretty lousy dad, hardly ever home with my wife and kids. Maybe this baby would be better off without me. Still, that was hard to come to terms with.

Well, I did run into Adina a few more times, by plan, before the baby was born, and later she got word to me that both she and the baby were doing just fine. I followed her career over the years, and many years later, quite by chance, I literally ran into Adina and her—our—beautiful daughter at an art gallery opening back in New York City. Since my wife's passing, we've kept in better touch.

There is one thing I'm very proud of, and that would be what I've done over these many years to make things right with Adina and our daughter and to prove to myself that I wasn't a total heel. As soon as I was told that Adina had given birth, I arranged with her younger brother to let me set up a savings account for the baby, knowing full well that the baby would be well provided for without my contribution. I guess my big ego couldn't or wouldn't be satisfied until it knew that our child would still be touched, somehow, by the love of the father she would never know.

At the various parties and events that Sally and David invited me to, I connected with as many people as I could. These were G-rated parties: The people there talked shop, dished out gossip, made connections for work and projects and industry events. It was at one of these parties that I first heard the term "networking," which I really liked, because it seemed to perfectly describe everything I was doing to find a permanent position as a studio designer.

After a while, I had brushed shoulders with so many stars and famous people that my horse was getting higher and higher and my head bigger and bigger. I started doing some really stupid things, like spending even less time with Lena and just not taking the care I used to with my work. I was still on the outs with Mr. Jelm because of the Eddie Monday fiasco. I guess he still felt that I had been disrespectful and had tried to undercut his authority.

It seemed like the only occasions we communicated at all were whenever he came into my workroom to plop down a note about my poor work ethic or to ask why I was taking so long to finish a project. A scribbled note! Most of the time, he wouldn't even stop long enough to discuss what the problem was, and when he did, it was clear from his tone that my days there were numbered.

I was tempted more than a few times to just walk away from my job there and make a clean break. But first, I wanted to find a permanent position somewhere else. The puffed-up part of my brain just seemed stuck on the idea that with all the hobnobbing, screwing around, and partying that I was doing, I would land an interview with a studio or television bigwig who would be dazzled by my talent. I would be offered a dream job, and soon enough my design talents would be splashed on the big and little screens twenty-four seven to amaze audiences everywhere.

Finally, something happened that showed just how much my high-horse attitude had screwed up the great opportunity that Mr. Jelm had given me. I was too full of myself to see that being right in a certain situation isn't always enough. *How* you handle being right also counts. Nobody likes a backstabbing know-it-all.

Mr. Jelm had arranged for Flowerama to have free advertising spots on a Los Angeles-area television station in return for supplying the station with real and artificial plants and flowers to be used on the sets of local television shows, like the evening news, weather, kids' shows, and other locally-produced entertainment. Probably the most popular items with the television station's display guys were the artificial palms, which were so much easier to handle and held up better under the hot studio lights than the real thing; there were no burnt leaves, no heavy palms to lug around. The decorators would come into our showroom to check out our selection and see what they might be able to use.

I'm not sure what the station's guys chose, but one time, in addition to the palms, Mr. Jelm sent over some of his brother's old raggedy flowers. The station refused them, and when the lead set guy brought back the rejected flowers, he started in on me about the "crappy, falling-apart flowers" we had sent over.

Mr. Jelm came out of his office, and the guy lit into him. "Carl, I told you specifically that we wanted Danny to do some fantasy flower arrangements for the cooking show set. His arrangements are always a big hit, and we get so many calls and letters from viewers telling us how beautiful they think our sets are. This time, we had an oriental motif, and the flowers we wanted Danny to make would have been perfect. So what's up? What happened? Why didn't you let Danny make the flowers? Why did you send us these crappy old flowers? Do you even have a clue how much you'd have to pay for all the advertising time we give you? We wound up just using the living plants that you sent over, not the old crap."

Well, I guess the decorator had talked to Mr. Jelm directly about what he wanted, and Mr. Jelm never even told me about the order.

The studio decorator told me in front of Mr. Jelm that he had wanted me to make some of my fantasy peonies, from three-inch buds to twelve-inch open blossoms. "Mr. Jelm never told me about what you wanted. I guess he decided to work on the arrangements himself," I blurted out. The look I got from Mr. Jelm pretty much told me how angry and hurt he was by my two-cents-worth comment.

I had seen those wilted-looking paper flowers before. At one point, I had actually thrown them into the dumpster while cleaning out one of the stockrooms. Rather than let me handle the cooking show flower arrangements, Mr. Jelm had put together some arrangements from the stuff that I had thrown away in the dumpster, some of Hollis's flowers that Mr. Jelm had tried to recycle into new displays.

The studio guy droned on and on, and at one point, he got up in Mr. Jelm's face and jabbed a finger at him. "I'm very unhappy with the quality of your work, Carl, and I'm really disappointed that you think so little of our business arrangement that you would try to push this crap off on us!"

Wow, he didn't have to put Mr. Jelm down like that in front of me and the other employees. This guy was being very rude and disrespectful!

Mr. Jelm was fuming. "Well, you can just cancel all of my spots! I don't need your damn business, or the money, or the hassles. Or the audacity and impertinence you have to talk to me in this manner. Goodbye to you, young man." Very formal, very cold, very right on, as far as I was concerned. As always, Mr. Jelm acted like the classy gentleman that he was.

Mr. Jelm had been right about not needing the station's business. He must have been a millionaire many times over. He didn't need me or my superior attitude for that matter, since he had a contract with 20th Century Fox to supply all of the live foliage, trees, and lawn wraps for their films and television shows. The designers who worked with the live stuff had been doing that for years and rarely needed any input from me. It seemed like I spent more and more time sparring with Mr. Jelm over the details of whatever job I was working on. In the meantime, I'd look out toward the back lot to our loading crew preparing shipment after shipment of all kinds of nursery plants for Fox, loading everything into large trucks, sometimes a half-dozen at a time. Mr. Jelm didn't really need me or the clients I brought in.

After this latest incident, Mr. Jelm just stayed in his office most of the time. He seldom walked through the work areas, and when he stopped to see how we were doing on an order, he continued to just plop down a note or speak quickly. Then, he would turn on his heels and hurry back into his office, often pulling down the blinds in the big windows that overlooked the work areas.

It got back to me that Mr. Jelm thought I hadn't stuck up for him enough with the guy from the television studio. And before that, I had made the situation worse with Eddie Monday by getting all preachy with him and Eddie.

Looking back on my time with Flowerama, I still wonder how what started out so well had come to such a painful end. Mr. Jelm had such an emotional attachment to the old arrangements that his deceased brother Hollis and his team had put together back in the day. It was almost as if Mr. Jelm wanted to continue the design business in memory of Hollis. He loved the faded old flowers and limp foliage that Hollis and his crew had created.

Mr. Jelm still did some display work for old clients, and he would put together ragged-looking arrangements that the clients often sent back. I tried to get rid of a lot of the old stuff, but Mr. Jelm would sneak out to the dumpsters to rescue and try to recycle what he could. I'm not sure why: maybe for sentimental reasons, or just to prove that he still could cut the mustard as a designer.

After the fiasco of the old raggedy flower arrangements being returned by the television station, I tried to work with Mr. Jelm on incorporating the old flowers into new arrangements. When I had time, I would try to rehab some of the flowers that Mr. Jelm seemed particularly fond of and attached to. I wanted them to last for as many gigs as possible, because Mr. Jelm seemed to enjoy seeing them being used and appreciated. I wish that I had asked him about his treasures: when they were first created, for who, for what movie, event, or occasion.

These flowers were so special to Mr. Jelm that he never allowed them to be sold, only rented for a short period of time. Eventually, a lot of the rental floral arrangements were in pretty bad shape when they were returned by the clients. So I would quietly and discreetly dispose of them, often trying as best as I could to copy the original flowers. I was walking on eggshells, and was way out of my element when dealing with Hollis's stuff. I felt like the aging and forgotten silent film actress's butler in the 1950 movie *Sunset Boulevard,* grasping a handle of the coffin containing the faded star's dead pet chimpanzee, walking beside her respectfully and silently as they carried the coffin from the actress's decaying mansion to the chimp's final resting place.

I was at a loss about how to deal with Mr. Jelm's sullen attitude and his going out of his way not to have any real communication or contact with me. So the King Bee took the coward's way out: I pulled out of the Flowerama parking lot one last time late one Friday night after after I finished work, leaving on Mr. Jelm's desk detailed notes about the few projects that he had recently given me to work on.

15

Into the Fire

I called up my favorite client from Flowerama, Sally Kaspersky, and told her that I was ready to accept her offer to make me her partner in a design business. As we had already discussed, I would provide the creative talent and know-how, and she and her husband would take care of the finances. She asked me to come by her house and pick her up, and she would show me where our design studio would be.

Sally lived just off of North Robertson Boulevard, in Beverly Hills. It was such a swanky area. As I pulled up in front of her beautiful home, I felt classy already! We drove into Hollywood to the Wilton Apartments, whose owners were friends of the Kasperskys. Once upon a time, in the golden age of Hollywood, the apartment building was called the Wilton Hotel, and Sally told me that its restaurant and bar had been some kind of Hollywood hot spot.

Because Sally was a friend of the building's owners, they were going to let us use a tiny showroom in the lobby. And I do mean *tiny*. It looked as if there would barely be enough room to move around when the shelves, tables, and displays were all set up!

"Well, kiddo," Sally said, wearing her infectious smile, "we gotta start somewhere. The only place to go from here is up!"

After the way I had left Flowerama, I needed to work off my guilt somehow, so when I saw where Sally and I would be setting up shop, I didn't squawk. I felt that I was getting exactly what I deserved. Sally had bought a lot of really nice furnishings, display tables, shelving, and materials for the new space, so with the help of the building's maintenance crew, I went gangbusters getting everything ready for our grand opening.

Looking at the small space we'd be opening in, it was kinda hard to think of grand as being the right word. We pushed some of the displays out into the lobby and even managed to add some classy finishing touches, including a small skirted table just outside our tiny display space. On the tabletop, we put a sign with the name of our new business, Fascinations, written on it in fancy calligraphy. Doris Day, Nat King Cole, Frank Sinatra, and other big-name singers had recorded a song called "Fascination." It was still popular when we were opening our design studio, so Sally and I thought that the name we chose would stick in people's minds.

I got in touch with Los Angeles-area television and radio stations to get some publicity and advertising slots to promote Fascinations. Some of the television outlets wanted to use me and Sally in person for the advertising spots. I tried to get the various TV stations to focus more on the floral pieces than on Sally and me, because I definitely had some reservations about how well we would do on camera! I was a very nervous and sweaty contestant on the radio-broadcast version of *Strike It Rich* years ago back in New York City, and I was uncomfortable on camera when I was in the more recent floral arrangement spots I did on live TV to promote Flowerama.

I wasn't sure that Sally would do any better than I had on camera. She had a habit of talking a mile a minute whenever she got nervous or flustered. She had a little poodle that went almost everywhere with her, and Sally said that if we were going to be in the advertising spots, she wanted to do them holding the dog. I was having waking nightmares about what would happen if we were on the air and the dog got loose and ran around the studio, yapping at everyone and peeing on the floor displays.

Sally had some good ideas of her own about promoting our design business, and she went ahead and called B'nai B'rith and some other organizations, offering to list them as sponsors for the televised grand opening and the various interviews. *What the heck,* I thought, so I contacted Mrs. Samuel Goldwyn, who had been so happy with my work for her personally and for her husband's studio. I wanted to ask if I could mention her as a satisfied client.

Mrs. Goldwyn's assistant answered the phone and said that Mrs. Goldwyn would be fine with us using her name. I asked if she thought it might be possible for Mrs. Goldwyn to attend our grand opening the following Sunday, and if so, what kind of floral arrangement could I do to thank her for her support. The assistant said sure, she'd ask Mrs. Goldwyn to stop by, and one of her favorite arrangements for her desk was African violets in a little china tea cup.

Thanks to Sally's and David's connections in and out of show business, our opening turned out to be pretty grand after all. In the design field, maybe more so than in many others, word of mouth—and who knows you—can make a business successful from the very beginning. Many celebrities, and shops carrying luxury goods, fine retailers, night clubs, restaurants, people in the entertainment industry—like Mrs. Goldwyn—are keen on being seen as embracing the latest trend. I guess that whole mindset is sort of a twist on the old adage that you are known by the company you keep.

The day of the grand opening arrived, and I was sweating bullets, chain smoking, and too nervous to eat much of anything. Sally brought one of the beautiful antique cups and saucers that her mother had left her. I ran out and bought some fresh African violets to add to the beautiful little cluster of porcelain and silk African violets made in France that I had found in a fancy gift shop. Things started out pretty good.

Her chauffeur pulled Mrs. Goldwyn's big fancy car up in front of the design studio. There was an entrance from the lobby and another door from our shop out to the sidewalk. Mrs. Goldwyn entered through the apartment house lobby. Our little shop was already crowded with some of Sally's friends, television cameras, sound equipment, and tables holding some of our featured floral designs. Sally's gaggle of friends just sort of froze and stood there gawking when Mrs. Goldwyn entered.

"Oh, Danny, you have so many beautiful arrangements here!" Mrs. Goldwyn turned toward me as I introduced her to Sally, who was beaming. I was afraid that she was going to try to pigeonhole Mrs. Goldwyn and introduce her to her friends, who by now were chattering away to one another and saying real loud, "It's Mrs. Samuel Goldwyn!"

The poodle started yapping, jumped out of Sally's arms, and ran out through the open lobby door. I ran after her—on camera—and found her peeing on the skirt of the little table just outside the door. I grabbed her and wiped her off with some tissues. A television crew guy took her and stood holding her off to one side. Mrs. Goldwyn didn't seem fazed at all, and she grabbed both of Sally's hands as she said "My dear, you have one talented guy here! I wish you both the best of luck in this new design adventure!" Then Mrs. Goldwyn headed out to her waiting car through the front door, which I held open for her.

To my shock and amazement, Mr. Carl Jelm glided past me into the shop through the open door. I stood there holding onto the door like I was going to fall over. Mr. Jelm tipped his hat to Sally, reached out to shake her hand, and said, "Best of luck and great success, my dear." As he headed back out through the door, he shook my hand, "Good luck and much happiness to you, Danny."

Then, Mr. Jelm disappeared through the front door. Boy, did

I feel like crap! I was speechless. Mr. Jelm had done so much for me and my family, and I had repaid him by walking out on him in a huff and taking several of his best clients. And yet, he showed up that day to wish Sally and me luck. I felt like a real heel, behaving as I had on so many occasions, when all he was trying to do was to get me to focus on my work, live up to my promises, and just stop once in a while to listen to other people's suggestions and ideas. Carl Jelm was probably the most gentlemanly and generous man I had ever met, and I had treated him like dirt.

That same afternoon, I went down to a television station to do a live demonstration of me making a floral arrangement during a couple of spots for our design shop on *The Wink Martindale Show.* Since the name of our shop was Fascinations, I was going to make the arrangement while a recording of Nat King Cole singing the hit song "Fascination" played in the background. But before showing how quickly I could complete the arrangement, for the first spot, I did a run-through. I explained to the viewers the various flowers and greenery, and how the flowers and foliage were trimmed and placed to make the finished arrangement.

The whole idea was to give the viewers some practical ideas and tips for doing some simpler arrangements, while also promoting Fascinations for those special occasions when folks needed more elaborate arrangements.

I guess I did ok, because the television station received a lot of calls and letters from viewers saying how much they had enjoyed my demonstration. Some viewers asked me to do more shows, maybe one with me demonstrating how to make some of the fantasy flowers that I had mentioned during the show. And we received a lot of phone calls at the shop, asking where we were located, could we do wedding florals, how long would it take, etc.

I finished the actual arrangement the very split second Nat King Cole finished singing our namesake song! I don't remember exactly what I said to finish up the spot, but as I walked out of camera range, I heard a woman's deep, resonant voice: "Very impressive, Mr. Danny Miller! Just wonderful!" That sexy voice belonged to Miss Della Reese, the popular singer. I had seen some movement behind the camera lighting while I was doing the spot, so I guessed that Miss Reese had been sitting just off stage during my demonstration. After I finished, I went backstage and walked over to Miss Reese, offering her my hand and then my business card. I invited her to come over to the design studio and choose a flower arrangement as our gift to her.

Wow! When I got home late that afternoon—for once, right when I had said I would be there—it was like gangbusters: kids and family hopping around, talking over each other as they rushed toward me. I had told Lena about the grand opening and that afternoon's demonstration, and she had kept the kids home from school. Everybody seemed so proud of me. Sally was there too, grabbing me by both hands, then giving me a big hug. I told her to expect a visit from Miss Della Reese, who had watched our two advertising spots from offstage.

"Fantastic, Danny! Della Reese is my favorite female vocalist! And we all want to know how you managed to end so perfectly, to finish the arrangement just when the song ended."

"It just happened that way," I said. "I was lucky, I guess."

Lena said that she was so proud and had called family and friends and told them to be sure to watch the show. "But they put too much makeup on you, Danny. You looked like a dead guy!"

Still, too much makeup and all, I was so happy and proud when I came home that afternoon. My family, friends, and neighbors were so excited about me being on TV. Sally couldn't have been happier about everything that we'd accomplished in such a short time.

But, soon enough, the old feelings of guilt about all of my screw-ups and indiscretions returned. So much guilt was weighing down my shoulders.

I felt guilty about screwing up the great opportunity that Mr. Jelm had given me, leaving him high and dry. I had basically just walked away from my career at Flowerama and hurt Mr. Jelm, that saint of a man, that generous gentleman and friend who had done so much for me and my family. My stubbornness destroyed a friendship that would have been a positive influence on me and my family for the rest of my life. I just couldn't get the whole guilt thing out of my head: guilt over being unfaithful to Lena, guilt over getting my lover Adina pregnant, guilt over so many things.

I made a conscious effort to do the best I could to help Sally succeed in the business. I hired a new designer to help out, and she turned out to be a real hard worker with a lot of great design ideas. She was the daughter of Sally's neighbors just down the street, and she knew how to patiently listen to and deal with these rich people's design ideas.

In Los Angeles, more than any place else, I felt that I was drifting professionally and personally. When we started Fascinations, our clients were mostly Sally and David's friends and social connections. I really felt more comfortable working in a retail setting, as I had at Flowerama, Silvestri, and the companies I worked for back East.

Yes, I had a good business partner with plenty of money, contacts, and influential friends who were potential clients. But, I just couldn't shake the feeling I had that something wasn't right in my life. I decided to ask Lena what she thought about moving back to Chicago, going home to our family and friends. Lena told me that, like me, she felt out of her element in Los Angeles. She missed our extended family and the many friends we had back in Chicago. She said that she was really looking forward to getting back to Chicago, back to familiar surroundings.

I finally decided to tell Sally that I just couldn't stay in Los Angeles any longer, that me and my family needed to get back to Chicago. Sally was a trouper: She pulled me into an earnest and heartfelt hug that showed what a perceptive and kind lady she was. "I know, kiddo, I know," Sally said, her eyes bright with tears. She stood back, holding onto my shoulders. "You've been a good friend, and you'll do just fine once you're back home."

Now I was feeling guilty about packing up and leaving Los Angeles, pulling out of my partnership with Sally Kaspersky. I felt guilty about having screwed up so many times in my life, starting with forcing myself on Lena and marrying her illegally. Oh, Lord, would these screw-ups and guilt ever end?

Have you no pride left, no spine? I asked myself as I dialed George Silvestri's phone number. I asked for my old position back. I was sweating bullets and had two cigarettes going at the same time. I was so nervous that I had forgotten there was one already burning in the ashtray.

Mr. Silvestri sounded happy to hear from me. "Gosh, yes, Danny, your timing couldn't be better! Next month we start doing the Christmas display work, so you're just in time. You did such an incredible job supervising the Miracle Mile lights!"

We sold all of the furniture and turned the house over to a friend to take over the payments. In California back then, it was still legal for a third party to take over a money or real estate obligation, like mortgage payments and such. Lena and the kids were so happy to be going back East, back home to our friends and relatives in the Chicago area.

I had bailed on Mr. Jelm with no notice and had waited until the last minute to tell Sally that I was heading back to Chicago with my family. I was hoping to leave behind my guilt as well. But in the short term, I wound up adding more guilt, worry, and bad feelings about myself.

16

Lessons Still Not Learned

We arrived back in Chicago on a vividly cold December day, just a few weeks after that year's NADI (National Association of Display Industries) show that featured display-design ideas for the coming spring. The yearly show was an opportunity to see what new display-industry ideas, trends, and products were out there, and it was a good place to network with other design professionals and to check out what the competition was offering. The show that year had been held in Chicago and alternated yearly between Chicago and New York. The show's catalog that year was stunning: elegant typography, color illustrations, good quality photographs, and short but informative articles about some of the new display trends for spring.

My high horse was getting higher and my ego getting bigger by the minute because George Silvestri hadn't hesitated to put me back on the company payroll. I had to wonder what he was thinking! I had come and gone before, so why did he think this time around would be any different? He told me on my first day back that I was one of the best designers he had ever hired and that he planned to make the most of my talent for as long as I would stick around. Maybe he considered me to be a kind of creative shot in the arm that would put some new life in Silvestri projects, get things moving creatively and in new directions before I took off again. He probably thought of my time there as a yearly boost of new display ideas and outside-the-box ways of doing things.

Yes, I was feeling pretty damn important, just thinking how I had managed to write my own return ticket after really mucking things up last time. Not only had I just up and left with no notice, but I had taken two other valued employees with me on my creative wild-goose chase. He had taken them back, no questions asked, no sermons about life's lessons learned. And now he was giving *me* yet another chance.

I was grateful for the opportunity to prove myself, but I was still clueless as to the importance of thinking things through and considering all the options. Listening to what others have to say has never been one of my strong points. I've always been a strong-willed, stubborn, real-life know-it-all, not one to take advice from other design professionals in the know. I don't think it's necessarily a Gypsy thing. It's probably just my inclination to believe that if I really want something, it will happen if I'm willing to follow my own gut feeling and stand my ground to make it happen.

Anyway, when I left before, I didn't leave Silvestri flat. The company had other, more flexible and really talented designers. My talents just added a twist to what others could do. My niche had been creating what I call my fantasy flowers: hand-and-machine-made flowers and foliage that started with what Nature had created and took off from there. It turned out that I was a good addition to the seasonal display-design team.

After I had left the last time, Silvestri actually put their summer design lineup on hold. On my return, it was re-introduced, and one of my first projects was to design an entire array of brightly-colored butterflies, from three inches to three feet in size, to be suspended or otherwise placed in a variety of natural or fantasy window or floor display settings. It was the 1960s, and the mod revolution was underway in art, fashion, and music. The design industry, always tuned in to what's happening in popular culture, made the most of the new trend. Polka-dotted fabrics were real popular back then, so some of my butterflies had polka-dot designs in psychedelic colors, which were soon seen in stage props and backgrounds.

For fall, I came up with different kinds of leaves, again from three inches to three feet, and artificial flowers—like hip-looking chrysanthemums, goldenrods, and other fall favorites—in a variety of wild colors. We also produced promotional banners in psychedelic colors that really stood out when black light fixtures were used for lighting. We did a series of modern art plaques that reflected what was new and trending in the New York and Chicago art scenes.

This use of then-popular colors and designs in seasonal window and floor displays was soon widespread in the fabric industry, home and office settings, and advertising. Bean-bag seating in bright red, green, orange, and other intense colors became real popular. These 1960s trends carried over into our broadcast and stage work as well. More and more stage productions of classic works were updated and brought into the modern era with sets and wardrobes that modern viewers and playgoers could relate to. Our display-design work not only reflected what was happening in popular culture—what people saw around them—but we also produced trendy display items for retail settings, plays, and broadcast use that added maybe a new twist to what people were used to seeing.

By the mid-sixties, Silvestri had quite a few clients out West, where display items were less seasonal. In Southern California, for example, there was little demand for generic autumnal displays with different East Coast leaves, foliage, flowers, etc. Halloween, Thanksgiving, and an early push for Christmas displays took precedence. The further north you headed—into the San Francisco Bay area and up into the Pacific Northwest—the more retailers' display trends mirrored what we were doing back East. In Northern California and points further north, there were even different seasonal weights of clothing.

For the Christmas season in Southern California, there was less variety in street decorations—garlands, street lamp decorations, etc.—but the shopping centers and department store branches still went all out, like retailers did in the Midwest and East. Florida and the South were kind of a mix, with very few autumn-themed retail displays or use of the brighter autumn color palette. When I was living and working in Los Angeles, one thing I really missed was the variety of seasonal displays that we had in the East. Even though the stores, shopping malls, and maybe the main streets were decorated, overall there seemed to be less seasonal decoration than back East.

While we were living in California, my brother Bill died real sudden like. That was really a shock, because he was never sick a day in his life. He never drank alcohol or smoked cigarettes, and Bill was real careful about what he ate, long before healthy eating was a big thing. He had some kind of leak in his heart and just fell over dead one day at work.

Bill and I weren't that close for a long time because he was fifteen years older than me, the first male great-grandchild born after my dad's family came to America from the Old Country. All the rest were girls until Bill showed up. Bill and I got along well enough whenever he came to Chicago to visit. When we talked about non-family stuff, we actually discovered that we had some of the same interests and talents. Bill was so different from the rest of the family and was lucky to live far enough away to not get caught up in all the family drama that seemed pretty much a regular occurrence. I admired that, but I was more than a little envious of his freedom.

Like our grand-uncle Stefan, when he was old enough, Bill

moved away and distanced himself from the Gypsy lifestyle and our crazy family life. Years later, my nephew Richie explained a word to me that he said described my extended family: dysfunctional.

Bill had moved to California, got into an auto mechanic apprentice program, and really enjoyed the work. When he went into the service later, he trained as an airplane engine mechanic. After WWII, he worked for Delta Airlines in Atlanta, Georgia. He worked there for many years as a turboprop and jet engine mechanic.

Bill married a beautiful and very bright gadji, and they had four kids over a period of about fifteen years. None of them took up the Gypsy lifestyle or really had any interest in it until they were older and wanted to learn more about their dad's people. Bill's son Sammy—the one I refer to as "my born-again-Gypsy nephew"—lived with us when he was in college and became real interested in and curious about the whole Gypsy thing. He gets on my nerves though sometimes, focusing on real small details about Gypsy customs and holidays and such, and asking why I do things different from how they're described in the books about and by Gypsies that he reads. He still gets all holier-than-thou at times because I prefer the word *Gypsy* to the terms used by many Gypsies and politically-correct gadje.

Sammy and his brother and sisters are good kids, and they're very smart like their parents. With the money Bill left his family, his kids were able to go to college—graduate school even—and Sammy and his siblings all have good careers.

Just a few months after Bill died, my sister Edie passed away a week or so after having a heart attack. When we moved back to Chicago several years after Edie passed away, we took in her sixteen-year-old son, Reggie. He fit in with no problems, at least at first, because he already took our kids as his own brothers and sisters and said that he had missed them a lot during the time that we were out in California. My kids thought of him as their big brother. As the weeks and months passed, however, Lena and I realized that Reggie was not the best role model for our sons.

Reggie's dad, Pete, remarried about a year after Edie passed away. The new wife didn't take to Reggie, and he didn't like her bossing him around. After he got into a real doozy of a knock-down fight with his oldest stepbrother, Reggie's stepmom called the cops on him, and he wound up in detention until my dad came and rescued his sorry behind.

Reggie moved in with my mom and dad out in Cicero. That didn't work out so well, as far as stopping Reggie from making friends with hoodlums, druggies, and alcoholics in the greater Chicago area. My dad was never real big on disciplining his kids or grandkids, probably because his own dad ran roughshod over him when he was growing up. Dad didn't want to follow in his own dad's footsteps and be resented for being too strict. My folks didn't do much to encourage Reggie to make the right choices during the couple of years he lived with them, and they both gave him a lot of leeway. Neither of my folks was real keen on "spying on" their favorite grandson and keeping tabs on what he was up to. That turned out to be quite a lot, most of it bad: petty theft, drug use, selling pot and pills.

This bad streak of usually going with wrong when Reggie had a choice between doing right or wrong had started years before. My sister Edie told me once that Reggie had been caught smoking in the boys' bathroom in grade school, and she wondered what the big deal was. That's a typical Gypsy attitude that even today seems to encourage kids to make a lot of bad choices in life, because they know that their folks will go out of their way to cover for them, even lying for their kids, if it comes down to that.

To hear my folks talk about Reggie, any trouble he got into at school and with the cops was always someone else's fault, or a setup, or because of prejudice against Gypsies. Well, again, this attitude goes back to the Gypsy mistrust of cops and other gadjo authority figures. Sadly, it encourages parents and family members to go out of their way to shield young people from any consequences of their unfortunate choices in life.

Before leaving California to move back East, Lena and I had more than a few discussions about what each of us thought would be best for my folks and Reggie. We couldn't get a real take on the situation with Reggie during our brief visits to Chicago and Atlanta for Edie and Bill's funerals. It was only when we returned to Chicago for good that we realized how troubled Reggie was, and how hard it was for my folks to keep tabs on him. My mom and dad were getting too old to be saddled with an out-of-control wannabe hoodlum. Lena thought that everything would work out for Reggie if he could just find a stable home with parent figures and hang out with decent kids who would keep him on the straight and narrow.

I had my doubts about Lena's optimistic view of Reggie's future, but decided that we should try to help. Friends and neighbors over the years had asked us how we managed to raise such wonderful, polite, and well-behaved kids. I had clung to that as proof that I must not have been such a bad dad after all.

We called my folks and Reggie from California and invited him to live with us when we moved back to Chicago. We loved him, cared about him, and wanted him to be part of our growing family. I felt guilty that we didn't stay in Chicago longer after Edie's funeral. With my work schedule at Flowerama, there was no way that I could take a long enough break so soon after my brother Bill's death to spend more than a few days in Chicago. I just didn't have enough time to get involved in yet another family situation.

Well, I should have done! Maybe then I would have realized just how far gone the situation was with Reggie! Like my parents, I gave Reggie a lot of slack when he was living with us, which turned out not to be such a good idea after all. In hindsight, it would have been great if I had taken time from my work and after-hours screwing around to spend more time with Reggie. And, of course, I could have always taken him with me to some of my freelance jobs. But no, that never happened. We wound up spending even more time and money in the end trying to deal with the legal consequences of Reggie's many screw-ups. I don't know how many times I thought about how savvy Reggie's stepmom must have been to spot a rotten egg and get it out of the house as soon as possible, before it could stink everything up.

Whenever I looked back on everything that had happened since I forced myself on Lena all those years ago, I felt overwhelmed by a whole mess of guilt. By leaving home, marrying Lena, and going back on the road with her, I had hoped to do right by her and our unborn child. Just disappearing like we did really hurt our families. After that, there had been so many missed opportunities, bad decisions, messed-up kids—victims of my serial adultery and all-consuming desire to be the best display designer that money could buy.

Me and my damn high horse! I had gone to Los Angeles to find fame and fortune and instead came crawling back to beg for a job that I had thought was too small for me. I felt real bad being so far away when my brother Bill and my sister Edie died and not being around for very long to help my folks deal with things. Feeling guilty about being away when all this happened, I started obsessing over other things that I still felt guilty about: forcing myself on Lena and making her pregnant; leaving Silvestri, Flowerama, and Fascinations; being unfaithful to my wonderful wife more times than I could count; getting my lover Adina pregnant.

Oh, on and on. How I carried on inside myself! The guilt was always somewhere in my mind. Maybe being busy with my work blocked it out for a while, but when my mind wandered away from my work, the guilt was back, tormenting me. Some nights at bedtime, when it seemed that Lena was in the mood for a little romance, I would beg off, saying I was just too bushed. I was so tired carrying around this burden of guilt.

Now I was back in Chicago, living and working in my favorite city. I had really high expectations. I hoped that putting so much energy into my work this time around—really overachieving—would finally alleviate my guilty feelings.

Everyone at Silvestri who remembered me from before was excited that I was working there again. Mr. Silvestri himself couldn't have been happier or more enthusiastic that I was back on the payroll. He would give me a pat on the back, grab me by the shoulders, look me right in the eye and say—so many times—"Oh, Danny, please stay around a little longer this time!" Even the office people, cleaners, and people who worked upstairs—like in the printing plant and the photography studio—gave me a hug or shook hands with me when they ran into me.

Yes, I was happy to be back at Silvestri. But as happy—excited even—as I was when I first returned, this time around, my design talents were put to much less use. The Silvestri Italian lights and other popular lighting treatments had been so successful that now Mr. Silvestri was focusing on expanding his retail decorative animation and lighting lines and designing new products. The Italian lights were eventually manufactured in Taiwan for commercial and retail use. Later, they were marketed not only to the retail trade but also to consumers for home use.

The first big boost for the lighting end of the display business had come back in November 1959, when Silvestri Italian lights made their big debut in public on the barren winter trees lining the street in front of the Saks store on Michigan Avenue. Mr. Silvestri and Joe Kreis, the display director at Saks, had put their heads together and came up with the idea of putting strings of the tiny Italian lights on the bare branches of the trees in front of Saks.

Each branch of the trees was covered with strings of the Italian lights. Each tree took about a day to do. When the switch was finally flipped on, the side of the street in front of Saks was bathed in a bright silver light. Pedestrians stopped to look, and cars slowed down. There were more than a few traffic jams, and the cops showed up to keep the traffic moving along. Within a year, other Michigan Avenue merchants joined Saks in lighting the trees in front of their stores.

This time around, back on familiar and forgiving turf, I wasn't thinking of leaving Silvestri, but I was hoping to find some freelance display work on the side that would take advantage of my own unique design skills. By this time in my career, I was known as the "go-to flower guy." I had also done a lot of work using willow and birch tree branches to make my own fantasy trees for general retail-display use as well. I had really high hopes that I could find some display work again at Ber-Tals, whose owner had been so happy with my freelance work there for three display seasons the last time I was working in Chicago.

I heard from Mr. Silvestri himself that the elderly owner of Ber-Tals had passed away suddenly while I was working out in California. His talented daughter had taken over the company and had put together her own display crew. So, dead end there.

I spent a lot of time trying to reconnect with the other freelance people that I had worked with in the past. Not much success with that. As I've already said, design folks are a pretty mobile group. They tend to move around a lot, staying with one company just long enough to learn some new skills before heading out to either go solo or find a better opportunity. This meant that I had to work a lot harder and put together a new network of contacts. I struggled, but finally landed a contract to produce two really hot retail Christmas display lines for the next two seasons. The spring lines just seemed to fall into place, and summer and fall weren't too shabby either.

I partied less and had more of a home life. Lena was always ready to lend a talented hand when I needed help with whatever I was working on. As good as things were going, of course my old high horse rode into town, and I got itchy feet to strike out and find a steady position that my ever-growing ego thought might be worthy of my creative talents. A guy I had run into at several display-industry trade shows called me and said that he was retiring from Austen Display in New York City and would be moving to Florida. He asked if I would like him to set up an interview for me with Mr. Austen. Mr. Austen actually called me, conducted a mini-interview over the phone, and he wound up inviting me to his Manhattan offices for a more formal interview and to show him my design portfolio.

I flew into Manhattan, and Mr. Austen seemed really impressed with the photos of the designs that I had recently added to my portfolio. He said that he was already familiar with my work, and that any display company would welcome a veteran display designer from Silvestri, because Silvestri was revered in the trade by all of the better New York City display houses. I told him that the reason I was leaving Silvestri was that most of my extended family lived in the NYC area and I wanted to be closer, to be there for some of the older generation who were in poor health. Boy, did I fib! I didn't think that he wanted to hear the real reason: that I had itchy creative feet and thought it was time to venture out.

Mr. Austen was impressed with my work and said that he respected my decision to be closer to my family. Then, he stood up, walked around his desk, grabbed my right hand, and pumped it up and down as he said my favorite words: "You're hired, Danny!"

The Miller family was soon on its way to New York City, for better or for worse: I was hoping for better this time around!

17

The More Things Change . . .

Austen Display, New York City
George Zafero Design, Philadelphia

We bought a nice row house in Sheepshead Bay, in the southern part of Brooklyn. Everything went great bangs. At the first staff meeting I went to at Austen Display, Mr. Austen walked over to me before the meeting got started and introduced me to a very handsome thirty-something guy with a bushy mustache. "Danny, this is Hal Walker, who worked on a line of crepe-paper Christmas flowers last season."

"Glad to meet you, Hal! So how did the flowers sell?"

"Well, Danny, you're hearing it from the horse's mouth: not so great. Mr. Austen says that maybe you'll have better luck. But I'm telling you, I've been there, and it's probably not worth your time. I only had three very small orders, and they added up to a grand total of one hundred and fifty dollars. I'll say it again: Making a line of crepe Christmas flowers is probably not worth your time. I know for me it was a waste of my time." Wow, Hal Walker was something else. Talk about a snooty guy with a bad attitude!

Mr. Austen cleared his throat, then pursed his lips into a pouty little smile. He got real close to Hal, leaned into him, and said, very sarcastically, "Well, Hal, I did pay you—and very well, indeed—for your efforts. Certainly more than enough to make up for all of your precious wasted time. And Danny, I can assure you that I will be glad to pay you as well for your time!" Yikes!

Mr. Austen turned around and headed over to the large work table that doubled as a desk. He sat down and called out, "Ok, folks, it's time for the meeting to get underway. First order of business, and my pleasure, is to introduce to you our new lead flower designer, Mr. Danny Miller, who comes to us from Silvestri Design in Chicago."

There was quite a buzz in the room, shouted greetings, and applause. Wow, looking back, I'm surprised that my oversized ego didn't ride my high horse right up through the skylight! Anyway, in those days—and for many, many years—Silvestri was known as the Cadillac of display-design companies. When other companies started a new display line, the designers were told from on high to make the new line look like it came from a Silvestri design studio. Competitors would send their design staff to check out the floor and window displays we did for our many clients in the Chicago area. They didn't out and out try to copy our designs, but the better companies managed to give their display line some of the elegance and professionalism that had made Silvestri Design so successful.

Well, that first year, I headed the two teams that produced the entire line of holiday display items. We had a factory in Mexico where skilled artisans supervised the production of about 75 percent of our holiday line. Back in New York City, I taught about twenty skilled workers, mostly Jamaicans, how to make the special fantasy flowers by hand and how to use the new stemming equipment we'd bought to automate part of the process. My team produced about 25 percent of all the orders. Austen sold over a million dollars' worth of holiday display items that year, quite an impressive amount back then.

One of the Austen sales reps, a very pretty young lady, came into my studio, grabbed me, gave me a big hug, then looked at me straight in the face and said, "Well, Mr. Danny Miller! I hope that your Christmas will be as special as mine! I just bought my very first Cadillac with my sales commission check!" Then she kissed me right on the lips and danced out. Well, yes, my family and I also had a wonderful Christmas that year, and for years to come.

After that first year, our stock seasonal display items were produced primarily in Hong Kong, with specialty and special order items made in-house. We had the latest machines to do wire stems, garlands, foliage, ribbons, and other items that used to be made mostly by hand. At first, Austen imported from Germany and Austria whatever luxury fabrics and materials we needed to produce our specialty items in-house or locally. After about five years or so, a lot of our display inventory, including the specialty items, was manufactured for us in Germany, where the labor costs were lower and the workmanship excellent.

Just as George Silvestri became well known in the trade for his Italian lights, display animation, and flame-resistant decorations, Austen became well known in the display industry for innovative display lighting and knock-down and modular types of display fixtures, which could be easily adjusted and modified for any size floor or window display. These fixtures could also be further adjusted for stage and set use.

In my travels since I retired from full-time work, I've visited trade shows and retail stores showcasing Austen-inspired florals, garlands, manzanita trees, and modular types of display and lighting fixtures. Many incorporated Austen Display innovations adopted and modified by other companies, all—including the many display-design products introduced by Austen Display—influenced over many years by the design genius of George Silvestri.

I didn't run into Hal Walker again for probably two months, and believe me, that was just fine with me! He had come across as an arrogant and self-important brat. Mr. Austen reassigned him to the photography and graphics department, located in the basement of our big building. There was a freight elevator that went down there, but it sat unused a lot, waiting for the elevator repair guy to get it running again. I finally saw Hal again when he brought up some proofs of the photos the photographers had taken of my crepe-paper Christmas flowers and foliage. He looked pretty much the same, but his whole demeanor and body language had changed. He was friendly, relaxed, and seemed really happy.

"Wow," he said, "I see now what Mr. Austen meant when he said he'd be glad to pay you for your time. Your fantasy flowers are absolutely phenomenal! I've never seen anything like them, Danny! Kudos! I brought up some cameras and lighting to take some more photos." Hal and an assistant started unloading a large cart piled high with lighting and camera equipment, and the three of us talked while they finished setting everything up.

"I feel ashamed and embarrassed for wishing you luck the day you were introduced to the staff here at Austen. I apologize for acting like a fucking idiot. You don't need me to wish you luck," Hal finally said. "Your kind of talent isn't based on luck, and I can see that right here as I look through the viewfinder." He straightened up, smiled, then reached over and shook my hand.

"I'm glad that Mr. Austen hired you, Danny. I never really fit into the display-design end. Mr. Austen and my dad have been good friends since college, and when I finally finished art school, Mr. Austen took me on to make use of my photography and graphic design studies.

"I never did get along with the old guy who was my boss back then. I tried to share with him some newer ways of doing things that I'd learned in school, suggested upgrading equipment, etc. I got tired of him not listening to me, of him calling me college boy and fancy pants. Rather than stick it out, calm down, and maybe actually learn something from him, I decided to just throw in the towel and try my hand at display design."

Gosh, that sounded familiar! How many times had I decided to pack it in when I didn't get my way on a job? *I don't need to put up with this crap,* I'd tell myself. *I can find a better job where they'll appreciate me.* I tried to sound sympathetic to Hal, and I asked, "But you studied design, right? Did you actually do any display-design work, like build sets or put together window displays?"

"Well, not really; not when I was in school anyway. I did a lot of design sketches, models, etc. I liked that, but in display design, you have to be a jack of all trades and a master of at least one." We both had a good laugh over that!

"And here at Austen, I wound up getting moved around a lot. I think that being sent back to the tech processes department was the best thing that could have happened. I think this time we've got it right! Mr. Austen gave me so many chances; each one turned out to be just more rope to hang myself. But this time around, I'm really happy. I like working with just a few other people, not rushing around so much. As busy as we are, I take time to read the trades, and I keep up with all the changes in photographic trends and equipment."

After my very first encounter with Hal, I thought that he was just another typical New York City display designer, with more money and attitude than talent, using family connections to move around from job to job. These spoiled guys treat a design career like some kind of hobby. The successful display, stage, and set designers are the ones who put a lot of effort into their work, appreciate the feedback they get, and gain a lot of valuable experience—the backbone of a successful design career. Some of them aren't as artistic or talented as others, but because of their experience, the ability to communicate well and learn from others, they tend to be put in charge of the most important projects.

Hal turned out to be a nice guy after all, like a whole different person: more relaxed, more confident, no longer coming across as a guy who has to one-up everyone else. He was obviously very happy in his work, having finally found his creative niche. I wanted to get to know Hal better. No, this wasn't a gay thing. There was just something about him, a certain manner he had about him that would put me at ease, calm me down, and relax me.

I jumped at the chance when he invited me and Lena over for dinner. I had met his pretty wife several times already. Like Hal, his wife, Gina, was a good listener and had a wonderful ability to put people at ease, to make them feel special by taking a real interest when they talked about their work, their families, what they thought about this or that. I'm genuinely interested in other people's ideas, concerns, etc., but sometimes I have to really struggle not to add my own two cents' worth and steer the conversation off course.

When I told Lena about the invitation, she was like a teenager all over again, in a really good mood: humming, singing, and dancing around. Free time—a chance for the two of us to just relax or enjoy a night out on the town—that was already something that neither of us had a lot of. Lena was so excited to finally have an evening away from the house and the kids. She had just finished making a beautiful green dress and was anxious to show it off to someone besides me.

Lena was a pro-level dressmaker, and that had come in handy in my years in window and floor display, because when I freelanced, I could bring Lena in to help with the mannequins. She could take a bolt of cloth, drape it around a mannequin, fold it, pin it, and make the mannequin look like something out of *Vogue* magazine. She made fantasy dresses for the mannequins, just like I made fantasy flowers for my display projects. The problem with the dresses was that when ladies saw them in the window and came in to try them on, they were as unreal as my fantasy flowers. They only existed in the window display.

The day we were going over to Hal and Gina's, I left work early so that Lena would have time to go out and have her hair done, get a manicure, and buy anything she needed. Lena had asked some neighbors if they would watch the kids. She spent hours getting ready, putting her hair up in a bun herself, which was my favorite way for her to do her hair, and had been since we were on the carnival circuit together. Lena went out to get a manicure, bought a new pair of shoes and an elegant new purse and belt. I hadn't even thought about how long it had been since we had spent time alone with another couple, without the kids fighting and whining in the same space.

We had a great evening at Hal and Gina's! Lena talked about

our kids, current events, and plays and shows that she wanted to see. She was all smiles as she described some of the display projects that she had helped me with. While Gina was preparing dinner, she and Lena chatted about their home lives and husbands, like dealing with Hal's and my crazy work schedules.

Anyway, we enjoyed ourselves, and Lena had made a new friend. Gina and Hal didn't have kids and didn't want kids. That was a new concept for Lena, and listening to Gina talk about her life with Hal without kids in the picture gave her a lot of what-ifs to think about. Maybe Lena could find ways to make more time for herself when I was at work or away.

In early 1967, we found out that Lena was pregnant. After a difficult pregnancy, she gave birth prematurely to our son Earl. Lena was having trouble breathing even before she became pregnant, and during the pregnancy, she gasped for air and had to go to the hospital for breathing treatments. Lena and I were both heavy smokers at the time, and that probably had a lot to do with Lena's medical situation and the fact that Earl was born early.

In the United States, as was the case elsewhere around the world, smoking was socially acceptable and widespread for many years. Back in the day, like other folks, a lot of doctors smoked, even when they were with a patient or making rounds at a hospital. A lot of print and radio ads featured "doctors" promoting the benefits of smoking a certain brand of cigarette over another. The famous Italian singer Galli-Curci was even featured in an ad for Lucky Strike cigarettes. She said that Lucky Strikes were so easy on her throat and her singing voice. Other celebrities said that they would often "reach for a Lucky instead of a sweet." hahaha!

Times and bad habits have changed, and these days most people are more health-conscious and don't smoke. But, smoking is still really widespread among Gypsies. Many young Gypsy women still smoke way too much and continue to smoke even when they're expecting. In my own extended family, except for a couple of nieces, a daughter-in-law, and my older daughter, Varda, who was a light smoker, I can't think of any mother who was a smoker who didn't continue to smoke while she was pregnant.

Tobacco and smoking are even incorporated into customs and rituals, like putting cartons of cigarettes into the deceased's coffin at a funeral. Often, someone visiting a grave will take with them a pack of the same brand of cigarettes that the deceased smoked. As part of paying respect to the deceased, the visitor opens the pack, takes out a cigarette, lights up, puts the cigarette pack on the grave, and places the lit cigarette on top of the pack. As of 2012, this is still a pretty common custom among Romanian Gypsies.

Anyway, Lena smoked way too much, and over the years, her heavy smoking caused a lot of health problems. Earl was never a child that was easy to deal with. I think maybe his brain didn't get enough oxygen while Lena was carrying him.

I was happy enough at Austen, had a lot of interesting assignments, and even had time to do a bit of freelancing to make some extra money. I had worked at Austen for quite a while now, and everything was going fine until my nephew Reggie got himself into some real trouble at the car repair shop in Manhattan where he was working. His boss, Nick Lattanzio, had found out from a couple of cops on the auto theft detail that a car that he had bought from one of Reggie's buddies was stolen. Reggie had already switched out the engine for another one. Nick told Reggie that he wouldn't be getting any commissions on repairs until he recouped the money for the car that the cops had seized.

Reggie, being of unsound mind, came back one Sunday when the shop was closed, got into the key safe, and stole another car. He hid it in a garage in Philly belonging to one of his shady friends. After hours, the garage was a chop shop. A chop shop is a place where stolen vehicles are taken apart so that the parts can be sold or used to repair other vehicles. Reggie was hoping to get part of the proceeds. He just dropped out of sight, so of course Nick figured that Reggie had taken the car.

Nick knew that I had been Reggie's legal guardian, so he called me up and told me that since he had had good business dealings with me and Lena, and he liked and trusted both of us, he would give Reggie forty-eight hours to return the car before he called the cops on him.

Long horrible story, but the upshot was that Reggie was laying low, and we didn't know where he was staying or with who. I called a couple of his low-life friends and asked them to relay Nick's message to Reggie and have him call us and tell us where we could pick up the car, if it was still in one piece. Finally, some nebun called and gave us some phone numbers to call and said maybe those guys would know where Reggie or the car was. After about a half-dozen calls back and forth with some real hoodlum-sounding guys, we found out that the car was in Philadelphia.

Lena and I had to take the train to Philadelphia to pick up the car that Reggie had stashed in his buddy's garage there. By taking the car across state lines, he had only added to his legal problems. We were so worried that we would be stopped driving the car back into Manhattan and be arrested for car theft.

We got the car back to Nick, barely within the forty-eight hours he had given Reggie to return it. But my nephew's problems weren't over, not by a long shot. Another moonlight customer of Reggie's decided that he would report a car stolen that he told the cops Reggie had worked on. Turns out that the customer reported it stolen so he could file a false insurance claim for the car and for a bunch of expensive stuff that he said was in the car when it was taken. His car insurance company investigated the theft and finally found out that the crooked customer had hired some mugs to take the car over to Jersey and dump it. But before the insurance investigator filed his report that the reported theft was part of a scam, Reggie wound up with an arrest warrant out on him for grand theft auto.

When Reggie finally called us after we had returned the car he had stolen, I read him the riot act. But I couldn't bring myself to tell him that he was on his own, that we'd had enough of him and his low-life friends. I already felt guilty because we had been out in California when his mom died. Now, because of the arrest warrant, Reggie couldn't come back to New York where we could keep an eye on him. That hadn't worked out so well before, but we were willing to help him as much as we could to make up for not being there for him when his mom passed away. Lena and I spent a lot of time agonizing over what to do about Reggie.

Turns out that Lena and I didn't have to do a whole lot. Reggie had met a nice gadji, Tina Colazzo, in his meanderings around Philly, and Lena was hoping that Tina could talk some sense into him and help him settle down into a decent job and a life below the police radar. I was pretty skeptical because I'd watched so many troubled, screwed-up guys hook up with women who just made things worse. Ducks of a feather . . .

Lena and I talked quite a bit on the phone with Tina and finally met her while Reggie was still hiding out. She seemed like a real nice gal, well-spoken, and with a good sense of humor. Tina was a widow lady and seemed to find the good in Reggie that up until now he had done a pretty good job of hiding from other people. Tina seemed determined to make a go of it with Reggie. He treated her like a queen, she told us, and was real good with her two kids and with making repairs around the house.

Tina had a good job as a bookkeeper's assistant, and she told Reggie that he would have to make some big changes in his life before she would agree to marry him. He had to stop hanging out with his hoodlum friends, get into an alcohol and drug rehab program, and sign up for job training in a line of work that had nothing to do with car repair. Lena, of course, thought that things would work out for Reggie. I honestly didn't think he could pull it off. But I was wrong.

This whole situation of being on the run and constantly looking over his shoulder had hit Reggie hard, and he seemed genuinely interested in getting his life together. With the information that the insurance people provided about the phony car theft, Reggie's Legal Aid attorney went to court and got the arrest warrant recalled. Reggie decided to stay in Philly though and make a new life with Tina and her kids. He got into a heating, ventilation, and air conditioning repair program at a trade school. After graduating, Reggie found an apprenticeship with one of Philly's oldest and most respected HVAC companies, putting his mechanical savvy to an honest use. I guess that Reggie really was happy to be with Tina, and he did everything he could to be a good husband and dad. All these years later, he and Tina are still doing fine.

I already had a job offer in Philadelphia I couldn't refuse, from George Zafero, who owned a well-known display company that did a lot of work in Philly, New York City, and Chicago. I had run into him at a restaurant in Philly when Lena and I were first trying to track down Reggie. I had done some work for him before, and my fantasy designs fit in with his upscale and imaginative approach to display design. So now we were going to try to make a home for our family in Philly. I told Mr. Austen that I had to move to Philly because an aunt had left me a house and a gift shop business there.

With the profits from selling our place in Sheepshead Bay, we bought a row house in a nice neighborhood in Philly. Lena was so happy again in her new house, which was sixty years old and in great condition. We bought all new furniture again. Lena turned to me after the last piece of furniture had been delivered and set up, shook a finger in my face and announced, "This is it! No more moving. We still got kids at home, and this is where we're going to raise them. Right here. No more moving!"

Display, per se, wasn't George Zafero's cup of tea. He earned a good living doing display design, but that was secondary in his mind to doing reproductions of period pieces and selling antiques. In 1967, George made fiberglass reproductions of fine furniture and antiques for the movie *Funny Girl,* and we designed, manufactured, and installed the large columns and other display items for the Ziegfeld Theatre set in the movie.

As much as George loved doing his antique reproductions, truth is that we were hard pressed to keep up with the demand for our display-design services. The bread-and-butter display-design business at Zafero Design was on the upswing over the next several years. George negotiated a contract to design and install spring displays in Lane Bryant stores coast to coast. Lane Bryant is a plus-size ladies' clothing retailer dating back to the early 1900s.

This was the first nationwide account that George ever got, and we were busy designing, manufacturing, and shipping display items all across the United States. It felt great being so busy again. We were doing so well that I bought a brand new 1970 Chevy Monte Carlo in September 1969. I think that I got the last Monte Carlo that would be sold in Philly for months, because the UAW strike at General Motors showed no sign of ending any time soon. Dealers all over the country were running out of the more popular 1970 models from GM.

George had a design portfolio of projects spanning the retail market from middle ground to high end. Major retailers on our client list were Wanamaker's, Strawbridge's, Gimbel's, Frank & Seder, and Macy's. Zafero & Company display crews did Macy's Christmas decorations and sales-floor and window displays for well over a decade. Matter of fact, it was one of our trees that someone riding up an escalator chugged a lit cigarette into, causing a massive fire.

We had to close down our display-design division for a few months because the building we were in needed major renovations. During the renovations, I did some work for RK International, a company that specialized in animated displays featuring figures of all sizes, the kind of lighted and mechanized figures that you see in bridal shops and department store window displays: elegantly dressed women, boys, and girls—the boys wearing tall top hats, the girls with velvet muffs. At the time, RK was still owned by Ron Kowalski and his delightful wife. Both were two of my favorite folks to do business with. I often recommended RK to my more upscale freelance clients when I thought that innovative animated figures might complement the seasonal displays that I was creating.

I had been back at Zafero & Co. for a little over a year when we found out that Lena was expecting again. Of course, we had mixed feelings about the news. We were worried because of the awful time Lena had when she was carrying Earl. This time around, Hal Walker's wife, Gina, came to stay with us for a while. Gina took Lena to a nutritionist and helped her plan and prepare healthier meals. The nutritionist lady also gave Lena tips on how to take time for herself to relax and to go on short walks around the neighborhood. With Gina's help, Lena had more time to relax and—lo and behold—she stopped smoking! Lena went cold turkey, which even today when I think about it, still seems nothing short of amazing, considering how long and how much she had smoked. As a pre-teen, Lena was already hooked on smoking cigarettes. She would buy cigarette papers, take cigarette butts out of ashtrays, separate out the tobacco, and roll her own smokes.

Putting up with Lena's mood swings and cravings wasn't the easiest thing I've ever done, but she was determined to avoid all of the problems that she had when she was carrying Earl. I don't think that this time around she even needed to go to the hospital for breathing treatments. A full nine months later, we were blessed with our wonderful, talented daughter, Drina, who was our pride and joy from the day she was born. She slept a lot, rarely fussed, and when she cried, her tears were soon replaced by a big smile when she was picked up, rocked back and forth, and talked to.

I don't think that Drina ever gave us a moment's trouble, and when she was older, she became the family peacemaker, really good at stepping between her brothers when they were fighting over something. By second grade, she was already reading recipes aloud and explaining the steps to her sister Varda, who had difficulty making heads or tails out of even simple instructions. Her mom or me had to help Drina with some words, but she was real good with amounts and measurements.

Lena remained an ex-smoker for a little under three years. I came home from work one evening, and Lena was puffing away. As much as we talked about her taking up smoking again, I'm still not sure what happened. Maybe stress and being the only one over twelve not smoking at family gatherings finally got to her. Even though she had started smoking again, I had to admire her for having stopped smoking when she did and for not smoking for so long.

In 1972, the NADI spring display industry show was going to be in New Orleans. We designed a twelve-foot-tall figure of a lady with a chicken wire skirt that I made at the show and filled with solid flowers. It was an 1880s look. I also had the honor of escorting the beautiful and classy representative from Lane Bryant Stores, Melanie Saenz, to the elegant dinner in her honor on the occasion of her retirement, held the first night of the show.

Miss Saenz had been the display director at Lane Bryant for over three decades and was somewhat of a legend for the quality of her displays for an apparel store catering to plus-size ladies, a market that most display folks didn't give much thought to.

I still had a lot of time on my hands to freelance, so I did some display-design work for Gordon Becker, located in Baltimore, Maryland. Mr. Becker's specialty was designing and installing seasonal displays for malls, shopping centers, and other businesses throughout the United States. Since I had a good track record with Silvestri and other major design companies, Mr. Becker was happy to have me on his design team. We sold complete Christmas trims for the common areas and exteriors of shopping centers. Installation of the displays generally went without a hitch, but when there *was* a problem, it sometimes affected the entire project.

One of Mr. Becker's sales reps sold dozens of double-sided Christmas wreaths to a large mall in Birmingham, Alabama. They were going to suspend them to hang perpendicular to the outside walls of the mall and also to line the interior space along the store fronts. By mistake, the manufacturer sent single-sided wreaths, which meant that one side of the trim would be blank, with no lighting or decorations.

Gordon Becker was a firm believer in doing whatever it took to make a client happy. In situations like this, he went so far as to say that money was no object, and that we had to come up with new designs on site and hire additional people to complete the project in plenty of time for the Christmas season. Back then, most of the store decorations were put up starting on Thanksgiving Day. That's when stores and malls were crowded with display crews crawling up on ladders and scaffolding, trying to get everything ready for the day after Thanksgiving, the start of the Christmas season.

I ran around Birmingham with my crew a few days before Thanksgiving and bought up almost every live and fake poinsettia that I could find. We put together a lot of loose artificial flowers and foliage to create enough wreaths to put on all sides of the mall, plus decorate the inside as well. We bought hundreds of feet of Silvestri Italian lights to put in and around the wreaths.

The mall management and individual stores were real happy with how my crew and I managed to put together a one-of-a-kind display treatment that really stood out. The company that owned the Birmingham mall was extremely pleased with what our crew did in the mall's fountain area. I had designed a display with an array of poinsettias in different-sized pots on a bed of blinking Italian lights.

The mall management company even decided to feature the decorated fountain area in newspaper ads and color posters encouraging folks to bring their families down to the mall to have their pictures taken with Santa Claus. I was so proud of the work that we did, and I still remember how much my crew and I enjoyed working with the mall employees to get the decorations up in time. The mall owners and local folks showed us so much fine Southern hospitality.

There was a popular country western song, "Don't Take Her, She's All I Got," that I really liked. I was pretty vocal about how much I loved that song, so much so that the display crew from one of the large anchor department stores in the mall played that song over and over on the loudspeakers while we worked putting up the decorations. I loved these folks so much: they didn't seem to have the attitudes that the display people back East often exhibited. Everybody—bosses and workers—pitched in and turned what could have been a disaster into a great success.

That's one group of people that I wished I had stayed in touch with. I don't even remember the name of the mall. So strange, not to remember the name of a place where I completed one of my most memorable and challenging display design projects! I guess like everywhere else, it was the people I worked with who I remember the most. I enjoyed working with Gordon Becker and his team so much that I continued doing holiday display projects for him whenever I had the opportunity to do some freelancing.

I really don't have a lot of favorite coworkers or clients in all of my years of working in display design or production design. I guess that might be because I was often stressed out dealing with prima donnas and tight, sometimes unrealistic deadlines. But when it comes down to the nitty gritty, I don't think that I've met any designer anywhere who enjoyed his craft as much as I did. I was obsessed with my design work, maybe even driven to doing what I had to do to see each project to completion.

I was well-liked by my coworkers, who would often come to me for advice when something they were working on just didn't look right to them, like maybe design elements that didn't quite come together to create the intended effect. One example comes to mind: At one point, I was doing some work in Chicago for George Silvestri when I got a call at Silvestri from Pancho Collados, a buddy of mine who owned The Dream Shop on the North Side of Chicago. Pancho specialized in life-sized replicas of fine art pieces—paintings and sculptures. He asked if I had time to come by and check out a display he was working on. Something didn't seem right to him, but he wasn't sure what it was. Sometimes a designer just can't put his finger on what looks kinda off in a display. He goes ahead and changes elements that are fine just as they are, overlooking the one small detail that throws the whole display off.

Mr. Silvestri and I headed over to The Dream Shop to see what the problem was. Pancho was in one of his large workrooms with some display buyers from Lord & Taylor, just in from New York City. He was working on a series of window displays for their Fifth Avenue store. One display featured a large barn with fields in the distance and thirty-inch figures dressed as medieval peasants. There was a large post with a scythe propped up against it, with little piles of wheat, bales of hay, bushels overflowing with autumn leaves, etc. The light was dim, like natural light at dusk, and one of the figures held a lantern with a flame going up and down. That was one of the new, just-on-the-market flickering light bulbs.

I looked at the whole tableau from different angles and finally said to Pancho, "Everything looks fantastic, except for the flickering light bulb, which is too large for the lantern!" We looked at each other and laughed. The folks from Lord & Taylor were beaming and looked at one another and over at the lantern just a few feet away, while Mr. Silvestri was wearing one of his trademark "gotcha" smiles. All eyes finally turned to Pancho and me. "Well, Danny, you hit the nail right on the head," Pancho finally said. "The Lord and Taylor folks love the concept and the look, everything except for the light bulb, which, as you pointed out, is just too damn big for that small lantern. That's the only size the bulb comes in, so we're just going to have to scour the display-supply places for a bigger lantern, but one still the right size for a half-life-sized figure."

During my years as a designer, whether I was following instructions provided by a client or working with an original design plan, I developed an eye for almost everything, from size and proportion to color and texture. Even when bringing to life one of my own designs, there were many times when I gained a new perspective by listening to a client's suggestions. If only I had been a better listener earlier on in my career!

I can't count the times that the competition tried to hire me away, or at least have me design something on the side for them. I came to the conclusion that my designs were sought after because of their originality and fantasy qualities. Even a small change in the design of a flower or tree can make it stand out, look familiar, and yet have a not-seen-before quality.

Most display designers sit down and make sketches of their designs and then send the sketches to the display assistants who create the finished design. I did make sketches to show my coworkers and the client, to give them an idea of the finished design. But if at some point the client was at my studio, I enjoyed doing a live demonstration of what I had in mind for their project.

I did a lot of hands-on design and worked directly with my crew and the client to produce, right in front of their eyes, live samples of the ideas in my head. Taking the time to meet with the client in person, to give them something that they could look at up close, feel the texture of and see the details, etc., usually got us the job!

18

Sins of the Father

My career was going great guns, but even when I was doing display design locally in Philly, I worked from 10 to 14 hours a day. When I finally got home, I just had a small meal and went right to bed. When we had a retail client with stores in multiple cities, I was often away for weeks at a time. The same was true when we did production design or art direction for an out-of-town movie or television show. The work was interesting but required a lot of fine-tuning and problem solving, both of which often required staying on site until all of the wrinkles were ironed out. With the overtime and traveling around, I was actually away more than I was home.

It was my wonderful wife, Lena, who bore the brunt of raising and trying to discipline our increasingly out-of-control younger boys. Lena had developed some serious physical problems: kidney disease, asthma, COPD, long bouts of fatigue. Ever since Lena had started smoking again, it was like non-stop. Now, when I look back at her manic smoking, I'm reminded of the frantic, full-speed-ahead pot smoking of the druggies in that cult movie,

Reefer Madness. She spent a lot of time wheezing, gulping air, and coughing up mucus. It probably didn't help, I guess, that I still smoked like a chimney, and almost everyone over twelve or so around Lena was a regular if not a heavy smoker.

Lena spent a lot of time resting in bed, less time keeping tabs on the kids and where they were at any given time. To be honest, Lena had tried to be more of a friend than a parent to our kids and nieces and nephews. She rarely raised her voice, and when our boys got into trouble at school or with the police, she always seemed more discombobulated or surprised than angry or eager to get to the bottom of whatever happened. She saw our boys more as victims of prejudice, profiling—whatever—than as the hoodlums they had become in my absence. Well, truth be known, my wonderful wife had never been good at dishing out discipline. So the inmates basically ran the asylum, as the old saying goes.

I was no help dealing with the kids. Between working long hours, being out of town a lot, and screwing around, I was pretty much an absent father. And I have my doubts that things would have worked out any better for my kids if I had been around more, because I usually followed Lena's script and avoided disciplining our kids. It was as if Lena and I believed that our good intentions alone would make our kids turn out ok.

Our oldest son, Andy, had spoiled us by more or less raising himself. He singlehandedly gave the lie to the old adage that if you spare the rod, you spoil the child. My good friend, Miss Ruth Janis of New York City, used to say that Andy must have been born with a built-in owner's manual. He has always been a delight. As a young kid, he was shy and pretty much kept himself to himself, but doted on his younger sister Varda.

By middle school, Andy had opened up a lot and enjoyed being with the friends he easily made. He excelled in most of his classes. In high school, he was popular and involved in a lot of extracurricular sports activities: swimming, basketball, track, and football. Andy wasn't really home enough to spend much time with his brother Lash, who was quite a bit younger. On weekends, Andy would shoot hoops with Lash, but that was about it.

Andy was the first in our entire family to finish high school. He excelled in science and sports and won all kinds of academic awards as well as ribbons and medals in swimming and track competitions. Lena and I were so proud of him, and I managed to hold on to his diploma through all of our moving around and family misadventures. I bought a nice frame for it, and it's still proudly displayed on the wall in my workspace, along with some of his medals and awards, and photos of him and his partner, Ray.

Andy has always done fine on his own, and always seems to make the right choices. He did well in his academic classes, but really enjoyed working with his hands as well as using his brain. Andy decided after he finished high school to study welding at a local trade school. He did really well, and had more than a few job offers. But instead of going to work right away, Andy went on a road trip with a pal to San Diego, where he enlisted in the U.S. Navy. With his welding training and his love of water and swimming, it was no surprise that Andy became a Navy diver.

During his long career as a Navy diver-welder in an Underwater Construction Team, Andy cleared underwater debris from harbors and maintained Navy ships, berths, and docks. After he retired from the Navy, he started a marine welding business with Ray and a couple of Navy buddies. I read how dangerous underwater welding can be, but Andy and Ray are doing just fine.

Except for Lena and me and his sisters, Andy distances himself as much as possible from the rest of the family. He never knew his great-uncle Stefan, but seems to be living his life according to his own version of his great-uncle's take on how to live a happy and successful life: Don't have kids, and distance yourself from family bullshit.

When Andy graduated from high school, Lash was almost thirteen years old, and Earl was going on five. Lash was already hanging out with a bunch of young wise guys from middle school who were bad news all around: into drinking, smoking pot, doing street drugs, and stealing to support their bad habits.

While visiting us in Philly in the late 1970's, my cousin Peggy Boswell went to use the bathroom and discovered Lash in the bathtub with a pal, sniffing spray paint from a plastic bag. This was just one in a series of events that eventually made me think that my kids needed a full-time dad in their lives.

By the early 1980s, my youngest son, Earl, aka Earl the Pearl, was old enough to imitate some of his older brother Lash's bad behavior. Lash would egg Earl on, daring him to do things like grab a lady's purse and run for it when they were at one of the local malls. Earl would creep up behind the owner of the local bodega to steal packs of cigarettes while Lash was at the counter making small talk. It wasn't long before he graduated to sniffing spray paint from a sandwich bag and smoking dope. When Earl was thirteen, a neighbor came home unexpectedly and caught his daughter and my boy having sex. Soon enough, he had a group of little wannabe hoodlums following him around.

Both boys were now pretty much out of control, and Lena's health was getting worse. I knew that I couldn't go on burying myself in my work and hoping that somehow everything would work out. Lena and I were thinking that maybe getting out of Philly, leaving behind the drug use and bad influences that our boys were so drawn to, would help our boys regain control of their lives and give us more time together as a family. Lena and I even talked about going back on the road for awhile, because the traveling-show circuit had worked wonders for our family life years ago.

When I was young, traveling shows were great places to raise kids and have a decent family life. The family unit was very strong on the traveling show circuit. You worked together, lived together, and ate together every day. Everyone looked after the kids. It was pretty rare that parents didn't know where their kids were and what they were doing.

Traveling show life provided great learning opportunities and role models for kids. My family traveled all over the United States when we were on the road with my grandparents' traveling theater or with the Sherman Bros. Carnival. We experienced all that big exciting cities had to offer and enjoyed the slower pace of life in small towns. We met carnies from all over the world, played with kids who spoke different languages, learned about their family life and customs, and heard stories about where they were from and how they came to America.

Everyone had a job, whether it was keeping house and raising kids, performing under the circus big top, operating rides, running a game booth, setting up for special events, selling tickets or food, repurposing or repairing equipment, and setting up/taking down the midway. At an early age, kids started learning about the work that their folks did. As we got older, we mastered the skills that would one day help us be self-sufficient and earn a good living.

Even before I could read or write, I was put to work making artificial flowers, foliage, and arrangements for my grandparents' traveling dinner theater. I also helped with the cleanup whenever the men were making theatrical sets or outdoor furniture. As I learned more and took on more responsibility, I settled into a routine that became a path to a good career. I worked as a display designer and eventually became a broadcast art director.

My brother Bill started his training as a mechanic by being "in charge of the tools" when our dad was repairing cars or equipment. He was soon working right alongside Dad. During WWII, Bill trained as an aviation mechanic, a career that he pursued in civilian life after the war.

If someone became too old or ill to work, they were taken care of by their family. I never heard of any older or handicapped folks living on their own or being put in a care home.

Then a bunch of "enlightened" and know-it-all social workers came along, and told the school authorities that carnival people didn't know how to raise their own children, and that the teachers who traveled on the carnival circuit didn't teach us "useful" subjects. I guess that the "education reformers" knew more about raising kids than our parents did! Traveling show kids wound up being raised by school teachers, school counselors, and social workers—strangers who didn't know anything about our customs and way of life.

My daughters learned that dressing and speaking differently made them outsiders to be physically attacked and called every name in the book. Our sons learned how not to have much respect for others or themselves.

Well, anyway, you can't go back to the way things used to be, and our sons needed help *now.* We decided that moving to a small town might be the answer, someplace where we could put down roots, where the young people weren't into heavy drinking and drugs. After talking with friends and family and spending some time with family there, Elkton, Maryland, seemed like it might be a good choice. We had cousins in a licensed and well-respected blacktop and sealcoating business there, and other relatives who made all kinds of lawn and porch furniture in the spring and summer months. I had built outdoor furniture and done paving work before, pretty much since I was a teenager, but those were temporary jobs, or work that I helped with when we were visiting family. This time around, if at some point I decided to do some seasonal display work, Elkton was just a short drive from the city of Newark, Delaware, and just over an hour from Baltimore.

We rented out the house in Philly to one of my coworkers, and the rent we got just covered the monthly mortgage payment. We bought a mobile home and headed to Elkton.

What I had made in one week doing display and set design, my relatives made in just one day doing asphalt and blacktop work and sealing driveways. It wasn't long before I got used to the regular hours and work routine. Business was good, and I had more time to spend with Lena and the kids. Every day was quite a heavy load on my brain and body, almost like learning how to walk again.

It was a new and challenging way of life for my family. There was a lot of hard physical work, but I felt that now I was being a better husband and partner to Lena, and a better father to my kids. I started taking Lash with me to sealcoat driveways and parking lots.

Most people don't know much about sealcoating and asphalt work, and unscrupulous paving companies take advantage of that to make what is actually a straightforward process sound like rocket science. An oil-based sealer is used on asphalt driveways and parking lots so that rain doesn't seep through to loosen the underlying layers, freeze, and cause the asphalt to expand and crack. The asphalt sealer actually waterproofs the asphalt and beautifies it. The older asphalt gets, the grayer it becomes. It loses its resilience and starts to crack. The sealer leaves a beautiful black finish on the asphalt and protects it at the same time. If the work is done right, it will last for several seasons. We always used the best quality asphalt sealer. We used it straight, without mixing water in with the oil. A lot of fly-by-night itinerant pavers try to save money by diluting the sealer. So we tried to reassure potential clients by showing them our paperwork and testimonials with addresses of completed jobs so that they could check out the quality of our work.

We did jobs in a lot of different neighborhoods in and around Elkton, but I wouldn't be honest if I didn't admit that sometimes it was a hard sell. In good weather, most folks were happy enough with what they had: gray driveways and parking lots with fading stripes. But after we sealed a few driveways here and there, the neighbors would see the beautiful black color and want their parking area or driveway to look the same. Most shopping centers already knew the advantages of seal coating and were glad to deal with a local company that would give them a fair and honest bid and do quality work. Some had been burned by dishonest out-of-state pavers; they were a hard sell until we showed them pictures of our work and gave them references from people that they knew.

On the side, I helped my in-laws make wooden lawn and patio furniture, using two-by-fours and one-inch wood. Sometimes we would head out to get some birch and make fancier chairs, tables, and benches for homes with covered porches and verandahs.

Like I said, I had a lot more time to spend with my family. But after just a few months, Lash wasn't home any more than he had been in Philly. As soon as we finished work, Lash disappeared, usually saying that he was going over to so-and-so's place to shoot some hoops. Lash was pretty good at sports, so I didn't give it much thought.

I'd been doing sealcoating for almost three years now, and we thought that we were doing fine. Then, my niece Effie Wheeler came to town for a music festival and told Lena and me that she had run into Lash at an after-party there and had seen him smoking some weird-smelling crap with a couple of guys who looked and acted real spaced out. Soon after that, our next door neighbors spotted our boys out in front of a notorious druggie hangout downtown, smoking with some guys who looked like hoodlums. Over the next few years, Lash was pulled in at least once a month by the cops for questioning about one petty crime after another. Lash and his buddies were excellent liars and covered for one another. The cops didn't manage to make any of the charges stick.

Finally, Lash's luck ran out, and he really screwed up. Lash and a doper buddy hatched a scheme to steal a bunch of commercial laundry equipment from a nearby warehouse where the buddy had worked long enough to learn the routine—like at what times during the night the rent-a-cops made their rounds—and managed to get a set of keys to the place. They rented a flatbed truck, and one night with the help of some buddies, they stole a lot of the washing machines and other heavy-duty cleaning equipment, loaded up the flatbed, and drove off toward Newark to sell the stolen property to a *fence* (a person who buys and sells stolen goods) there.

When the truck's differential went out, Lash and his pal left the truck on the side of the road and caught a ride home with their buddies. Lash went back the next morning for the truck with a tow truck. The cops were waiting for him, and he wound up doing some hard time for grand theft.

Lash cut himself off from the family during his time in prison. He didn't want us to visit him there, never asked for money, and never wrote or called on the telephone. Lena was heartbroken, and I was disgusted with Lash for shaming the family. Once again, it seemed that my sons' behavior proved that I had been a pretty lousy dad.

I started to think that maybe this move to a smaller town hadn't been such a great idea. Lena and I shared with each other what each of us had been thinking for quite a while: that our well-intentioned decision to leave Philly had in fact been a really bad one.

I missed my design work, and Lena was in bad health and only getting worse from trying to take on too much. She had to have breathing treatments, and at one point, her kidney function went way down. Lena was having difficulty with cooking and housework, and Earl was acting up at home and at school and seemed to be on the same path that his brother had taken to becoming a wannabe outlaw.

I thought that we were at the lowest point—making daily visits to Earl in juvenile detention after his arrest for trying to buy street drugs from an undercover cop—when I was injured on the job. My right leg was badly burned when it got splashed with hot asphalt. Now we we in a situation where I wasn't going to be able to work for a while. It was really difficult not to tempt fate by asking myself, *what else could go wrong?*

I was about halfway through a long course of physical therapy on my leg when I received a life-changing telephone call from Daniel Finzi-Baccaglini, one of my favorite designers at Silvestri Design in Chicago. Daniel asked me if I would be interested in coming to work for him as the lead designer in the display-design division at Affinity Design, his display-design and production-design company in Chicago. He said that he would provide any help and equipment necessary for me to come to work for him as soon as possible.

I couldn't say yes fast enough! As soon as my doctor released me to do light work, Lena and I sold the trailer in Elkton, put the house in Philly up for sale, and headed back to Chicago with Drina and her pet menagerie in tow. Earl would join us in Chicago when he was released from juvenile detention in Elkton. I felt guilty about leaving Earl behind, but I also wasn't looking forward to him coming to live with us in Chicago. I figured that if Earl was going to get set up and arrested in Elkton, Maryland, of all places, he was probably brain damaged enough from sniffing model airplane glue and spray paint to try, try again anywhere we lived.

You can't run from your problems; we should have realized that by now. When your kids get involved in drug use, finding a place where street drugs aren't easy to get is pretty much impossible. Drugs were, and are, everywhere. So the cycle of drug use and stealing that started in one place just starts up again wherever you wind up. What we found out was that drug birds of a feather flock together, whether you live in a big city or a small town.

Lash and Earl hooked up with local drug users, dealers, and petty criminals anywhere we lived or visited for any length of time. Lash also had a nasty and expensive habit of getting involved with older women who were either druggies themselves or enjoyed the steady flow of money that my sick boy, even while still at home, earned from selling drugs and stealing to pay for his bad habits.

Some wag once said that "there are no victims, only volunteers." Well, that's probably too broad a statement to always be true. But in my case, I had been so focused on my work that, like a fool, I gave both of my younger boys enough money to get high on drugs and wind up in bad company and bad relationships wherever we lived. When they got into trouble with the law, I threw away more money trying to pay fines or get them out of jail, always thinking that this time around, they had learned their lesson. All they learned was that, like so many other Gypsy parents, Lena and I would do almost anything to get them back home, where the stealing and drug use continued to impact all of us.

19

The Tree That the Acorn Fell Far From

My dad, Tom Miller, passed away twenty-one years ago today, on August 19, 1979. He was ninety-nine years old and still pretty sharp. He lived in our big old house in Cicero, Illinois, with my mom and a caregiver. No way was my dad going to wind up in a care home that smelled of poop and Lysol. My mom, my wife and me, my siblings, and visiting relatives made sure of that! My dad enjoyed being the center of attention and took full advantage of the almost daily presence of family and friends who came to visit and do for him.

Doing for someone, being there for them when they're ill, or just pitching in to help them around the house or with a job (making furniture, taming horses, doing black top, etc.,) is an old Gypsy custom. My dad never took to city living and missed his life on the road with traveling shows. On the road, there was a sense of purpose and camaraderie that living in the city just seemed to stifle, for Dad anyway. When my dad was younger and healthy as an ox, he was quick to get out of the everyday rat race at a moment's notice to head out onto the open road with me and my brother Tony in tow. Most often, we'd pitch in to help uncles or cousins make and sell wooden lawn furniture, repair awnings, finish a sealcoating or blacktop job, or do for a sick relative.

As he got older, my dad spent more time propped up in bed, especially in the winter when his arthritis acted up. He passed his time reading, listening to music, and reminiscing with family and other visitors. Well, he also took a lot of naps, short ones, because he said that he was afraid of missing something. Boy, did my dad's eyes twinkle whenever a pretty visiting nurse came by to check up on him! And Dad's eyes really lit up, and he smiled and sat up as straight as he could whenever my mom came into the room he was holding court in. As shy and quiet as my mom was, she was always kind and welcoming to visitors. Dad wasn't at all shy or quiet, and he totally relished his role as the family patriarch—always on, always kicking up a little trouble whenever he had the chance.

My business partner, Mike Cohen, is back in New York City attending yet another display-design convention, so tonight I'm doing my own reminiscing, remembering a lot of the stories my dad used to tell me when we took off to do for a family member or to earn some extra cash.

It was on these trips and day jobs that I learned so much about the Miloradovich clan, their lives over in the Old Country, and everything my dad saw and experienced when he set out on his own as a young man to travel around Western Europe. He would get so excited telling me about his adventures on the road that sometimes I had to reach over and grab the steering wheel because his hands were up in the air, going every which way. The details changed sometimes as he retold his stories over the years. Except for when he told me how he met my mom, joined her family's traveling theater show, and finally won her hand in marriage. Whenever my dad talked about my mom, the details—her beautiful singing voice, her shy smile, his love for her—those were spot on every time

My Dad's Story, in My Own Words

The Miloradovitch clan was originally from what is now part of Romania, and for generations the Gypsies had been slaves there.

No, they weren't serfs or anything like that; they were actual slaves—the property of wealthy landowners, nobles, and Orthodox monasteries—until sometime in the 1850s. After they were freed, my dad's people went on the road and finally settled in northwestern Bosnia, in Eastern Europe, where my dad was born. Even today, some Gypsies whose ancestors lived for so many generations in Romania refer to themselves as *Ludar* or *Ludod* or *Ludad*—Romanian Gypsies.

Mosha (Grandfather) Dragosh Miloradovitch was a well-known fiddler and bear trainer in Bosnia. This was way back when Bosnia was part of the Ottoman Empire. Gypsies had to pay a special tax to the Ottoman officials. While there was some discrimination, the situation for Gypsies was generally better than in many West and Central European countries during the same period, where Gypsies often faced severe persecution, expulsion, and pogroms.

Mosha Dragosh came from a famous Romanian clan of musicians, horse traders, and animal trainers. He wanted my dad to follow in his footsteps as a fiddler and bear trainer, but one time when my dad was feeding a bear, the bear swiped at his left hand with a paw, and he lost the pinky finger.

Dad had never been particularly gung-ho on becoming a bear trainer, so he used his injured hand as an excuse not to have anything more to do with training bears or any other animals for that matter. He had a real passion for playing the fiddle, and he set out to play as best he could without the missing pinky finger. It wasn't all that easy, but with a lot of self-discipline and help from a fiddle player from a nearby village, Dad adjusted just fine to playing the fiddle without a left-hand pinky finger, and he enjoyed playing all kinds of music his entire life.

From time to time, Dad helped his cousin Esme and his grand-uncle Rodak build sheds, put up fences, repair wagons, carts, and vardos, and he really enjoyed the work. So when Grand-Uncle Rodak offered him a job as an apprentice carpenter, he went that route. At first, he was sort of the cleanup guy, but as he learned the ropes, he began working right alongside his cousin and uncle. Dad set his mind to learning everything he could about woodworking and carpentry. He spent most of his adult life on and off the road working with wood: making repairs, working in construction, and making very fine rustic willow or birch furniture. Somehow along the way, he also developed a real aptitude for working with canvas and rope: repairing traveling-show tents, nautical sails and rigging, and making, repairing, and installing awnings. His talents were much admired and sought after in traveling shows, where a good deal of maintenance and repair work is needed to keep the show on the road.

When my dad was a teenager over in Bosnia, he was taught how to read and write by the Catholic priests in his village. My dad was shy when he was young. He was very intelligent and a devout Catholic to boot. My dad's confidence and ego grew later when he left his village and traveled throughout Europe. My Aunt Ina told me once that the priests were impressed with my dad's strong faith and smarts and took him under their wing because they hoped that someday he would follow in their footsteps and become a priest. That never happened, in part because my dad liked the ladies too much and wanted a family.

Dad became an avid reader, and through the years, he gained a lot of general knowledge from reading and having conversations with folks from different walks of life. Even as an old guy, my dad kept abreast of politics and world affairs. Although he never actually attended a real school, he could hold his own with people who had.

When my dad turned sixteen, my grandparents decided that it was high time for him to get married. There was no casual dating, no courting back then. Young Gypsy men and girls were kept strictly apart and never spent time alone together unless they were related. Most of the girls in those days were—like my mother—thirteen to sixteen years old when they got married.

Back then, in Europe and even in America, Gypsy marriages were near one hundred percent arranged, either by the families or by a real actual matchmaker. Today, arranged marriages are still the norm, but marriages based on a romantic relationship are becoming more common.

Arranged marriages can happen several ways: If a family is new someplace, they might opt for the services of a matchmaker who knows pretty much all of the families with a young man or young woman the right age. If the family is an established one and has a lot of connections in the local community, the parents might take it upon themselves to find the right match for their son or daughter.

Parents could begin the process when a boy and girl were not even teenagers yet. They might approach the parents directly, saying something like: "You have a nice girl. We have a nice young man. We know each other, our families." You respect their family, admire their people, so you say, "Well, when the children get older, maybe they can get together and get married."

My grandparents were close to another family in their village, and they were set on one of the younger daughters as a match for my dad. Mosha and Baba were all ready to invite the parents over for a special meal and ask them if they would agree to a marriage between their daughter and my dad.

Dad wasn't interested at all in this girl that his parents were going to go and ask for. And he knew his cousin Dervo had talked with her at village gatherings and had romantic feelings for her. Dad loved his cousin like a brother and didn't want anyone or anything to come between them. My dad figured if he wasn't there, this girl and his cousin might get married, which they eventually did. Dad hadn't been happy with his family life for a long time, and now that his folks were trying to marry him off to a girl he wasn't interested in, he knew that he had to do something pretty quick to avoid more problems for himself and Dervo.

For a couple of years, my dad had been giving serious thought to leaving his scruffy little village as soon as he finished his carpentry apprenticeship with Grand-Uncle Rodak. He fell asleep almost every night dreaming of traveling around Europe with a circus and seeing with his own eyes what the world beyond Bosnia had to offer.

Dad told Cousin Dervo about his dream of joining a traveling show and seeing Europe, and he told him that he hoped to leave soon. My dad shared with Dervo what to tell his parents after he took off: He wanted to see as much of the world as he could before he got married. He would be back someday, after he found a better place for himself and the family to live.

One night, after a terrible argument with Mosha Dragosh, Dad just up and decided that was the night that he would leave home to try to make it on his own in the world. He gathered together in a canvas knapsack his small nest egg, some bread and fruit, some clothes, the fiddle that Uncle Rodak had helped him make, and a few of the books that the village priests had given him. My dad crawled through his bedroom window onto the first floor roof, then carefully lowered himself to the garden below.

Dad walked quietly along the garden wall, then quickly made his way down the hill to the road that led to the provincial capital. From there, my dad headed to the Bosnian coast, catching rides on farm wagons on their way to or from market or on Gypsy circus wagons heading to their next spot. Dad did day labor on the way, already feeling a sense of freedom and distance from the poverty and monotony of his village. When my dad finally arrived on the Bosnian coast, he crossed the Adriatic Sea by barge to Italy.

Dad fell in love with Italy and the Italian people, their culture, ways, and food. Dad joined a traveling show, a circus that was run by a Romanian family. My dad worked with a crew of carnies responsible for the upkeep of the big top, the ropes and rigging, and all of the equipment that was used by the performers in the various acts.

While traveling with the circus, Dad met, courted, and married a beautiful Italian Gypsy girl, Violetta Orfei, a talented acrobat who performed with her dad and two brothers. Unfortunately, his young wife died giving birth. My dad said that he was so distressed and heartbroken about the deaths of his wife and baby that he thought he was going to go crazy with grief.

My dad left the circus and traveled around on his own for a while. He finally went back on the road, traveling with several different carnivals and circuses. Dad traveled through almost every country in western Europe, even as far as England and

Ireland. He was pretty quick to pick up what he could of the different languages and learned as much as possible about the countries he traveled through.

Dad was on the road with various traveling shows for over five years. He sent home letters and postcards describing his new life and his many adventures on the road. Almost no older folks in those small Bosnian villages could read or write, and this was especially true of Gypsies. So teachers from the village school or a priest would come to my grandparents' house for Sunday dinner and read the letters to my family.

By the time my dad decided to come back to his people, he had learned a lot about the world outside his little village in Bosnia. In his travels, Dad had learned some English, French, and German, and became fluent in that most beautiful of languages, Italian! He met circus people from all over the world. Some had relatives and friends who had immigrated to the United States, and my dad heard enough about life in America to make him want to learn more.

He talked to all kinds of people he met in his travels, asking them what they knew about life in America. When the circus played a larger town or city, Dad would visit bookstores and lending libraries and find books about life in America. He started dreaming about what life must be like in America, just as back in Bosnia he had dreamt about joining a circus and traveling around Western Europe.

No, the streets in America weren't paved with gold, which was an actual rumor, I guess, but it was a place where anyone willing to work hard, including Gypsies, could own land, a house, and earn a good living. Finally, his mind was made up: When he returned home, he was going to try to persuade his folks and siblings to go with him to find a better life in America!

My dad's clan wasn't all that happy in Bosnia. They were far better off than they had been in Romania, but there was a lot of discrimination from some members of the other ethnic groups. After a lot of back and forth discussion when my dad returned home, his folks, brothers and sisters, and some aunts and uncles decided to come to America. The plan was for the rest of the clan to follow if everything worked out in America for my dad and his family.

In the last decades of the nineteenth century, and into the early 1900s, when steamships made travel across the Atlantic Ocean faster, safer, and cheaper, many Gypsies worked whatever jobs they could find to make enough money for a boat ticket to the East Coast of the United States. Among the lucky arrivals in the New World in July 1903 were my dad, his immediate family, and other members of the Miloradovitch clan from Bosnia.

My dad and his family put down roots in Chicago and became what Gypsies call settled people, no longer on the move from place to place. The Miloradovitch men among the new arrivals were circus and traveling-show people, musicians, animal trainers, metal and wood workers—wood carvers, carpenters, furniture makers—builders, and painters for the most part. The Miloradovitch women were mostly what we call today homemakers, busy with keeping house, cooking and baking, and raising kids. Some also did fine hand sewing, weaving, peddling, and fortune telling.

Dad and his older brother Gheorghe hired out as day laborers, started putting money aside almost from the get-go, and eventually started an awning and outdoor furniture business. After a year or so, my dad married an Italian Gypsy girl whose family had hired him and his brother to do some remodeling at their home and to make awnings for their small grocery store. The marriage didn't work out, and it didn't last long at all because my dad's new wife turned out to be a flirt and then some!

After she married my dad, the young woman became interested in another man, an older and wealthier gadjo, and shamed my dad, our family and hers by openly having an affair with the older gent, like sometimes staying overnight at his place. Well, back then, that kind of behavior was pretty much unheard of, whether the woman was married or not. It was the old double standard: Some Gypsy men had affairs, usually very discreet, and almost always with non-Gypsy women.

There was no chance that anything serious would come of these affairs, because marriage between a Gypsy woman and a non-Gypsy was pretty much forbidden in the Gypsy community. A Gypsy woman who married a gadjo would be disowned by her family, shunned by other Gypsies and be forced to leave, never to be mentioned again. Any child would wind up being raised by grandparents or other relatives.

Anyway, my dad, to save face and to not get stuck with a kid fathered by some other guy, divorced his wife. And so, my dad might very well have been the first Gypsy in America to actually go to court and get a divorce. These days, like affairs, it's not so rare, and it's fairly common in communities of settled Gypsies, who have left the road to put down roots in a town or city. Dad was probably not even thinking about marrying again until he saw my mom for the first time. I guess it was sort of a one-sided infatuation because it was quite a while before my dad actually met my mom!

In its third season on the Midwest Circuit, the Vano Family Travelling Theatre had a long run in Chicago's Lincoln Park. It was there that a frequent visitor to the dinner pavilion—Tom Miller, my dad—first saw a slender and pretty young Italian Gypsy girl with the most beautiful singing voice he had ever heard—Elena Vano, my mom! Whenever she and her sisters were the featured act in one of the shows, my dad would sit all by himself at a table near the stage. After taking in just a few of the shows, my dad was already telling himself that he was going to marry the beautiful young woman with a voice like a singer on a radio show.

The whole setup at the Vano Family Travelling Theatre—being entertained while you ate a fancy dinner in a beautiful setting—was pretty exotic on the traveling show or carnival circuit back then.

My mom really stood out in the song and dance numbers and musical plays because of her beautiful singing voice. Mom was only fourteen at the time, but my dad didn't find that out right away. In fact, she was really mature-looking, and he just assumed that she was probably in her early twenties.

Dad went to a bunch of the vaudeville shows and even some of the musical plays while the traveling theater was in Lincoln Park. Whenever he tried to invite the talented young lady's folks to dine with him, the request was politely but firmly refused.

The traveling show was due to leave in a few weeks when my dad decided that he had to make some kind of contact with whoever was in charge of the entertainment, make an attempt to meet the parents of the young woman he was infatuated with and tell them of his interest in her. Well, knowing my dad, I guess he was pretty insistent, and finally her folks agreed to join him at his table one evening between performances.

That evening turned out to be the clincher in his decision to ask my mom's parents for permission to marry her. I remember hearing as a teenager that the first time my dad asked if he could marry my mom, her people said no. They wouldn't even consider promising to give their fourteen-year-old daughter to my dad when she was old enough to marry. They didn't think that my dad was suitable because he had been married before, twice over, with the last marriage ending in divorce. But they liked Dad, and they were impressed with his honesty and his many skills, which they could make use of in their traveling theater show.

Nonna Rosa and Nonno Manfri put my dad to work as a carpenter and mechanic for the rest of their stay in Chicago. After only a few weeks, they were impressed with his ability to build sets, rehab concession stands, repair everything from broken furniture to ripped canvas tents, and anything mechanical. In that short time, they grew to really like and trust my dad, and offered him a job on the road with the traveling theater company.

Over the next year, my mom's parents grew fonder of my dad and came to respect him and the sincerity of his affection for my mom. Finally, after my dad had carried the torch for my mom long enough, I guess, in their eyes, her folks finally gave in and let my mom and dad get married.

With my dad's help, Nonna and Nonno made a lot of changes to the traveling theater over the years. They added attractions that families could enjoy for not a lot of money, which appealed to families with kids. When I came along, the show was still following a popular circuit, going from east to west through the Midwest, then west to east, heading to South Carolina or Florida for winter quarters, where the company would make repairs and take on new performers and acts. The furthest west we usually went, I think, was Kansas City. This route took us to the small towns where we were a popular source of family-oriented entertainment.

After my grandparents retired and my family moved to the Chicago area, my dad got the travel bug from time to time, and we'd go back on the road for a while. But Chicago was always the place we returned to, and it was the place we called home.

Show and Tell

Right around the time of my daughter Drina's eighth birthday, Lena and I took Drina and the rest of our little brood to spend a few days with my folks. My mom and a couple of aunties prepared a huge Italian feast, and Mom baked and decorated Drina's favorite treat, a chocolate cake with buttercream icing.

Dad sat in his favorite chair in the living room and paged through the Vano family photo album that Drina had fetched for him from his study. "All right, you *hotchi-witchies* (hedgehogs), git over here and settle down. I want to show you some photos taken over the years of your Nonna and Nonno's traveling show, and picture postcards from all over. Most of these photos was taken in the early nineteen thirties, and we developed the photos in our own traveling darkroom. They was all black and white, because that's all we could work with. Color didn't become popular until the late 1940s, and for color photographs, folks had to go to a real photo shop. But your grand-uncles did a real good job, and folks could take home family pictures the same day.

"The Great Depression was getting worse and worse. Times was bad, real bad, and folks was short on money to spend on having a good time, getting out of the house and forgetting the rat race for a few hours. Not everybody had the money to enjoy an evening of entertainment and a fancy sit-down dinner. So I sold your Nonna and Nonno on making some changes to the traveling show, changes that would attract more families that didn't have a lot of money in their wallets but still wanted to treat their kiddies and themselves to a good time now and then. I designed a new amusement area. It was small, but there was something for everyone. There was carnival rides, food booths, a bandstand for special events like weddings and family celebrations, games of skill, and even some of what is known as *thrill acts*."

Drina raised her hand—like she was in school—and asked, "Mosha Tom, so what's that, the last thing you said?"

"Oh, you mean thrill acts? Well, those are still around, even today with television and all. We had fire eaters, sword swallowers, and contortionists—folks who could twist themselves all up into a ball—and knife throwers. A pretty gal who was part of the act stood against a wooden background with her legs and arms and the fingers on her hands spread apart, and the knife guy threw knives in a pattern that missed all of her body and even landed like between her fingers. Well, folks tried to figure out how he did that."

Our son Lash was quick to ask, "Well, Mosha, how *did* he manage to do that? I'll bet if I saw that, I could figure it out."

My dad turned all solemn-looking and sat up straight as he turned to the next page of photos in the old album. "Lash, my boy, some things is just like they seem. Sometimes there's nothing to figure out."

Lash scowled and shifted his feet around until Lena leaned over and in a loud whisper told him to be still and behave.

Drina smiled her shy smile and said, "Mosha Tom, what are games of skill? That sounds like some kind of contest!"

"So, Drina, by far the most popular game of skill is still something called the *high striker*, a game where players swing a mallet to hit a target at the bottom of a wooden tower, sending a weight up a wire to ring a bell at the top of the tower. The force of the swing determines how high the weight goes. The high striker is a very good concession for a carnival. It's a big money-maker, because there's always some young man who wants to show off and impress his girl with his strength."

Drina was perched at Dad's side and reached down and

pointed at a photo of a tent that looked like a tiny big top. "Mosha Tom, what's this? It's not much higher than those ladies standing in front of it. Gosh, is that Bisnonna (*Ital.:* "Great-Grandmother") Rosa, all dressed up for Halloween or something?"

Dad chuckled and reached up and tried to tug on Drina's right ear. She pulled back, laughing, and steadied herself against the arm of my dad's big overstuffed chair. "Hah! Missed again! That was no Halloween costume, Drina. That was your bisnonna Rosa dressed for work! She was a very respected clairvoyant. She was no fake storefront fortune teller. She had a real, God-given gift for seeing into other people's lives and giving them good advice.

"Wherever we had a spot—wherever we was playing—we would set up a colorful little tent with big tassels at the four corners and a lighted glass globe at the top of the roof pitch. We put up a sign that said 'Madame Rosa will show you your life's path' in beautiful calligraphy. That's real fancy handwriting that older kids learn in art class at school. Your grandma Elena's mom, your great-grandma Rosa, was known as Madame Rosa. She told fortunes for many years—the first time, I think, at the 1904 world's fair in St. Louis. Years later, when the President's wife, First Lady Eleanor Roosevelt, went to Linda Vista, California, to dedicate one of the first real shopping centers in the whole United States, she had her palm read and her fortune told by your bisnonna Rosa. Over the years, your bisnonna had a lot of important clients: politicians, politicians' wives, other bigwigs, even some movie stars."

I had to stifle a laugh. My dad was a religious man, so I don't know how he reconciled that with his mother-in-law's career as a clairvoyant and psychic. I do know that there are a lot of people—and not just ladies—who even today believe all of that hocus-pocus stuff and are willing to pay a lot of money to journey into The Great Unknown. Hahahaha! Well, I suppose that the believers of this or that "true religion" have killed a lot more people—probably up into the many millions by now—than folks who have followed the advice of a Gypsy psychic.

When we left the traveling theater to settle in Chicago, Nonna

Rosa and—years later—my sister Nettie, put advertisements for their clairvoyant services in ladies' magazines and all of the local newspapers. When I was old enough to get a driver license, I used to take Nonna Rosa to meet with her fancy lady clients who lived in some pretty swanky neighborhoods in and around Chicago. I never listened in or nothing, but I got the impression that most of these clients were widow ladies who were just lonely.

Well, anyway, we finally got the kids into their winter coats, checked Lash's pockets for anything that might have "fallen in" there, said our adoos, and headed home. It was just a short drive, and in warmer weather, it was a pleasant walk on wide sidewalks, under leafy old trees along streets lined with nicer older well-tended family homes. My folks had done more than okay in life. Although theirs had not always been an easy life, it had been for many years now a good one.

Mom told us later that my dad hadn't enjoyed a visit so much in a long time. She said that he fell asleep that night with a little smile on his lips, a smile that was still there the next morning, when he wouldn't wake up.

20

Just Good Buddies

I used to say that my screwed-up druggie ex-son-in-law, Curtis Wheeler, had fathered "four kids, plus two": four kids with my youngest daughter, Drina, plus two born to two other women while he was married to Drina. I guess he'd get too drunk, or too high on street drugs, to manage putting on a condom without breaking it or rolling it up into a useless little ball of latex. Curtis was, in his own father's opinion, a loser: "He showed up with a small dish when the brains was handed out, so he doesn't have a lot up there to work with," his long-suffering father would say, as true the hundredth time he said it as it had been the very first time, when Curtis was caught sniffing model airplane glue in the boys' bathroom at St. Rose of Lima School, in Chula Vista, California.

Soon after Drina and Curtis settled in Scott's Breech, Curtis started hanging out with his good buddy, Terry Skinner, another loser, who he had met on a roofing job while working as a day laborer. Some losers have big plans which never seem to pan out, and they always wind up back at square one. Not so with Curtis and Terry. Their big plan, as it became obvious over the years, was to go hunting and fishing as much as possible, work as little as possible, stay high, and commit serial adultery with any woman in the tri-county area who was dumb enough to fall for their romantic bullshit. That plan actually worked out pretty well for them!

Before marrying Curtis, Drina had a lot going for her and was on track to be the first girl in the family to finish high school. She was popular with the other kids at school, even though she chose not to socialize one-on-one with her male classmates away from school. So how, you might ask, did Drina—artistic, bright, and talented—wind up married to Curtis?

Drina and Curtis are third cousins on my dad's side of the family. Being family, it was ok for Curtis to give our girl a ride, take her shopping, or go to a movie with her and not raise any eyebrows. At one point, Curtis had dropped his niece Selina off at Sunday school and offered to give Drina a ride home from church. They wound up going to the movies with a couple of my nieces a few nights later. On the way home, my nieces went their way, and Curtis and Drina got out of his truck at a nearby park and sat at a picnic table to talk about a big wedding that they were both helping set up.

To cut to the chase, Curtis forced himself on our girl right then and there in the park, in a maintenance shed. Drina told Lena and me later—after she found out that she was pregnant—that Curtis had started kissing on her, and that before she knew what was happening, one thing had led to another.

Well, Lena and I weren't happy about Drina and Curtis getting married, but we felt at the time that our hands were tied. Abortion was out of the question, and we didn't want Drina's predicament to be grist for the Gypsy rumor mill for years to come, spoken of in whispers every time a truck full of Gypsies in the know drove by the park where Curtis forced himself on our girl. Curtis seemed genuinely remorseful, and Drina was looking forward to being a mom.

Drina gave birth to a beautiful baby girl about eight months after the wedding, and settled into her daily routine of keeping house, cooking and baking, gardening, and doting on her firstborn. She had a lot of help from her sister, Varda, and her cousins. Drina even found time to babysit, do fine sewing and alterations, and teach Sunday school.

Curtis and Terry would take off and go hunting as often as they could manage to get away. They lived in different counties, but in or out of whatever hunting season, they'd spend as much time hunting as they could. To get extra money for their hunting trips, Curtis would make outdoor furniture with his dad and take Drina peddling in the poorer neighborhoods every month, after the folks there had received their government checks. Curtis and Terry both spent a lot of money on fancy big-game firepower: rifles, shotguns, and crossbows.

I had been a partner at Affinity Design for some years now, and still had no desire to retire or cut back on my workload. I was busier than ever, working on projects throughout the entire United States. But through the years, I visited Drina and my grandkids as often as I could for holidays and family get-togethers. I was around enough to notice that Curtis and Terry sure went hunting and fishing together a lot. They must have been the unluckiest hunters and fishermen in all of North America, because the big top-loading freezer on the front porch at Drina and Curtis's place was usually pretty empty.

I started to wonder what Curtis and Terry were up to one time when I was visiting Drina and the kids with Mike Cohen, who at that point was one of my project managers. This was my birthday week, and I wanted to spend some time with Drina and my grandkids. Mike and I also planned to meet with one of our production-design teams working on set construction and decoration for a new television series to be shot on location about a half-hour's drive from Scott's Breech.

Mike and I were staying at a nice motel but were over at Drina's most of the time when Curtis wasn't around. Curtis and Terry returned from a long hunting and fishing trip with only a few ice chests sloppily packed with doves and fish, not much to show for more than a week away from home.

One morning Drina asked me if I would go with her to

pick up some supplies. She always had a creative project going, and I was happy to do what I could to help out. Drina was the sweetest, most trusting, and God-fearing girl you could ever hope to know. She was a wonderful and talented homemaker, a great mom, the best cook and baker anywhere, and had become a very fine seamstress, dressmaker, and tailor. No drinking alcohol or smoking cigarettes for her!

Drina and I got into the truck. Even before we had settled into our seats, we noticed a terrible smell. We just sat there, afraid to move, confused, making faces at each other. The truck cab smelled real strong of fish. We tried not to gag on the smell. Drina and I felt around under the seat, but only managed to come up with some shriveled french fries, empty booze bottles, flattened cigarette packs, a few falling-apart half-smoked marijuana cigarettes—nothing that could have caused that God-awful smell! We finally looked behind the seat and found a pile of slimy butcher paper. What the hell? When we asked Curtis what was up with the smelly wrapping paper, he just said that the fishing had been real poor and that he didn't want to disappoint us after being gone for so long.

Well, this happened a couple of months before our next visit, when Drina came over to the motel one night, sobbing, crying hysterically, tearing at her clothes and hair, saying over and over how munca she felt, and how angry she was with Curtis. Drina was all sore and itchy in her bad place, and between sobs, she managed to say that Curtis had made her sick down there before. My girl had sent the kids over to stay with an auntie and locked that bastard Curtis out of their trailer. Drina was in a terrible awful state. I was so prayerfully thankful to God that my beloved wife was at peace and not around to see and hear all these goings-on. This was just another example of why we should never have let our Drina marry that piece of shit.

The next morning, Mike and I bundled Drina up, put her in our truck, and headed down to see the doc. As we walked into the waiting room, we saw Terry's wife, Jeannie, sitting there, crying her eyes out. She had driven all the way from Clarkston, just so she wouldn't run into anyone she knew. There we were; and there she was, all crumpled up on a little couch, wailing about being touched by her husband's sin. Days later, I was still shaken up by all this ruckus. Was it just a sad coincidence that Drina and Jeannie had gotten the clap at the same time? Were Curtis and Terry sharing a lady friend? Or were they screwing each other—and one of them had got VD from someone else? Yikes! Well, that would explain a lot.

I reckoned that I had nothing better to do with my free time than watch both Curtis and Terry real careful and maybe ask around about them, starting with their work buddies. Problem was, over the years, I had spent a lot of time in Scott's Breech, had done quite a bit of consulting work in the area, and was pretty well known by the local construction companies. A lot of people in Clarkston and Scott's Breech knew I was Curtis's father-in-law. I asked Mike if he would mind helping me get the goods on Curtis and Terry. Mike took Drina as a daughter, and was eager to do anything he could to help.

Mike and I came up with a plan, inspired by Curtis's own history as a master bullshitter to get what he wanted, whether it was to get laid or high. Mike would use his old business card, come up with some cock-and-bull story that he was looking for a few good men to add to the set and road construction crews a television production company was putting together. The local hires would be building sets or doing blacktop and paving work for a new television series that would be shooting on location in the area. Mike's story would be that Terry and Curtis had been recommended by someone, and the human resources guys at the production company wanted Mike to check them out, maybe recruit some extra guys as well. Hell, they might even be hired as extras when shooting started. We came up with a line of crap right up there with some of Curtis's best efforts!

Mike decided to focus first on Terry and find out what his bosses and the guys he'd worked with thought of him. Terry moved around a lot and never really settled into a job for long. In addition to hitting the out-of-town construction companies and

Gypsy and gadjo asphalt outfits, Mike headed for some of the places Terry had worked before he moved his family to Clarkston from Scott's Breech.

I was mad as hell at Curtis, so I put off going back to Chicago just yet. We had a good team there that could handle anything that came up while Mike and I were away. Mike went to talk to Stan Stanley, the foreman at the latest of the few decent jobs Terry ever had, doing roofing. Most of the time, he hired out as a day laborer, lucky to make forty bucks a day. Stan told Mike that he had to let Terry go because he would show up late to the job, high or hung over. Also, there was a potential morale problem.

Some of the guys Terry worked with had seen him hanging around the truck stops and rest areas out on the interstate, and they didn't feel comfortable working the same job with him. "My guys just don't want to work with a queer; they're afraid they might catch somethin' from him, I guess," Stan confided. Wow! I guess my suspicions weren't out in left field after all!

Mike continued his undercover work and made the rounds of some of the places Curtis had worked. Boy, did he get an earful! The older guys on the job didn't take too well to Curtis because they said he didn't do his share of the asphalt or roofing work. Seems like he was always complaining about something: needing to get laid, his back, the heat, the long hours, the mosquitoes. A lot of the guys Curtis had worked with said that he had a habit of looking like he was working real hard when he saw the bosses heading through the job site. But all in all, Curtis really didn't pull his own weight.

On the other hand, some of his work buddies, especially the younger guys, sort of looked up to him as some kind of trailer-park Casanova, always ready to share stories of his latest conquests. Curtis apparently was quite a talented bullshitter on the job as well as off.

Sometimes he'd take a couple of guys aside and offer to set them up with one of his lady friends. "Come huntin' or fishin' with me next time, and I'll have some ladies for you to meet jus' off the interstate." But when the next hunting season opened and one of his work buddies asked if he could come along and share driving and expenses, Curtis said, "Nope, Terry beat you to it; don't need no extra company this time around."

I had asked him several years back if I could tag along on a dove shoot, and he politely said, "No thanks, Danny. On huntin' trips, three's definitely a crowd. And we talk about all kinds of shit. Wouldn't want to have to worry about disrespecting you, seein' as how you're a lot older and you're Drina's pops."

This time around, just after Mike had finished his undercover work, I got a call from Daniel Esterhazy, my lead designer, asking if I could head back to Chicago right away to look at some set designs and fantasy floral treatments for an upcoming television special. The production company had pushed forward some meetings with our people, and Daniel wanted my feedback on our progress. When I ran into Curtis down at the QuikStop, I told him that I would be going back to Chicago in a few days and that he should stay the hell away from Drina.

"That's fine, Danny; no worries there! You and I ain't on the best of terms, but I sure do appreciate everything that you've ever done for me and Drina and the kids. I'm heading out myself in the morning. Deer season opens tomorrow up in Pearson's Reserve, and we want to get an early start."

The following day, in the afternoon, we got a call from Curtis's mom in Indianapolis that his dad had taken a bad fall and had broken a leg. He was back home from the emergency room but had been asking to see Curtis.

This was before cell phone use was affordable and widespread. I had no other way to contact Curtis, so I decided to set out to catch up with him and tell him the bad news. This may sound like a stupid idea, but when something like this happens in a Gypsy family, everyone's normal everyday life grinds to a halt and we head out to do for whoever needs help. This was one reason I brought Mike on board as a project manager years ago. With his design background and business savvy, he could handle just about anything in my absence. This time around, he caught the next plane back to Chicago to help Daniel take care of business while I shifted into high gear to track down Curtis and Terry.

Just over the county line, I saw the exit toward Pearson's Reserve. I got off the expressway and almost immediately came across Curtis's truck and Terry's van parked all crooked just off the road next to a wooded area. I pulled in behind Curtis's truck and headed down a gravel path into the woods. I wandered around a bit and finally found their campsite. In the fading light, I almost stumbled over them, fast asleep and all tangled up together in a sleeping bag.

I poked at them with a stubby little branch and yelled out, "The honeymoon's over, fuckers!" Terry came tumbling out of the sleeping bag, naked as a jaybird. He stood up real straight-like and blurted out, "We needed to pull over to get a few winks, Danny. We was just cold, that's why we was in the sleeping bag together. We ain't queer or nothin'!"

Curtis hopped up, wearing just a pair of socks. He lit a cigarette and nervously took a drag. He shook his head. "No, Danny, we ain't no Nancy boys! Why are you here? What's going on? Is Drina ok? The kids?"

I stood there biting my tongue, angry as hell. They tore at the pile of clothes off to the side, holding everything up to see what belonged to who. "Curtis, your mom called and said that your dad fell and broke a leg. They fixed him up in the emergency room. The doc wanted to put him in the hospital, but Harry insisted on going home. He's been calling for you non-stop. Let's get goin'! I'll follow you in my truck. Terry, you'd better get your sorry ass to your van and head back home."

They finished getting dressed, trying real hard not to look at each other, glancing over at me like they expected me to poke them again. Terry finally mumbled something and headed back toward his van. I helped Curtis get his stuff together, and we made our way back out to the road.

"Danny, please don't tell . . . "

I cut him short. "Curtis, I don't give a damn who yer fuckin', or who's fuckin' you, because I'm telling you again what Drina told you when she threw your lying ass out of the trailer: that you will never get a chance to make my girl sick again."

"Danny . . . "

"Just shut up and listen to me. You've been a lousy husband to my girl, but you've always been decent to me, so I'm goin' to give you some advice. You know, if you get the clap in your ass, it don't stay in your ass: It travels around in your body, and you can give it to the next guy or gal that you screw. I've even heard that if you're getting screwed and the other guy takes too long back there, all that friction can give you butt cancer."

"What the fuck? Wha—no way! Well, that may be, Danny, but like I said, I ain't no fuckin' homo, and I don't get buttfucked."

"Well, maybe you're a down-on-your-knees kinda guy with your good buddy Terry. Herb Walker told Mike that he's seen Terry making the rounds of the stalls out at the truck stops, checkin' out the bulls' cocks at the urinals."

"Well, what's old nosy-ass Herb doing out there? Anyways, I told you, Danny, me and Terry ain't homos. We're just good buddies, best buddies even. We ain't fags. And it ain't right for Drina to refuse to let me sleep in the same bed with her, tellin' me that I made her sick down there. That ain't right, shutting me out like that. And I'll say it now, Danny, right to your face: It wasn't me that made Drina sick. She must be foolin' around. I'll tell you, Danny, she just ain't the good girl no more that you raised her to be."

That was it! I went crazy, grabbed Curtis's bag and threw it to the ground. I pushed him back, made a fist and slugged him so hard on the jaw that his whole body jerked up, then collapsed in a heap onto the gravel path.

I stood over Curtis, shaking my fist at him."Fuckin' bastard," I hissed, "if I ever hear that you've been in my girl's trailer again, I'll finish what I just started. I will fuckin' kill you with my bare hands. And when I tell everyone that I found you two fuckers naked together in a sleeping bag, I'll have plenty of backup!"

I left Curtis crumpled up on the ground, trying to sit up, rubbing his messed-up jaw, sobbing quietly as I turned around and continued to walk back to my truck. I knew that I would never tell anyone what I had seen that day, never do or say anything that would bring shame on my girl and my grandkids.

Curtis had his broken jaw wired shut and went alone to visit his dad in Indianapolis.

He never returned.

One evening, Terry told Jeannie that he was going out for a pack of cigarettes.

And he never returned.

Postscript

The latest word we had of Curtis and Terry was that they were on the road with the Sherman Bros. Carnival on the Southern Circuit.

Drina went back to school and got her high school diploma, then took up quilting. She has made quite a name for herself as a talented quilter, creating many beautiful and intricate designs that fetch high prices at the soft-goods store up in Cutler and at the Arts Consortium Gallery over in Winton.

Drina bought the land just behind her place, had a new triple-wide trailer brought in, and opened a Gypsy guest house, offering room and board to Gypsies on the road and gadje who want to relax in an authentic Gypsy setting.

My girl never ceases to amaze me.

Decorator Tree

Notes

www.ingramcontent.com/pod-product-compliance
Lightning Source LLC
LaVergne TN
LVHW090548110826
845146LV00001B/68

* 9 7 9 8 2 1 8 5 0 5 1 1 0 *